THE POWER OF FLOW

THE POWER OF *Flow*

PRACTICAL WAYS TO TRANSFORM YOUR LIFE WITH MEANINGFUL COINCIDENCE

*Charlene Belitz
and Meg Lundstrom*

THREE RIVERS PRESS ✦ NEW YORK

Grateful acknowledgment is made to the following for permission to reprint material: Connirae Andreas, from *Core Transformation: Reaching the Wellspring Within*. Moab, Utah: Real People Press, 1994. Bantam Doubleday Dell, from Frances E. Vaughan, *Awakening Intuition*. New York: Doubleday-Anchor Books, 1979. Paulist Press, from Brother David Steindl-Rast, *Gratefulness: The Heart of Prayer*. Mahwah, N.J.: Paulist Press, 1984. Samuel Weiser, Inc., from Phyllis Krystal, *Cutting the Ties That Bind Workbook*. York Beach, Maine: Samuel Weiser, Inc., 1995. *The Record* of Hackensack, N.J., for "Déjà Vu All Over Again," February 4, 1996. David K. Reynolds, for *A Handbook for Constructive Living*. New York: William Morrow, 1995. David Spangler, from *Everyday Miracles: The Inner Art of Manifestation*. New York, Bantam Books, 1996.

Published by Three Rivers Press, 201 East 50th Street, New York, New York 10022. Member of the Crown Publishing Group.

Random House, Inc. New York, Toronto, London, Sydney, Auckland
www.randomhouse.com

THREE RIVERS PRESS and colophon are registered trademarks of Random House, Inc.

Printed in the United States of America

Library of Congress Cataloging-in-Publication Data
Belitz, Charlene.
  The power of flow : practical ways to transform your life with meaningful coincidence / Charlene Belitz and Meg Lundstrom.—1st pbk. ed.
Originally published : New York : Harmony Books, c1997.
1. Self-actualization (Psychology). 2. Coincidence. I. Lundstrom, Meg. II. Title.
BF637.S4B4257   1998
158.1—dc21   98-25300

ISBN 0-609-80197-X

10 9 8 7 6 5 4 3 2

*We dedicate this book to you
and to all those whose lives you touch.*

May all beings be happy.

Contents

Introduction

Awakening one morning in his sunny Austin bedroom, Caylor Wadlington heard himself saying out loud, "So I'm moving to Denver?" The words were part exclamation, part question, and they woke him up completely. As surprised as he was, he also experienced a happy, pleasurable feeling. But by the next day, he had dismissed the whole thing as just an odd dream. After all, he was cozily ensconced in Austin, where he had lived eight years, and he knew hardly a soul in Denver.

Then, out of the blue came a phone call from an officer of his national professional association, who invited Caylor to participate in a week-long work meeting—in Denver. *Hmm . . . maybe there is something to this,* Caylor thought, and without further hesitation he said yes.

In Denver, as the meeting ended, Caylor was chatting with another participant, a man who ran a school in the city. "Caylor, if you'd ever want to live here, I'd like to hire you to teach for me," he said. Caylor thanked him calmly, but inside he was stunned: *This is amazing! Walls are coming down to open the way for me to move here!*

To leave Austin, however, would require selling a professional business that was so specialized he figured it would take at least a year to find a buyer. Quietly beginning to look around, Caylor invited a friend to Sunday brunch and, over coffee and pastries, laid out the prospect. His friend was not interested, but just as he said no, a colleague of theirs walked in. Caylor had not thought of him as a buyer, but, struck by the timing, told him his business was for sale. The colleague was more than interested—he was thrilled. "Don't tell another soul!" he said excitedly. "I definitely want it." *This seems to be happening all by itself,* mused Caylor. Then he received a letter from his landlord: Caylor's condominium was going to be put on the market. A dream, an opportunity, an offer, the boot—the message was unmistakable. Caylor willingly closed down his life in charming Austin, and moved to Denver.

Caylor wears no wings, sees no auras. But to him, life works in magical and surprising ways when he's connected to a deeper force in the Universe—and he knows he's connected because he feels it physically, as a soft, warm feeling inside that links him to a sweet expansiveness. When he's in that state, he experiences meaningful coincidence after meaningful coincidence. "They add magic to my life, and tell me that the action I'm taking is safe and true and right," he says. And they point the way to new opportunities: "Although I loved Austin, I was starting to feel bored and a little stuck professionally and personally," he says now. "I thought that Denver might open the way in my life to some important changes."

Caylor lives in *flow*—and through it he has come into a fuller, truer existence. Flow is the natural, effortless unfolding of our lives in a way that moves us toward wholeness and harmony. When we are in flow, occurrences line up, events fall into place, and obstacles melt away. Rather than life being a meaningless struggle, it is permeated with a deep sense of purposefulness and order. Flow has tremendous power to transform our lives, for it is dynamic and moves us unerringly toward joy and aliveness.

Most of us have had experiences of being in flow. In those times, we know we're in the right place at the right time doing the right thing. We feel both exhilarated and at peace, somehow connected to something larger and greater than ourselves. Life is rich with meaning, magic, and purpose. We feel vital, alive, joyful. But for most of us, it doesn't happen often enough or for long enough. We feel glimmerings of flow, and then they fade away.

This doesn't have to be the case: people like Caylor have learned to make flow their way of life, the rule rather than the exception. The way they do it is through *synchronicity*—those meaningful coincidences in which outside events, seemingly disconnected in time and space, link up with our internal states and connect us with the greater whole.

When synchronicity happens, people like Caylor follow the direction it seems to indicate—and then they watch synchronicity happen more and more. They know they are deeply in flow when synchronicity is sparkling all around them. By using synchronicity for guidance, confirmation, and validation, their lives become a dance of energy with the Universe, a give-and-take with their environment that fills their days with insight and zest.

This way of life requires paying attention to meaningful coincidence. Caylor, for example, could have disregarded his dream and turned down the Denver job. But over time he had developed a strong respect for what he considers signs from the Universe, both subtle and unmistakable. He has learned that by paying attention to these signs, he reaches new levels of comprehension about his inner life and his role in the world.

"Synchronicity is lyrical—a little sprite of a surprise, a little gift," he says. "It can get so big that *everything* can start to talk to you; everything can suggest things. When you enter that dimension, synchronicity becomes part of your self-definition."

Think of the times synchronicity has happened in your life. It might be when you thought of someone and the phone rang with that person on the other end. Maybe you ran across someone from home in a faraway place when you were feeling lonely, or the same number repeated itself at significant times, or unlikely events dramatically converged to save you in a tight spot.

When you experience flow on a daily basis, synchronicities such as these are as natural to you as breathing. Although by its very nature, synchronicity cannot be created, controlled, or planned, when you live a life of flow, you can practically depend on synchronicity to show up.

Notice the words: it's *when* you experience flow—not *if*. That's because flow is always present and its power is absolutely attainable. To experience it requires first of all that you choose to undertake that process. Then you must develop the necessary skills, much as you do when you learn to ride a bike: it takes focus to learn the basics and practice to make it second nature—but once you know how to do it, you enjoy ease and smoothness and elation. Flow is a lifelong process that is rich with rewards all along the way, and this book shows you how to undertake it.

To understand how flow works, we interviewed fifty "flowmasters"—people highly engaged in the process of flow. They range in age from seventeen to ninety-six and include lawyers, dancers, secretaries, students, foundation heads, middle managers, therapists, professors, consultants, homemakers, teachers, activists, health professionals, a minister, a rancher, an inventor. We spent absorbing hours with them, delving into why their lives had purpose, inner ease, and joyfulness. We asked them about their turning points, their beliefs, their daily practices. We explored what makes life work so well for them, and what they do day to day to experience flow consciously and consistently.

The flowmasters did not have only one approach to life. Some were feisty and engaged in changing the world; some were gentle and relaxed; some had the exuberance of children; some had thoughtful, deliberate ways. But looking back over our discussions, commonalities emerged. The flowmasters were open; they stretched themselves to learn and grow; they had deep integrity; they felt steadfastly grateful; and they were dedicated to living by their inner truths. Being with them made us feel richer, and hours of engrossing conversation passed like minutes.

Valuable information came from two other sources as well. In response to magazine and newspaper articles, hundreds of people from all over the country filled out surveys on their experiences and beliefs. And we organized nine focus groups involving 98 people across the country who hashed through the topics, processes, and techniques we'd learned from the flowmasters. The flowmaster interviews, surveys, and group discussions were transcribed and sorted by subject matter into 241 categories. When printed out—a twelve-hour process—the reports filled nearly 1,600 pages.

Our conclusion from this research process is that flow is the ultimate feedback machine. Flow responds directly to our beliefs, behaviors, and actions. We can either enhance this state of perfect timing and flawless serendipity, or we can diminish it and even cut it off. When we become open, willing, trusting, we experience flow as fulfillment and joy, and synchronicities pop up all over the place. When we become fearful, doubting, controlling, flow diminishes, our day is filled with blocks and frustrations, and synchronicities cease.

In this book, we have distilled the major beliefs, attitudes, and behaviors of flowmasters into nine attributes that engage flow: commitment, honesty, courage, passion, immediacy, openness, receptivity, positivity, and trust. We have offered fourteen practical techniques to deepen those attributes in yourself; you'll find them in chapters 7 through 11. We based the techniques on established psychological and communication theories, and people in the focus groups tried them out in their lives. Their enthusiastic feedback assured us that, yes, we all have it within ourselves to move into meaning, lightness, and serenity. We don't have to be yogis chanting mantras in icy Himalayan caves to live in this state of inner peace. Because synchronicity is the key—and synchronicity occurs to absolutely everyone, including you—we all have it within ourselves to live in flow.

In the first part of this book, you'll see how flow runs through everyone's life. You'll see the power it has to shape and enrich your days. You'll read how people have used synchronicity to put themselves on the right path, ease the details of daily living, have a good laugh, and answer pressing questions.

You'll learn from the flowmasters what they do to experience flow continually in their lives and what steps they take to make it strong and steady. Among others, you'll meet John Beal, a Vietnam veteran who reclaimed his life by singlehandedly reviving a nearly dead salmon stream and who has a knack for showing up at the exact time and place that someone is dumping toxins into it. Lloyd Tupper, a minister who sees himself as "just an oboe in the orchestra," has risen from financial ruin to become an adviser in multinational merger talks. Carolyn North, a dancer, organized a food bank delivery service that has relied for a decade totally on synchronicity—on the right volunteers showing up at the right time, day after day. These flowmasters have charted the course we will follow on our journey.

Among the fourteen techniques, you'll discover tools to create changes in yourself to further your experience of flow and thereby enhance synchronicity. You'll discover how to be true to yourself. You'll determine your mission in life and your next step to fulfill it. You'll treat yourself gently and compassionately. You'll enhance your intuition so that you make better decisions. You'll stretch yourself and take risks. You'll see how gratitude fills your days with overflow-

ing compassion and how generosity becomes your way of
being.

As you take these steps, you will find yourself moving
into harmony, into oneness, into true aliveness. You'll be living life the way it is supposed to be: fun, light, purposeful, in
concert with the rhythms of life.

No matter where you are on your path, this approach
works. If you have been pursuing personal and spiritual
growth for years, this approach can provide you with feedback from the Universe that will lead you to understand
yourself even better. If you are just now turning your attention to life's deeper questions, it offers you an easy, immediate means of access into the workings of your consciousness.
If your world is devoid of meaning, here's a way to find significance in the commonplace. A bird flying across your path,
a book dropped at your feet, a postcard arriving in the
mail—all can improbably but definitively connect you to
deeper currents of existence.

You're about to embark on a journey that will transform your life. This book is your guide; synchronicity your
compass; flow your inevitable destination.

THE POWER OF FLOW

1 WHAT IS FLOW?

For thousands of years, before Descartes, Newton, and the beginnings of modern science, people believed that all of nature was a single organism and that everything was connected. Responsiveness to signs from the Universe was a normal part of daily life, for everything from passing clouds to passing events was perceived to speak in ways that mattered.

Struggling to define the essence of this underlying connectedness, people used words such as God, Atma, essential life force, universal mind. But these words fell far short of reality because, by their nature, words limit and contain—and the nature of this unified connectedness can't be boxed in or tied down. "The name that can be named is not the eternal name," says the *Tao Te Ching*.

In current times, quantum physicists encounter similar difficulties in struggling to define the basic nature of matter. They have found that the boundaries that isolate one thing from another exist only at the most obvious and superficial level; at deeper levels, all things—atoms, molecules, plants, animals, people—participate in a sensitive, dynamic web of information.

This interrelatedness is something for which we have an intuitive sense. Even if we have no formal beliefs about a higher power, the concept of being connected to a dynamic force beyond ourselves shows up in an ordinary, everyday phrase: "in the flow." "Go with the flow," we might say, or, "I'm really in the flow today."

When we try to define flow, it is also tough to nail. One approach is to study a readily observable aspect of it, which is what psychologist Mihaly Csikszentmihalyi did in defining flow as "optimal experience, a state of concentration so focused that it amounts to absolute absorption in an activity." In that state, which most often occurs during intense physical activity, we feel strong, alert, and at the peak of our abilities. This is connectedness—to an activity, to a moment.

Often when people speak of flow, however, they are alluding to it in a larger sense. They are speaking of a connectedness to larger patterns of events and meaning. And here a new definition is required:

Flow is the natural, effortless unfolding of our life in a way that moves us toward wholeness and harmony.

Flow is *natural* because we personally do nothing to cause it to exist. Whether or not we give it our conscious attention, it just *is*. Sometimes we may hardly know it's there: when obscured by our fear or anger it can run underground like a river. But when we move into greater awareness and trust, it emerges in all its strength and power.

Flow is *effortless* because when we learn to swim with it, its currents move us easily, smoothly and gently through life. Our stress, struggle, and uncertainty drop away, and our joy, peace, satisfaction, happiness, and effectiveness increase.

Flow is an *unfolding* because it furthers our potentiality—it brings us into life as it is meant to be lived. We often have an "aha" feeling of familiarity, of rightness, when we're "in the flow." And, flow does not only involve our personal unfolding but the unfolding of a larger pattern in which we play a part.

Flow has tremendous power to transform our lives. Like water, it is dynamic and still, strong and receptive, persevering and yielding. We can't push or force flow any more than we can a river; gently and surely, it has its way.

Flow speaks to being part of something bigger than ourself. It runs counter to the sense of being out there alone, of ending where our skin ends. Not only does quantum theory substantiate this interconnectedness, so do the findings of the major spiritual traditions. Western religions point to flow in stressing the need to be in harmony with a larger pattern of meaning and purpose, which they call God, Jehovah, Allah. By surrendering ourselves to this larger pattern, they teach, we come into joy and peace and our needs are taken care of. "The Lord is my shepherd: I shall not want," says the Twenty-third Psalm. Eastern religions perceive the Universe as a flowing web of consciousness in which everything is connected; by aligning ourselves with underlying patterns, they say, we come into harmony with our environment. "Let your nature blend with the Way and wander in it free from care," Zen tells us.

Flow runs through everyone's life, and proof of that interconnectedness is all around us. A good example is the time that Ann Medlock and John Graham of New York City first walked down the main street of Langley, Washington, population 845. They had been searching hard for a year across the country for a new place to live, and they came to Langley for a closer look after John spoke to a group there. At first, Ann wasn't impressed—too many tall dark trees, too cold a wind. But then they happened upon a high-quality letterpress print shop, exactly what Ann needed to do graphics for the feisty nonprofit organization they ran. At the tobacco shop, they spotted John's favorite pipe mixture, which he had only been able to find in one store in all of New York City. They saw a notice for church services for the same small denomination they attended back home. Finally they came to a dry goods store with a sign in the window that said, "Levi's For Sale." There, on top of the pile, were three pairs in John's size—a challenge to find because of his 6'5", 180-pound frame.

By then, they were howling with laughter. "We give up! All right!" they said to each other. Soon afterward, they found the land they wanted to buy. To complete the picture, when they returned to New York, they learned that one of Ann's closest friends had been in Langley the same weekend and had also decided to move there.

Some people would not have taken these coincidences seriously. But to Ann and John, they were no accident: each meant something to them, and together they amounted to the Universe giving them a loud, clear message that Langley was where they belonged. Months later, they were living there— and have been flourishing in the eleven years since, as has the Giraffe Project, their nonprofit organization that recognizes people who "stick their neck out" for the common good.

Flow is marked by two types of occurrences: synchronicity and fortuitous events. As the experience of flow increases in our lives, so do these occurrences. *Synchronicity* was coined by Carl Jung, who, after watching its effect on his patients, defined it as "meaningful coincidence that cannot be explained by cause and effect." He believed synchronicity to be the "acausal connecting principle" that demonstrates the dynamic interrelationship between our consciousness and the outer world. As he defined it, synchronicity often takes the form of the coming together of an inner and outer event in a way that has an emotional or psychological impact on us and that gives us a sense of being part of a larger whole. His definition includes not only coincidental happenings but also dreams that foretell an event and inexplicable knowledge we have of events occurring at the same time but elsewhere.

By its very nature, we cannot directly cause synchronicity to happen—and yet it responds to our needs. It boggles the mind because it seems as though the Universe swings into place to give us what we need. For Ann and John, seeing so much that was familiar and comfortable in a totally unknown town gave them the certainty that they were, in fact, home. And they had done nothing directly to cause it. They didn't query the Chamber of Commerce beforehand to locate the retail shops they needed, or plan to be in Langley the same time as Ann's friend. But when those things happened, they took them to heart and followed the direction they indicated.

Fortuitous events happen when things come together in ways that work out amazingly well, and they can be explained by cause and effect. For instance, the fact that Ann and John found land they wanted to build on in Langley can be easily explained: they went to a realtor, toured properties, and found one they liked. But what was *fortuitous* was that the site had the trees and mountain view they wanted, that it was within their price range, and that they found it the first day they looked. Soon after, there was a sharp increase in housing prices, which would have put the land out of Ann and John's modest price range.

We each have our personal route to flow. Ann's and John's journeys began with hardships. Ann, a bubbly and energetic writer, plunged into a depression when her first husband ran away with her best friend as she was undergoing an emergency cesarean. John, a gangly, intense foreign service officer and mountaineer, had experienced vivid nightmares and post-traumatic stress disorder after the Vietnam War and had also suffered a painful breakup of his previous marriage.

In despair, Ann began meditating. John became involved in spiritual and personal growth organizations. As each examined who they were and what they wanted, they stopped living by other people's expectations and began living by their own. They looked at when and how they were stopped by fear, anger, and pain, and they took steps to remove those blockages. They opened themselves to new possibilities and ways of thinking. They learned to listen to their intuition and to follow what it said. Their days became studded with synchronicities that brought them valuable contacts, work, housing, and their life mission. Flow had become their everyday reality.

Flow has been part of your reality as well. Think of a time when life seemed rich and shimmering with possibility and you felt wordlessly connected to something greater and vaster than you could imagine. Perhaps it was when you first held your newborn baby in your arms, or when you were watching a spectacular sunset on a beach, or when you heard music so beautiful it brought tears to your eyes, or when you gazed into a loved one's eyes. At those times, all the pettiness and worries of life dropped away, and something deep inside you was touched. When flow becomes your way of life, those moments pervade your days. You feel excited and full of wonder, and awe yet peaceful and calm. You feel creative, productive, safe, comfortable, and complete. Each moment seems perfect in and of itself.

Flow has certain characteristics that tell us when we're experiencing it at high levels. Some of these characteristics are concrete manifestations of its power; others are more subtle dynamics that indicate that flow is moving us forward on our path.

We experience the power of flow when:

✦ *Things fall into place, obstacles melt away, and whatever is necessary—money, time, work, people, opportunities—appears as needed.* Flow eases the way. It's like the intricate workings of a fine Swiss clock—all the gears and parts mesh smoothly to move things forward. This doesn't mean we sit back and take things easy when we're in flow: we are doing all our necessary daily activities and routines, such as making phone calls and running errands. But things happen naturally and easily, and before long, we can't remember living any other way.

Glenn Logan, after thirty-five years as an alcoholic, was celebrating his 90th sober day when his daughter-in-law asked him to drive her to a local university so she could register for a course. He impulsively enrolled in a beginning course on computer science, but was dropped from it because he was too advanced. As he was leaving the professor's office, he noticed a course catalog with "Ethics in Counseling" circled. He enrolled in it. His instructor was so impressed with him that he suggested Glenn apply to graduate school.

That's when every door seemed to open. The assessment test Glenn needed to take was being given the next day; all the college transcripts he needed arrived in a week; all his references sent in their letters the same day they were asked; and the faculty board convened just as he met all the requirements. The result? He was accepted seventeen days after he applied. Now, at sixty, he's an addictions counselor and in the midst of a Ph.D. program in clinical psychology.

This kind of meshing together of events can happen in ways both profound and mundane, depending on our tasks and needs at each point in life. Sometimes, in fact, flow is most validating when it is the small things in life that mesh together. When we have to get somewhere quickly, it is concrete proof that we've tapped into the power of flow when we hit all the green lights and find a parking spot in the most crowded part of town.

◆ *We find ourselves in the right place at the right time doing the right thing.* Coming into flow involves knowing ourselves deeply, which gives us growing certainty about what we need for our happiness and where we fit in the world. As we move in the direction of balance and wholeness, our choices are constantly affirmed by synchronicities and fortuitous events. If we start doubting, something may happen to bring us renewed confidence that we're where we should be—a phone call, a lucky break, a fresh opportunity, money out of nowhere.

Laura Putney of Mount Pleasant, Utah, wanted to stay home with her two sons while they were young, but at several points it appeared that she might have to go back to work to make ends meet. Each time something intervened, including an unexpected inheritance from a distant relative. "It reinforced our commitment to the way we live our lives," she says.

◆ *Perfect timing smooths the way in long-term and everyday logistics.* With the power of flow, one thing leads into another without wasted time or effort. This can mean reaching a friend by phone minutes before she's walking out the door for a week, or turning on the radio just in time to hear news that's important at our job that day, or arriving at the corner just as the bus does. Or it may mean that when we're delayed by traffic and arrive fifteen minutes late at a restaurant, the friend we're meeting arrives just then too. It can mean that we apply to a company for work and learn that an opening has just occurred because someone with precisely our qualifications has just quit. Or that we meet our future spouse at the only time in years that we are simultaneously available for a new relationship.

Sometimes perfect timing is due to what look like problems. Eric Sondermann, who has a public relations consulting business in Denver, planned to lay off one of his employees before the start of the workday, but he was delayed and reached the office too late to discuss it with her. At a 9 A.M. meeting with a client, he was handed a totally unexpected project that she was well qualified to do. It would have been unfortunate for both of them if he had let her go a half-hour earlier.

✦ *Life unfolds as a dynamic process.* We begin to experience, in a practical way, the fluctuating, constantly changing nature of existence. We understand that everything has a timing and a pacing of its own. Instead of struggling to get what we need, we relax into a situation. We follow our intuition and watch for feedback from life. We learn when to push and when to pull; when to speak and when to be silent; when to advance and when to retreat. We do our best in whatever we do, and we trust that what happens is supposed to happen. Then, free of impatience, guilt, and anxiety, we watch with pleasure as events unfold that are better than what we had conceived. One flowmaster, a lawyer, says that when he is working toward a goal in his life, he always asks himself, "Am I pushing or am I not?" If he's pushing, he stops. While negotiating for a car, he could have purchased one at a reasonable price, but when the situation started seeming full of effort and stress, he stopped the proceedings. Two weeks later, he made a single phone call and purchased the same car at a better price.

✦ *Events and actions mesh together in a coherent pattern of deep harmony and underlying order.* Life seems purposeful and integrated rather than chaotic and meaningless. Our actions and decisions arise from and merge into a larger pattern that affects others we come into contact with, and we in turn are affected by them. We realize that everything we do matters. In this larger scheme of things, the work we do—whether it's building homes, waiting tables, or raising children—gains added significance: it's our unique contribution. Understanding the mutuality of life, seeing how much we have been enriched by others, we have full hearts and we want to give back.

We find ourselves becoming flow messengers—vehicles for other people's synchronicities. When Ann Medlock and John Graham returned to New York from their trip to Langley, they immediately called an architect known for his innovative designs to ask him to design their house. Although he is usually unattainable, he and his partner were sitting in their office discussing the need to test their concepts on houses in different climates at the time he picked up the telephone.

We experience this underlying order in another way as we see how actions we take in the physical, mental, emotional, and spiritual areas of our life can create parallel events in the outer world. After cleaning out the basement, we find we are ready for a new relationship. Upon forgiving our father for his emotional distance, we hear our own child confiding a secret to us. We see the threads that tie seemingly unrelated events together.

✦ *Outside events link up with our inner thoughts and feelings, giving us a sense of participation with the Universe.* With flow, it's not, as the Anne Murray song goes, "You and me against the world," it's you and me *and* the world, or, even better, you and me *are* the world. We experience the interplay between us and the Universe, and the lines of separation between ourselves and others disappear. We feel connected at a deep level to everyone and everything. We see everyone—including ourselves—as being in the process of learning and growing and we don't judge or discount them. Struggle disappears; in its place is cooperation and ease. We are open to whatever the Universe brings. We are ready to do our part. In this state of receptivity, everything seems to support us in a way that enriches our life and helps us see our process and purpose more clearly. The names of places, numbers on houses, a series of phone calls begin to lace together in meaningful patterns. Slowly, the mundane threads of life become a tapestry of ongoing discovery, deeply absorbing and richly textured. The magic is in the moment—in this very moment.

Flow, in short, fills our days with meaning, purpose, and ease. And best of all, it has a very accessible entry point—synchronicity, which we can clearly see operating in our lives once we understand how it presents itself.

2 WHAT IS SYNCHRONICITY?

Because our scientific worldview is built on the concept of cause and effect, as a culture we tend to doubt and deny aspects of experience that aren't measurable and verifiable. So often when events coincide in startling ways, the first words we hear or say are, "Oh, it's just a coincidence."

Some people might think of it in terms of the odds. If there's a one in a million chance of that coincidence happening, why make such a big deal of it? After all, *somebody* has to win the lottery! This point of view has a certain validity: synchronicity is part and parcel of physical laws. It doesn't defy the natural order of events; it simply raises more questions than can easily be answered by a cause-and-effect equation.

The concept that everything has a concrete cause is so entrenched in our modern Western mentality that it took considerable courage for Carl Jung to take on the subject of synchronicity. He didn't discuss it in depth until the eighth decade of his life when, as he wrote in his preface to the *I Ching,* "The changing opinions of men scarcely impress me anymore." A dramatic incident clarified his thinking on the matter. He had been looking for some way to break through to a patient who was super-rational, had rigid, stock answers for everything, and therefore was not doing well in therapy. He writes, "I was sitting opposite her one day with my back to the window, listening to her flow of rhetoric. She had an impressive dream the night before, in which someone had given her a golden scarab—a costly piece of jewelry. While she was still telling me this dream, I heard something behind me gently tapping on the window. I turned around and saw that it was a fairly large flying insect that was knocking against the windowpane from outside in the obvious effort to get into the dark room. This seemed to me very strange. I opened the window immediately and caught the insect in the air as it flew in. It was a scarabaeid beetle, whose gold-green color most nearly resembles that of a golden scarab. I handed the beetle to my patient with the words, 'Here is your scarab.' The experience punctured the desired hole in her rationalism and broke the ice of her intellectual resistance." On the basis of his work with his patients, Jung said that synchronicity is more likely to occur when we are in a highly charged state of emotional and mental awareness—when, in his words, the "archetypes," universal images or themes underlying human behavior, are activated.

Before Jung, Austrian biologist Paul Kammerer documented another type of coincidence that he called seriality, in which things repeat themselves across time. He wrote of a case involving a Mr. Deschamps who, as a boy in Orleans, France, was presented with a piece of plum pudding by a guest of the family, Mr. de Fortgibu. Years later, Mr. Deschamps, now a young man, ordered plum pudding in a Paris restaurant, only to find that the last piece had just been taken—by Mr. de Fortgibu, who was sitting across the room. Many years later, at a dinner party where Mr. Deschamps was again offered plum pudding, he regaled his guests with the story and remarked that all that was missing was Mr. de

Fortgibu. Soon the door burst open and in came Mr. de Fort-gibu himself, now a disoriented old man who had gotten the wrong address and had entered by mistake.

When we talk about synchronicity within this book, we base it on Jung's definition—

Synchronicity is the coming together of inner and outer events in a way that cannot be explained by cause and effect and that is meaningful to the observer.

—And we include in our discussions Kammerer's recognition of seriality as a form of meaningful coincidence, which, while not considered by Jung, is encountered in such events as the significant repetition of songs, numbers, and phrases.

RECOGNIZING SYNCHRONICITY

Synchronicity is not a word we have grown up with. The concept may not be firmly in our minds, and because we don't have a label or mental framework for it, we may not notice it. Researchers in communication have found that when we lack a word for an object or a concept, we can't identify it—and this can happen in the most literal of ways. For instance, in China, there is only one word for red—and people literally do not distinguish between rose, crimson, pink, and scarlet. They lack the vocabulary and therefore the perception that red comes in more than one shade.

So when synchronicity happens, many people overlook it or call it something else. They might say, "I got lucky," or "That happened just in the nick of time," or "It came out of the blue," or "It jumped out at me." Later on, when asked if they have experienced synchronicity, they can't remember any. All those incidents are filed away in their memory, but under the category of luck or happenstance.

When you watch a 3-D movie, you put on special glasses and suddenly see images emerge that had been invisible before. Learning about synchronicity is like putting on 3-D glasses that allow totally new dimensions to pop out when you look over your life. Those dimensions have been there all along, but now you have the eyes to see them. Once you know what synchronicity is and how to look for it, you begin to notice it everywhere.

In order to understand synchronicity as it appears now, has appeared in your past, and will appear in your future, let's look at the circumstances in which synchronicity shows up in your life and at the patterns it takes—single incidents, strings, and clusters.

As you read the following descriptions, read actively. Scan your memory for similar events. Think of what's happened to you in the last few weeks and months and see what patterns emerge. This quiz will help you quickly look over the synchronicity in your life to date. Check the items that you say "yes" to.

HOW MUCH SYNCHRONICITY DO YOU HAVE IN YOUR LIFE?

☐ Have you thought of telephoning someone, only to have that person call you unexpectedly before you could get to it?

☐ Have you been late to get somewhere and found the way inexplicably seem to open in front of you so that you arrived just in time?

☐ Has the right amount of money shown up from an unexpected source just when you needed it?

☐ Has a toll lane or a cash register line ever opened up just as you approached it?

☐   When you are in a hurry, do you ever find a scarce parking spot right where you need it?

☐   In a desperate search for some piece of information or item you really need, has it amazingly shown up in some unexpected way?

☐   Have you run into a friend in an unlikely, distant, or out-of-the-way place?

☐   Has a lost object ever come back to you in an unusual and unexpected way?

☐   Has a series of coincidences happened to you that all seemed to be pointing you a particular direction?

☐   Have you been in the right place at the right time to rescue someone, or were you ever rescued by a stranger who just happened to be there?

☐   Have you run into obstacle after obstacle only to find out later that it was a very good thing you didn't continue in that direction?

☐   Have you thought of a question only to have it answered on the radio or by the people talking at the next table before you could ask it?

☐   Have you found that meaningful coincidence usually validates the direction you're going?

Total checked:_____

To learn your synchronicity rating, read through to the end of the chapter.

We experience synchronicity most often when we're open and aware, which in turn is affected by the outer conditions in which we find ourselves and the inner conditions in which we put ourselves.

✦ *Special circumstances* such as births, deaths, and times of upheaval are outer conditions that push us toward openness because, as the ground shifts beneath our feet, we feel more vulnerable.

✦ *Mundane circumstances* of daily life can be rich with synchronicity if we have the right inner conditions—if we make ourselves more open to the world through personal awareness and inner work.

Let's examine each of these.

SPECIAL CIRCUMSTANCES

Among his patients Jung observed that synchronicity often happens during circumstances of emotional intensity and upheaval, and often peaks right before a psychological breakthrough. These situations of an "aroused psyche" include such life-changing major events as:

✦ Births
✦ Deaths
✦ Falling in or out of love
✦ Turning points or personal crises
✦ Rescues from danger
✦ Travel

Our awareness and uncertainty is heightened during these times of turmoil, change, and challenge. When we're groping for solutions, or even learning how to appreciate unexpected joy, we are much more open to input from all sources. Synchronicity may reassure us, point us in a whole new direction, or give us the missing piece we need to make everything work.

Life passages such as births, romances, and deaths are times when the worries of daily life recede as we are drawn into the currents of a larger existence. Our ordinary routines are disrupted, our thoughts are focused on the changes in process, and our senses are wide open. We know that when the child is born, when the wedding is over, when the funeral is done, our life will be different in ways we can only dimly perceive now. We probably have a jumble of conflicting feelings. Along with our joy at a birth may come fear about our new financial responsibility; along with the grief of death may come relief at the end of suffering. We might be looking for direction, for answers, for reassurance that the good and right thing is happening. Beverly Fox Martin of Greenwood Lake, New York, tried to adopt an infant daughter for five frustrating years, and even had a name picked out—Kathleen, after her mother. On her mother's birthday, Beverly went to her grave and prayed for her mother to intercede for her in heaven. She walked inside her home to hear the phone ringing. It was the adoption agency with an infant daughter. And what name had the child's birth mother given her? Kathleen!

When we're in love, synchronicity seems to jump out all over the place. We feel light-headed, happy, open; the world is smiling back at us, giving the relationship a sense of destiny. Irvin Thomas placed a personal ad in the local seniors paper that Joy Thompson saw only because she was throwing away someone else's trash. They fell in love, and had to laugh at a peculiar coincidence: twenty-five years earlier, her children adopted a lost puppy and, out of the blue, named it Thomas Irving.

Synchronicity can also intercede at important points in a relationship. After a concert one night, Pamela LaTulippe of Boston broke up with her boyfriend. The next day walking down the street, she ran into the stranger who had sat next to them the night before. The woman told Pam what a wonderful couple she and her boyfriend made. Pam saw that as a sign she was supposed to work it out with him—and she did.

The death of a loved one can thrust in front of us life's questions, creating openings for new understandings and making us more receptive to synchronicity. When Pina McGee's mother passed away, Pina and her siblings found a letter to them in her Bible. In the letter she had included a poem. Two days later at the memorial service, the rabbi read a poem that he said had fallen from a book in a library years before. He said it seemed to him to apply to her. It was the very poem Pina's mother had included in the letter.

Turning points occur when we have come to the end of the old and are on the cusp of a new life: we graduate, or lose our job, or buy a house, or our child leaves home. When our beliefs or values change, we may be prompted to leave a relationship or career, or stop drinking heavily, or move somewhere different. Whether we welcome the change or resist it, uncertainty is often present: What lies ahead? What can we do about it? Often in these times, synchronicity appears in dramatic ways. It moves us along, and it gives us a sense of reassurance and certainty about what we're doing. Unsatisfied with his life and job in Kansas City, Raymond G. Spinnett was meditating one evening when he saw a clear picture of himself working as a laboratory technician in California. Two days later, he quit his job, hitchhiked out west, and took a bus to El Segundo to answer a newspaper want-ad. He couldn't locate the address on the ad, and, discouraged, stopped at a sandwich shop. The waiter said, "Wait! It's a misprint! This isn't an address—it's a phone number!" Raymond was the only applicant, and was immediately hired. "The typographical error in the ad reserved my new job for me," he says. It turned out to be the same job he had envisioned a few days earlier, thousands of miles away.

Stories of rescues—someone being in the right place at the right time to save the day, and maybe a life—fill our daily newspapers and television reports. The rescuer and the person rescued were on paths that converged at exactly the right time, and often at least one was in that spot for the first time.

Karen and Bruce Pane were driving to work through Brooklyn when they saw an apartment building in flames. Holding Karen's coat taut between them, they caught six-month-old Amanda Morales as her mother threw her from a fourth-floor window. They had never been on that street before, and were there only because they were circumventing a traffic jam.

Another time when synchronicity abounds is when we're on the road, away from home. Amid new surroundings, eating new food, talking to new people, we may find ourselves looking for clues in ways that we generally don't in our familiar workaday world. It seems to happen particularly with travel that involves risk: if our plans are open-ended rather than set in stone, if we're traveling alone rather than with a tour group, if we're submerging ourselves in a foreign culture rather than skipping over its surface, then we're more likely to have meaningful coincidences. Suzanne M. Rodriguez was traveling through India, and she was deliriously happy. On a small train chugging up a mountain gorge, she threw out her arms in a burst of ecstasy and cried, "India!" At that precise moment, the train passed a rock on which was painted in foot-high letters, "SMR, I love you."

MUNDANE CIRCUMSTANCES

When we're open, responsive, and attentive to both the world around and the world within, we set up an environment that welcomes synchronicity. Then we may find synchronicity occurring every day, in the most ordinary of places: on the telephone, at the office, at the grocery store or shopping mall, in the library, at school, in the car.

Renee Schwartz of Dundee, Illinois, drove twenty miles to a new shopping mall, and searched its enormous parking lot until at last she found a parking spot—which turned out to be right next to her mother's car. One night, Renee was sitting on the sofa talking with her twelve-year-old—named

Destiny because she was conceived when condoms broke three nights in a row. When Renee got up, Destiny asked, "Where are you going?" "Kansas!" joked Renee. Twenty minutes later, Renee asked her daughter where she'd like to live if they ever moved. Destiny got a piece of paper and drew two circles, one for Illinois and one for Texas, where they had traveled. She made an X halfway between and said, "Here, two states up from Texas." They opened an atlas to see where that was, and the X fell on Kansas City. The next day, Renee learned that the company she worked for would likely be moved—to Kansas City.

The more aware we are of our surroundings, the more likely it is that synchronicity will occur—and the surroundings can include such things as overheard conversations, articles in the newspaper, billboards, and songs on the radio. Steven Cooper of LaGrange Park, Illinois, was on his way to a country club to drop off cassette tapes he had duplicated for a cellist who was playing there. Driving down the highway, he crossed train tracks and didn't know which way to turn—until, at that moment, on the radio came an advertisement for the country club, and the announcer said, "Turn right at the train tracks."

DETECTING THE PATTERNS

Whether in special or mundane circumstances, synchronicity presents itself in many ways. It can be as dramatic as a firecracker or as subtle as the passing of a breeze across your cheek. You can understand in a flash what it means or its significance may engulf you months or years later. It can change your life forever or it can glance off you, leaving barely a trace of memory.

To understand how synchronicity manifests itself, we'll look at the three patterns in which it appears in our lives: single synchronicities; strings of synchronicities that drive home a point; and meaning-packed, multilayered synchronicity clusters.

SINGLE SYNCHRONICITIES

This is the simplest, most direct way in which synchronicity happens. The single synchronity has a beginning, a middle, and an end. It stands out in clear relief from the rest of our everyday lives.

For example, you are walking down the street, and you cross paths with a friend you haven't seen for many years. You do a double-take, stop, talk, say good-bye, and walk on.

What would make this encounter a synchronicity? Let's look again at the definition of synchronicity: the coinciding of inner and outer events in a way that can't be explained by cause and effect and is meaningful to the observer. Assume that there's no causal connection: you did nothing to arrange the meeting with your friend and had no idea he was even in town. Perhaps you were thinking of him just the day before, for the first time in years: Your thoughts would be the inner event, the meeting the outer event, and the meaning might be in the wonder you feel at how things are connected. Or perhaps he fills a need for you: you've been thinking of buying a computer, and it turns out he's just bought one himself and has some good tips for you. Your thoughts about your pending purchase are the inner event, the meeting and his advice comprise the outer event, and the meaning might be that now is the time to take the plunge into cyberspace. Or perhaps you've been trying to experience flow at deeper levels: your aspirations are the inner event, the meeting the outer event, and the meaning to you is that you're on the right track.

What, then, would make it *not* a synchronicity? According to our definition, meaningfulness makes the difference. Your meeting with your friend would be "just a coincidence" if it had no meaning whatsoever for you: you saw nothing special in bumping into him and made nothing of it. The unlikely encounter wouldn't lead you anywhere—not to inward searching, not to a nearby computer store, not to the power of flow.

Single synchronicities happen often in things like telephone calls, chance encounters, and lucky numbers. Bruce Kohler remembers how twenty years ago he had a sudden urge to call his father in Florida, whom he hadn't spoken to in several weeks. When he picked up the phone, before he touched the dial, he was flabbergasted to hear his father's voice on the other end—trying to reach him.

Information you need might come your way through some surprising route at the moment you need it. Dame Rebecca West told philosopher Arthur Koestler how she had been researching a specific episode of the Nuremberg war crimes trials: "I looked up the trials in the library and was horrified to find they are published in a form almost useless to the researcher. They are abstracts, and are cataloged under arbitrary headings. After hours of search I went among the line of shelves to an assistant librarian and said, 'I can't find it, there's no clue, it may be in any of these volumes.' I put my hand on one volume and took it out and carelessly looked at it, and it was not only the right volume, but I had opened it at the right page." Koestler writes that coincidences of what he calls the "library angel" are "so frequent that one almost regards them as one's due."

Just because a single synchronicity is simple in pattern doesn't mean it can't have a great impact. Looking back, you might find that a turning point in your life, such as meeting your significant other, was a single synchronicity.

STRINGS OF SYNCHRONICITIES

Synchronicities can happen one after the other, as though a point is being made over and over again. Perhaps the friend you bump into on the street was a high school classmate you once had a strong, unrequited crush on. Later that day, you hear on the radio a song that puts you right back into your high school days and the hopeless romantic longings you had back then. And two days later, you open the newspaper and read a story about a budding film star who originally had the same name as the friend you bumped into.

That would be a string of synchronicities. Depending on what you are going through in life at the time, it could have all kinds of meaning. Perhaps it brings your romantic ideals into focus, clarifying what you want from your current relationship. It might bring about a realization of how you've always put your friend on a pedestal and you decide to go visit the friend so you can develop a more realistic relationship. Or you might be pleased to realize that the type of rejection that caused you pain back then no longer does, and to you this is proof that you've grown stronger over the years.

Notice that it's the sequence of occurrences that make this a string of synchronicities. Meeting your friend on the street after so many years might be considered a coincidence by anyone's reckoning; hearing an old song on the radio or reading a name in a newspaper might not. But because the events occur one after the other, they resonate in your consciousness and have specific meaning to you in their totality.

Another way in which strings of synchronicities appear is in repeating numbers or words. A certain number may start to emerge as a signal of something important in your life. You may never have heard a word or phrase before, and then you'll hear it several times, in different forms and contexts. Sometimes the connection of the phrase to your life is clear and direct; sometimes it's a puzzle. Pam Makie went to an evening meditation class in New York City and found herself moved by a quote of Nelson Mandela: "Our deepest fear is not that we are inadequate. Our deepest fear is that we are powerful beyond measure. It is our light, not our darkness, that most frightens us." The next day, a successful psychologist who is a client of hers confided, "I'm having a really hard time. Everything is going really great—and my deepest fear is that of my own light." Two days later, another friend said to her, "Did you ever read that book, *The Unbearable Lightness of Being*? You've got to have courage. You've got to stop being afraid of your own light." Says Pam, "I got the message!"

You might find that your life repeatedly intersects or parallels that of another person. Judy Swierczek was visiting a friend in New York City when she saw "Marie Suzanne Rogers" on the apartment lobby mailbox. Since she knew someone by that name from grade school, she knocked on the door and introduced herself. She was the same Marie, and they discovered that they had lived a block away from each other in Boston at the same time and had worked for the same travel company there, but at different times. They had both moved back to New York at the same time and worked for the same video development company, but at different times. Marie now lives in Hawaii, where Judy once lived, and of course works for the same company—but at a different time.

CLUSTERS OF SYNCHRONICITIES

A cluster is like a string in that it involves a series of linked synchronicities, but its pattern is richer and more complex: It involves many different types of synchronicity with multiple levels of meaning that coalesce over time around a particular theme. Out of a cluster you may draw not just a single message or a specific direction but a broader and deeper understanding of some basic dynamic in your life.

Let's go back to that street you were walking down. You're amazed to see the old friend you haven't talked to since high school, and the coincidence is even more amazing because he's in town for only two days, and for the first time in years. He invites you to join him and some friends for dinner that night. You just happen to be free because a few minutes earlier, the meeting you were supposed to attend was canceled. Struck by the timing, you say yes. You don't mind being away from home for the evening because you'd had words with your spouse the night before: You had seen *Apocalypse Now* together, and you got into another heated argument over politics.

At dinner that night, it turns out that your friend's two friends are Vietnam veterans. Here, you think, is a chance to get some information you can bring back home to enlighten your spouse. You bring up the movie and find out the two disagree about it and everything else about the war. As they launch into a discussion of their differences, you realize they're exactly mirroring your fight from the night before. One of them says a phrase over and over that really hits you: "Let's get to the heart of the matter." You try to figure out why you feel tense, and then you recall that your father used to say those exact words to your mother when they were fighting. In fact, you notice that the man's name, Don, is the same as your father's. It brings back to you how much you used to hate to hear your parents arguing—and you start to wonder how much of your parents' dynamic is affecting your current relationship.

But as the two talk, you see something remarkable happening: they come to common ground, a realization of how they're bonded by the impact of their war experiences. On the way home, the radio plays, "Give Peace a Chance," a song you haven't heard in years; for the first time, you don't think of it politically but as a song about relationships, especially your own. It makes you thoughtful, and when you arrive home, you're no longer angry.

Let's look at the synchronicities here: the significant encounter, the timely cancellation, the mirroring argument, the repeated phrase, the key song. These could all appear singly or in a string, but when they appear in a cluster, they can be particularly revealing.

The overall theme that emerges is conflict. Jungians might say that your fight of the night before aroused in your psyche a need for a deeper understanding of the issue, and that this created a kind of psychic energy that drew to you the synchronicities. You can derive many meanings from the cluster, including that you need to handle conflict better in your life.

The more deeply you understand synchronicity, the more you'll be able to see the myriad ways that the Universe talks to you. Full comprehension of the language of synchronicity prepares you to recognize it in all its manifestations. In the next chapter, you'll see how to use this knowledge to actively access flow.

YOUR SYNCHRONICITY SCORE

Count the number of items you checked and find your rating below:

0 to 4   You are a *flowsnoozer*, not yet awake to the magic in your life.

5 to 8   You are a *flowbrowser*, starting to notice that something interesting is going on.

9 to 12 You are a *flowseeker*, following the signs and paying attention.

All 13   You are a *flowmaster*. You are ready to share with others your way of living.

3 USE SYNCHRONICITY TO ACCESS FLOW

Synchronicity is a powerful entry point to flow. By paying attention to it, we can make the exhilaration of flow the rule rather than the exception in our lives. Synchronicity has this propulsion ability because it has two simultaneous effects: It pushes us toward individualization and full expression of our uniqueness, and it connects us with a larger whole. When we know ourselves at deeper levels, we're able to go beyond ourselves to connect meaningfully with others and with the Universe. And when we're connected with the Universe, we are in flow.

Synchronicity pushes us toward individualization by speaking to us in ways we uniquely understand, with layers of meaning and resonance that apply to our own lives and no one else's. By validating our uniqueness in this way, synchronicity leads us to further self-awareness, self-acceptance, and self-expression. Earl Davis was trying to track down an out-of-print book called *The Adventures of Marco Polo*. He scoured two used book stores in New York City without success and caught a taxi to a third. The cabbie was unusually chatty, and Earl glanced at his ID placard. His name? Marco Polo! Earl, too, is an explorer—of the dynamics of synchronicity.

Synchronicity connects us with the Universe by being so far outside our conscious control that when it happens, we feel touched by forces we only dimly understand. We feel humbled. Life assumes fuller and richer dimensions, and it seems possible there is an order, a purpose, behind everything we perceive. Synchronicity works this way because we perceive the meaning in a "coincidence." Meaning doesn't just happen—it is a matter of personal choice and action. When we choose to see meaning in the coinciding of events, we open the door wide for synchronicity—and thus for the power of flow.

Meaning is important because it is part of our essential nature as human beings: psychologists describe the search for meaning as one of our basic drives. Numerous studies bear this out: people who see their lives as meaningful are happy, productive, and fulfilled. William Pearce, a contemporary communication theorist who has studied meaning as a process, says that when something happens, we evaluate it by examining external factors: the event itself, the parties involved, the circumstances it happened under, the place it occurred in, the conditions under which it occurred, what society thinks of it. Then we position it within our own life—past, present, and future. Finally, we interpret its significance for ourselves—we find its meaning.

With synchronicity, evaluating the external factors involves looking at the event in terms of the unusual coming together of things at a certain moment in time; positioning it relates it to our internal process. What this means is that synchronicity is in the eye of the beholder. Ann Medlock's special number, 111, appeared on the bank clock as she drove in to sign her divorce papers. The hour she was born was 1:11, and the papers signaled the beginning of a new life for herself—so seeing the numbers gave her the feeling she was getting confirmation from the Universe that she was doing the right thing. But for another person, even another person driving in to sign divorce papers, 1:11 would have meant merely 11 minutes after 1 o'clock.

Synchronicity creates a powerful dynamic of meaning in life, because it gives heft to what we once might have overlooked. We choose to explore, rather than to overlook. To explore the meaning of a specific synchronicity, three steps are required:

✦ Notice the unlikely coming together of inner and outer events.

✦ Position its importance.

✦ Interpret it in terms of your life.

Think of the process you ordinarily go through when a synchronicity happens—say, bumping into an old high school friend on the street. First you see him coming toward you. It takes your mind a second to click into the fact that it's him, and you're struck by the unlikeliness of the encounter: That's noticing the event.

As you greet each other warmly, you are alert to the ways in which this encounter is linked to other processes of your life, and that gives the event and his words more significance to you. That's positioning its importance in your mind.

As you speak to him, you are seeking its meaning, which might involve looking for lessons, linking it up mentally with other recent events, or applying it to your life either directly or metaphorically. That makes it a synchronicity. Let's walk through those steps, one by one.

NOTICE THE UNUSUAL EVENT

Synchronicity helps you understand yourself more deeply. Circularly, the more deeply you understand yourself and how you function mentally, emotionally, and physically, the more likely you are to see the synchronicity in your life. Recall the definition: synchronicity is the coming together of inner and outer events in a way that's meaningful. This means you have to be aware of your inner events: your thoughts, your feelings, your hopes, your fears, your potential. Understanding these gives you greater clarity and frees up your mind and emotions so that you can perceive better what is happening in your environment.

You're also more or less likely to notice synchronicity depending on the state of mind you're in at the time it occurs. If you're feeling distracted or downhearted or harried, you may not see your friend on the street; or if you do, you may not be available to a synchronistic encounter. For example, if you just had a fight with your spouse, you could be so absorbed in your angry thoughts that you could walk right past your old high school friend and not see him. If you're running late to an important meeting, you might see him and stop for a brief second, but have neither the time to let the interaction play out nor the space to appreciate its implications.

Noticing a coincidence is something you get better at over time. You can't miss the dramatic ones, but it may take days or weeks to realize that a subtler coincidence has occurred, and to move it in your mind from an unusual event to a synchronicity. As you become more skillful, you'll grasp synchronicity as it is actually happening, which will make it even more useful to you by allowing you to actively participate in its unfolding.

POSITION ITS IMPORTANCE

You establish the importance of an event by positioning it, which involves separating it from the stream of events that run through your everyday life and identifying its potential impact. This can involve a realization of the odds against it occurring. The more unlikely an event seems, the more importance it assumes. What is it that makes this occurrence so unique? What makes it stand out as a synchronicity? Again, both external and internal factors play a role here.

External factors are the objective odds determined by the context of an event, much as a statistician might see them. How likely is it that this event would happen? Has it ever happened before? If you live in the same town as the hypothetical high school friend you encounter on the street, and it's not that large a town, and both of you frequently walk down that street, running into her may not seem like that big a deal. However, if you live in New York and she lives in Montana and you run into each other on a back street in Bangkok, that would certainly grab your attention—and a statistician's.

Intersecting with this are the internal dynamics of the situation. What's going on inside you at the time? What's happening in your life? What associations come up from your past experiences, your present circumstances, and your thoughts of the future? An otherwise ordinary event can have deep resonance when it coincides with a physical, mental, or emotional process you're going through—and statistically speaking, that can also increase the odds against the synchronicity occurring. For example, even if you live in the same town as that old friend, unexpectedly running into her might be synchronistic if you're on the way to the emergency room with your choking daughter and she's a doctor, or if you're compiling a list for your high school reunion and you had just been fumbling around for her address.

INTERPRET THE SYNCHRONICITY

Within every synchronicity is a potentially valuable message or information for you. That is its gift, and you have only to reach out your hand and take it.

In practice, this involves spending the time and energy

to interpret what a coincidence means to you. How might it affect your next decision? Your understanding of yourself? Your relationships? Your life?

Interpret describes this process, because although synchronicity can speak in direct ways—for instance, when you bump into the person you later marry or who introduces you to a future employer—it also speaks in the language of metaphors and symbols, in pictures and actions that represent something else. It's your mind that interprets the meaning. In *The Waking Dream: Unlocking the Symbolic Language of Our Lives,* author Ray Grasse describes walking down a desert road with a Native American medicine man and talking about his fears that a project he was involved in was taking a different direction than intended. At that exact moment, he writes, "A bird conspicuously darted in front of us letting out a sharp cry, only to change direction abruptly and make a sharp right turn. Noting this event, my companion cheerfully remarked, 'See! There you are! Like you thought, things are going to turn out quite differently than you had originally planned.' "

Becoming familiar with synchronicity is similar to learning a foreign language. Some words have a direct translation in your native language. Other times, a word has several totally different translations, much as the word *bear* can mean either "carry" or "a clumsy, heavy mammal with shaggy hair." If you're reading a foreign newspaper and you come across a word you don't know, you consult a dictionary and try out the different definitions to see which one works best in that context. With synchronicity, the meaning is sometimes immediately and dramatically clear. But other times, it involves mulling over possibilities until one strikes you as likely, much as you might look for the meaning in a dream.

It works better to mull than to investigate. Metaphors arise and are interpreted by the part of your mind that perceives the relationship and interconnectedness of things. It's a creative process, and it works best when it's not forced.

When interpreting a synchronicity, it's best to relax into it, to play with it, to hold it lightly. What is your gut feeling about what it means? What immediately pops to your mind? As you play around with it, what associations come up from your past, your present circumstances, and your thoughts of the future?

One important point: The nature of synchronicity is that it is tantalizing, always unfolding, multilayered in its implications. At the time a synchronicity happens, you may know exactly what it says to you, or it may not be obvious for hours, days, or weeks—even years. Some aspects of a string or cluster may be immediately clear, and others not. Or you may have one interpretation at the time, and another one becomes apparent later. Exploring that richness is part of engaging in flow.

HOW SYNCHRONICITY MARKS FLOW

Like beeps from a feedback machine when we are doing something right, synchronicity lets us know we are functioning in flow. When there is synchronicity in our lives, we are on track. As synchronicity tantalizes us into flow, it happens more and more often, which in turn increases flow even more. Each builds on the other until our progress toward greater wholeness and harmony becomes almost automatic and our life is transformed. By paying attention to and interpreting the synchronicities that happen in our life, we consciously engage ourselves in this process.

Synchronicity is not the only path to flow. As you read on, you'll see that many spiritual and psychological paths can take you into its power. But no matter what your approach, synchronicity marks your progress and moves you deeper into harmony and wholeness.

Remember our discussion about the characteristics of flow in the first chapter? Often it is synchronicity that provides the perfect timing, the melting away of obstacles, the meshing together of events. Let's look at how this works in practice by reviewing the characteristics of flow and seeing the ways that synchronicity plays into them.

◆ *Flow is at work when things fall into place, obstacles melt away, our timing is perfect, and whatever is necessary—money, work, people, opportunities—appears as needed.* Synchronicity is often the means by which our way is eased. When we make a to-do list, people on it start phoning us. When we need the name of a good doctor, the very next day we overhear a coworker lauding theirs. When we need an appointment right away, one will be available because a cancellation was just phoned in. When we have a lot of work to do, the phone stops ringing; when we finish a project, it starts up again. Think of recent weeks in your life. Did someone give you a call just when you needed to talk to them, or vice versa? Did you find exactly what you wanted in a totally unlikely way? Did a book or article that was useful to you come into your hands serendipitously? If so, then this is the power of flow.

Synchronicity can mark flow for you in the most ordinary way. Cate Loveland had just moved to Washington, D.C., and didn't have enough money to buy bigger pots for her plants. One morning she walked out of her apartment to find a whole stack of pots awaiting the garbage pickup. Another time, she had a fierce hunger for a pecan pie. She was living with an elderly woman whose gentleman friend visited her each Wednesday afternoon. He usually brought her ice cream for dessert, but that week he brought her—of course—pecan pie. Pat Vine of Cresskill, New Jersey, roomed next to her friend Kathy at a week-long retreat. While unpacking, Kathy found she lacked an extension cord for her fan—but Pat had brought an extra one. Pat lacked earphones for her tape player—but Kathy had brought an extra set.

Sometimes a string of synchronicities can solve several problems at once. Carey and Barbara Lubow bought a cabin on twenty breathtaking acres of woods and meadows in upstate New York for a mere $20,000—the result of walking into a real estate office the day the cabin happened to go on the market. With the property came a wreck, a 1954 Mercury that was stuck in the woods. Prying open the trunk, Carey found the tools and tar paper he needed to redo the cabin roof. A month later, a neighbor agreed to mow their overgrown meadow, but his tractor broke down halfway through the job. A repairman arrived—a man who collected old cars. He spied the Mercury and asked Carey if he wanted to sell it. "You fix the tractor for free and I'll give you the car," said Carey. Everyone started smiling.

Sometimes a good laugh makes the way easier. Synchronicity has a whimsical side and it can come as a lark, as a wink from the cosmos. Art Patterson of Winnipeg, Canada, was sitting at his computer composing an E-mail message when his cat Coal jumped from his lap onto the keyboard. Before Art's startled eyes, as Coal shifted from key to key, his paws tapped out the word *emerson* on the screen. "To make it even stranger, I've been studying Ralph Waldo Emerson intently for the past year," he says. "My wife was sitting next to me at the computer. She's a witness, and if I'm sent away for being crazy, she has to go, too!" Emerson, an American Transcendentalist, wrote about the essential unity of all things.

When synchronicities happen and we're feeling grumpy or depressed, the underlying message may be to take ourselves less seriously, and the effect can put our irritations of the moment into a larger perspective. Gary

Smith of Atlanta was driving home late one night in complete anguish. His fiancée, Anne Larkin, had just broken up with him and he didn't know what to do. "Give me a sign, God, give me a sign," he begged. At the next cross street, he looked up at the signpost—it was Larkin Street. No, he groaned, not that kind of sign! But he drove on with a lighter feeling.

+ *Flow is our being in the right place at the right time doing the right thing with our lives.* When we're doing what we're supposed to be doing in life, synchronicity can help by fulfilling the needs we have along the way: by expediting our actions, putting information into our hands, allowing connections to be made. This may be obvious to others, who might comment that they've seldom seen the bureaucracy move so quickly or meeting arrangements come together so easily. Or it may not look that different to outsiders, but on the inside we feel confirmed that we're on the right track and therefore take any obstacles with equanimity and calmness, expecting them to clear up—and they usually do.

Conversely, obstacles may synchronistically arise to block our way when we're headed toward a goal. Time and events show us why. Donna Shallenberg of Chicago, broke her ankle jumping on a mini-trampoline and then got sick on an overseas trip that was supposed to be the kickoff for a new corporate division she was going to manage. Because she wasn't prone to accidents or illness, she took both as a sign that it was urgent she leave the business world and move on, even though she wasn't sure what the next step was. Her decision was confirmed when, after she put it on the market, her apartment was sublet within minutes by a couple who happened to be walking by. They needed it for exactly the eight months remaining on the lease. Today, after more synchronicities that included meeting her husband

and getting financial aid for graduate school, Donna is much happier as a pastoral counselor.

Signals such as Donna received may point us in a certain direction, but not always the direction we expect. In fact, they might run counter to the assumptions we've lived by in the past. If we've always sacrificed for others, we might find that synchronicity is urging us down a path that is more self-directed. If we've been absorbed in our own daily needs, we might find it pointing us down a path in which others come first. But what seems to be consistent is that synchronicity supports flow in moving us toward balance and wholeness. When we take a step toward what excites and energizes us, synchronicity often swings into a supporting role. Kathleen Young knew exactly what would make her happy with herself—a church "family," starting to sing again, and losing weight. But she was too low on energy to do anything about it. One Sunday morning, she woke up early and decided impulsively to go to a church whose services she had listened to on the radio the week before. Everything the pastor said hit home for Kathleen. She signed up after the service for church membership. Thumbing through the bulletin, she saw a notice seeking new members for the choir. Chatting with a church member, Kathleen learned that a new weight-loss group was just starting up, and the first meeting was in three hours.

Sometimes synchronicity points us down certain roads not because it's our final destination, but because it's part of the process we need to go through to get there. We can't always get from here to there in one step; we need to be shaped by the experiences along the way. Kathleen ended up belonging to that church for only six months, but her participation in the choir and the weight-loss group gave her the confidence to travel and seek a job promotion—and led her deeper into flow.

Another way that synchronicity keeps us on track is by setting us straight—fast! A lie will boomerang and hit us in the face. A bout of self-pity will be turned upside down. A round of righteousness will receive a symbolic rebuke. And the more we bring integrity into our actions, whether it's keeping our promises or picking up our litter, the more quickly we'll seem to get slapped on the wrist when we lack it—which is flow supporting our higher intentions. During World War II, Anton Oswald was temporarily stationed at a Navy base in Connecticut, which allowed him weekend trips to his home in Passaic, New Jersey. One weekend, he told his girlfriend he didn't have liberty and couldn't leave the base. But he had lied. That Sunday afternoon, as he turned the corner of 42nd Street and Times Square with his Bronx date on his arm, he ran right into his girlfriend from New Jersey. "Needless to say, I never saw her again," he says sadly.

✦ *Flow is experienced when life unfolds in a dynamic process.* Our lives, as part and parcel of a greater whole, have a direction and pacing to them—a deliberate unfolding. Comprehending this dynamic process is often easiest when we stand back and look from a distance. Then we can see how flow, through synchronicity after synchronicity, led us down certain paths to our calling. Peter Nicholson, an artist, spent hours one summer atop an ocean cliff mentally constructing a shimmering domed home of the future. Then the dismaying thought occurred to him that it held no place for artworks. "I heard some words inside my head—'Holography, young man!' " He knew nothing about the field, but the first stranger he bumped into upon returning to New York was a holographic scientist who ended up teaching Peter about the field. Years later, Peter, now an inventor associated with the Smithsonian, was traveling the country trying to link artists with giant corporate laboratories experimenting with holography. He overheard a Los Angeles scientist talking about "a key man leaving the world's biggest holographic effort at McDonnell-Douglas." The next day, Peter got a sudden urge to go immediately to McDonnell-Douglas. He raced to the airport and arrived at the company in time to learn from his sole contact there that the entire holography unit was being shut down, that this was everyone's last day, and that tens of millions of dollars of equipment was to be auctioned off. In a series of hurried calls, Peter was able to have the massive equipment donated to the Smithsonian—for his use. Today, he's the inventor of cutting-edge laser technology that can detect minute cracks in airplane wings.

Synchronicity puts us in touch with patterns of a larger unfolding by giving us information on how our actions of the present are related to the past and the future. It can happen in such a way that we get a sudden sense of what physicists mean when they say that time doesn't exist as we conceptualize it, with events occurring end to end; that in fact, the past and present and future are all happening simultaneously. In his book *Everyday Miracles,* David Spangler writes of how, driving down the highway after a difficult day, he uncharacteristically began gleefully imagining breaking plate glass with a hammer—and a second later a flying rock shattered his windshield. He considered the synchronicity of the rock to be a forceful manifestation of his inner thought, until a friend suggested that maybe his thoughts were a precognition of the rock breaking the glass. "What really is cause and effect in all this?" he ponders.

Sometimes synchronicity forecasts the future, if we decode it properly. Earl and Suzanne Davis were playing poker with Suzanne's father when Earl was dealt four aces. They were stunned by the odds. They shuffled the cards and dealt a new hand: Earl got four aces again. He turned to Suzanne and said with complete conviction, "Well, either I'm going to die or you're pregnant." Three days later, she took a pregnancy test—and it was positive.

When we're in the midst of trials, synchronicity gives us confidence that in a deeper sense everything is okay; our troubles are part of the unfolding of a larger plan. Twenty-year-old Janie, traumatized by a date rape and consequent pregnancy, was sitting in a clinic in anguish, waiting for an abortion that went against everything she believed in. Suddenly, the thought of her eleven-year-old niece came into her head. "An overpowering feeling came over me that all this would have meaning for her and benefit her later on. The thought gave me strength and I felt much more peaceful about what I had to do." Eight years later, her niece called, crying hysterically, and Janie knew immediately what was wrong. Her niece was pregnant. From the experience of her past trials, Janie was able to help her through her trauma. Says Janie, "It was the most profound synchronistic event of my life. It proved to me that all events in life are intricately connected."

✦ *Flow is evident when events and actions mesh together in a coherent pattern of deep harmony and underlying order.* In the course of flow, synchronicity often supplies the visible, ongoing evidence of how interwoven the fabric of life is. The elements in a meaningful coincidence can be as disparate as, in the case of New York writer Rebecca Kalin, handwriting from the past and an animal. Rebecca was researching the life of a mysterious woman, a famous writer's lover who had died tragically at a young age. Driving to Boston to view the writer's archives, Rebecca on a whim stopped off at the sprawling cemetery in the woman's hometown. She had no idea where to begin amid the hundreds of acres, so she drove a bit down the road and parked her car by some hedges. There, on the other side, was the woman's gravestone. On it was perched a rabbit, its pink nose quivering. At the sight of Rebecca, it started skittering around in circles. In Boston a few hours later, Rebecca was reading through the writer's diaries when, in the margin of a page, she came upon a few lines of curlicued schoolgirlish handwriting, which she recognized as the young woman's. The words? "Thank God for the rabbits and their funny little habits."

Synchronicity can show this underlying order in ways that are particularly helpful when we're facing an emotional or physical crisis. When Sarah L.'s mother died suddenly, Sarah's heavy drinking worsened. Soon afterward, every time she flipped through a magazine, it opened to an article about alcoholism. Every time she turned on the TV, there seemed to be a program on sobering up. The kicker came when she was in New York visiting her sister. They were in Rockefeller Center sightseeing when a woman swathed in mink approached them and offered them her two extra tickets to the Phil Donahue show, which was starting in five minutes. Out on the stage came Suzanne Somers and her family: the show was on how Somers's father, two brothers, and sister had recovered from alcoholism. A week later, Sarah entered a detox program, and she's been sober ever since.

♦ *The power of flow is manifested when outside events link up with our inner thoughts and feelings, giving us a sense of oneness with the Universe.* When we're seeking answers, synchronicity can move us into flow by feeding us information we need, sometimes from nature itself. Mary Ann Winslow was walking the streets of

London one morning, agonizing over what to do about her tortured relationship with her abusive boyfriend. A dead bird suddenly dropped out of the sky and landed with a plop at her feet. It was the perfect analogy for the way she felt, and she left her boyfriend immediately.

Sometimes the answers we get are more subtle metaphors and need decoding. In her book *The Tao of Psychology,* Jean Shinoda Bolen writes about being at a dinner party with friends when one woman raised a question. When she closed her eyes, frightening demonic images would occasionally appear. Should she confront them? Examine them? Immediately turn her attention elsewhere? As they discussed the matter, a skunk started scratching at a sliding glass door in front of them, trying to get inside. The hosts had never seen a skunk in the area, and after discussing how odd it was to see one trying to approach people, they joked about how unlikely it was that anyone would open a door for one. It was only later that Jean and her husband realized that the skunk provided a synchronistic answer to the question: Just as a skunk would stink up a living space, demonic images would do the same to one's inner space.

Sometimes the major message a synchronicity has for us is that we are not alone, that we are an important part of a larger, caring whole. When things come together almost magically in a way that meets our needs, we feel singled out and blessed, tapped on the shoulder, acknowledged. Depending on our beliefs, we can then interpret that connection in all kinds of ways. We might see synchronicity as God or a Higher Power speaking to us, as grace or miracles or answers to prayers. "Synchronicity is God wishing to remain anonymous," one saying puts it. Or we might believe that we are being helped by beings in other realms: angels, saints, enlightened beings, departed loved ones. When Jeanne McCarron's son called from college with a desperate plea for $100, she said yes, but didn't really have the money. She prayed to her angels, and the next morning, the clothes pole in her closet collapsed and threw an old winter coat at her feet. In a pocket was a $100 bill.

We might interpret synchronicity not in terms of connection with other beings but with other levels of consciousness beyond our usual waking state. We might see synchronicity as proof of our higher self acting for our spiritual advancement, or our unconscious directing us toward wholeness or manifesting what we need when our intention is clear. Lila Condax of Sacramento, California, experienced how this works when, after a week of looking in frustration in secondhand and used furniture stores for a chest of drawers, she began talking silently to herself and, as she puts it, "commanded the 'inner me' to get busy on this project because the 'outer me' was sick and tired of not getting results." Within an hour, unlocking her door, she overheard a conversation between neighbors about furniture for sale in a nearby apartment—and got exactly what she wanted at a very good price.

Or we might feel that synchronicity is a karmic reward for the positive actions of our past, especially if there's a clear correspondence between the details of the events. Sunny Schlenger's car was on its last legs, and although she didn't have $10,000 to buy a new one, she did have enough money to loan $500 to a friend who desperately needed it. Two days later, her parents told her they had unexpectedly received a coupon from Toyota—for $500—toward the purchase of a new Camry, and were going to give her their old one. Then she ran into an old friend who offered—of course—$500 for her old car.

MAKE THE POWER OF FLOW
STRONG AND STEADY

In this chapter and in chapter 2, you've seen how synchronic-ity is defined, its conditions, patterns, circumstances, and meaning, as well as how to recognize it. You've thought about it in terms of your own life, and soon now you'll be noticing an increase in the frequency and significance of syn-chronicity in your days, both in quantity and quality. As that happens, you will know that you are increasingly in flow. With the confidence and trust that flow gives, you will be more open and aware—which will again increase the syn-chronicity in your life.

Coming into deeper levels of flow, however, involves more than synchronicity. Synchronicity is a marker of flow, and it moves us into flow. But we can't create it or pursue it directly. What we can do is live life in such a way that syn-chronicity is a natural, effortless byproduct. To do that in-volves changing our attitudes, beliefs, and behaviors to welcome flow into our lives. By looking at how flowmasters have done just that, we can learn how to make flow rich and synchronicity abundant.

Flow Exercise

Keep a small notebook with you, and write in it a running ac-count of all the synchronicities and fortuitous events, both large and small, that happen to you. Review it regularly to see the underlying themes or patterns that are emerging at this point in your life.

4 THE NINE
ATTRIBUTES
THAT CREATE
THE POWER
OF FLOW

Research for this book involved, in addition to surveys and focus groups, in-depth interviews with fifty people who are committed to living life in flow. They range in age from seventeen to ninety-six, and were located through questionnaires, organizational contacts, published articles and networking. They live in big cities, small towns, suburbs, and rural areas across the country, and they work in offices, schools, stores, homes, clinics. Through their words and example they demonstrate what it means to have days rich with meaning and ease. They have learned—and are still learning—how to make flow strong and consistent, and they have much to offer about its dynamic, expanding nature.

From our discussions with them, we distilled nine attributes that you can develop in yourself to live deeply in flow on a steady, ongoing basis. They are:

- ✦ Commitment
- ✦ Honesty
- ✦ Courage

+ Passion
+ Immediacy
+ Openness
+ Receptivity
+ Positivity
+ Trust

In the following pages, you'll find each attribute described in detail, along with a portrait of a flowmaster who illustrates it in action. The fourteen techniques that follow in chapters 7 to 11 will show you how to increase these attributes in yourself so that you, too, access flow at ever-increasing levels. You'll see how along the way synchronicity lends a hand in developing these attributes.

The nine attributes are not unique. In fact, when you look at yourself, you'll find that you already possess them, some to a greater or lesser degree. As you move through this chapter, see where you stand and consider what attributes you would like to strengthen in yourself.

1. COMMITMENT

If there were only one personal attribute we need for flow, one that makes everything else possible, it would be commitment: to our own growth and expansion, to our family, to our chosen profession, to truth, and to the greater whole. With commitment, we say yes to life, and we don't just mouth the word. We take a stand for our deepest values, and we do everything it takes to live by them.

Flow involves three commitments:

+ *Commitment to self* means we are willing to risk, to expand, to be true to ourselves. With this drive pressing us forward, we reach deeper and deeper levels in flow until we know, beyond any doubt, that we are connected to everything that exists. On a daily basis, it means that we respect our bodies by eating well and exercising, our minds by staying uncluttered and positive, our emotions by paying attention to them but not being driven by them, and our spirits by daily silence, prayer, or meditation.

✦ *Commitment to others* means that we do no harm in thought, word, or deed. We see everyone we encounter as a teacher, someone from whom we can learn through sharing and synergy. Because we see everyone as connected, it's as though others are aspects of ourself, and we draw no lines between us. We are open and receptive to those we meet, with no judgments or expectations.

✦ *Commitment to the greater whole* means that our actions are guided by the understanding that there's a good purpose for everything that happens and that we have an integral part to play in the scheme of things. We dream about what might make our marriage, our city, our political party, or the world a better place, and then we plunge in to make it happen.

Commitment creates perseverance, discipline, and decisiveness. We apply steady, consistent effort to whatever is at hand, even when the outcome is uncertain. That sureness creates a fountain of inner strength; it carries us past obstacles that might deter another.

Commitment frames Carolyn North's life. It is evident in her occupation: at fifty-nine, she teaches her own style of improvisational dance six hours a day to a steady stream of students in her Berkeley, California, studio. But she didn't put on a dance shoe until she was forty-one. Before that, she had been raising three children and pursuing a career as a writer.

"I wanted to be a dancer so badly I hurt, but I didn't do it and didn't do it and didn't do it—and then I hated myself," she recalls. Finally, a friend said, "If you want to dance, dance! You don't have to be a professional dancer—take a dance class!" The idea was a revelation to Carolyn. When she tried it, she says, "That was the beginning of my real life." It took years of hard work for Carolyn to get her body supple, but the more she got into her dance, the more she experienced flow.

Carolyn's commitment to others can be seen in her marriage. Her husband, a chemistry professor, was skeptical of the notion of an underlying connectedness in all phenomena. In her book, *Synchronicity: The Anatomy of Coincidence,* Carolyn tells of the time, early in their marriage, when she requested a copy of the *I Ching,* the ancient Chinese oracle system, as a birthday gift, which he was reluctant to buy. Finally he did buy it, throwing the coins as prescribed in the book to demonstrate to himself it was irrational. But he found that the pages describing the hexagram were inexplicably blank— it was a misprinting. He returned the book, but Carolyn was given a copy by someone else. When they looked up his hexagram, it referred to the need to negotiate differences peaceably. Mystified, he threw the coins again: the hexagram said it was foolish to ask the same question twice.

"We've been together for thirty-eight years, and we've been struggling with this for thirty-eight years," says Carolyn. "I see our marriage as microcosmic. We represent extreme ends of the spectrum, and I think if we can work it out in our household, there is a chance for society. I think this is why I am in this world today—to bridge gaps, especially the gap between the mind-set that sees only physical reality and the mind-set that perceives more ephemeral aspects of reality. I believe it's a continuum and all part of the same whole; in reality, there's no separation."

Her commitment to the greater whole is evidenced in the food distribution program she organized in Berkeley in

1983 after she saw an elderly man eating a bread crust he'd salvaged from a trash container. Operating with no budget, her program organized hundreds of volunteers to deliver leftover food from restaurants, bakeries, and markets to shelters and soup kitchens. For ten years, she coordinated the work from her home. Synchronicity was its operating mode. One Christmas morning, a frantic call for food from the poorest shelter was followed only minutes later by a fortuitous call from a hospital with refrigerators full of extra meals. Carolyn says, "When I'm doing the right thing, it's almost like assistance is available. I never have to worry about funds or volunteers or legalities; everything I need appears at the door as I need it."

In another example of commitment, two years ago, she had another inspiration: to build a load-bearing rice-straw-bale house. It would deal with several problems in one fell swoop: shrinking forests, rice straw that can't be disposed of, and the need for low-cost housing. She knew it was the right thing to do because when the idea came to her, it *felt* right, and she knew from experience that when she felt that way, the Universe provides what's needed. Sure enough, as soon as she committed herself, the necessary people, information, and resources showed up, the local zoning officials came into agreement, and the house at the Shenoa Retreat and Learning Center slowly rose from the ground.

One afternoon during the building process, the stairway had to be drywalled, and neither she nor another volunteer knew how to do it. Just then, an interested tourist came by. After they showed him around, he said tentatively, "Gee, I wish I could do something to help you." "Well, we do have this drywalling to do today," said Carolyn. His eyes widened. "I'm a drywall man!" he said. "That's what I do for a living!" He accomplished in half an hour what would have taken Carolyn a day. The straw-bale house was deemed so successful that the technique is being duplicated by many people in California, including Habitat for Humanity. In

Mongolia, it was the model for a maternity hospital and workers' homes.

Think for a moment of the ways in which you, too, are committed and how you show it. Did you fix breakfast this morning for someone in your family? Did you do good work at your job? Did you eat vegetables? Did you cheer up a coworker who was down? Did you say a prayer? All of these are a way to say *yes;* all are evidence of commitment and caring for yourself, others, and the greater whole.

The more committed you are, the more you can experience flow at its deepest levels and unleash its power.

2. HONESTY

Honesty, like Janus, the Greek god of hearth and home, has two faces: one that looks outward and one that faces inward. Inwardly, as we enter more deeply into flow, we seek integration, the coming together of all of our sometimes-conflicting parts into one powerful whole. This requires a solid commitment to identify and break through layers of misconceptions, self-deceptions, emotional scars, limiting and self-sabotaging beliefs, outdated responses, internal conflicts, buried dreams, hopes, and fears—all the accumulated baggage of human existence. We are ruthlessly honest with ourselves, no matter how uncomfortable that may sometimes be. We pursue the truth because we know it will set us free from old wounds that interfere with our experience of flow. We question and probe our own inner world to see what's real, what's true, and what's not. The result of this quest for the truth is a deep self-understanding and a peace that can come only when we truly know ourselves.

In the way we express ourselves out in the world, we honor the truth we have found on the inside. Our appearance, words, and actions have an internal congruity: we are

all of one piece, and that piece is uniquely us. There's no acting, posturing, positioning, or hiding. When others look at
how we hold ourselves, how we style our hair, what clothes
we wear, the tone of voice in which we speak, it all ties together with our basic beliefs and attitudes. We are who we
are—not someone else's idea of what we should be, or even
our own idea of what we'd like to be.

Honor is our standard when we go out into the world.
Being in flow requires a steadfast adherence to our own
moral or ethical code, and this faithfulness stems from our
deep commitment to the truth. The more authentic we are,
the more energy we have, for it simplifies life. Pretending to
be who we aren't takes a tremendous amount of energy and
creates difficulties with others, because the truth within us
makes itself known. We tell a friend we'd love to have lunch
with her—but the flat tone in our voice says otherwise. We
volunteer to help out at a hospital, but something always
seems to come along that gets in the way.

But when we're authentic, people trust us. Because we
are honest, we do what we say we'll do, and people know
they can count on us. Our source of approval is within, not
without: we live up to our own expectations, not those of
other people, and our standards are higher. We appreciate
other people's approval but judge for ourselves how well we
do. Although we don't base our decisions on what others
think, we're respectful of their thoughts and opinions and listen carefully to their points of view. We do our best to treat
everyone with fairness and even-handedness.

Honesty prompted a turning point in flowmaster Ron
Chin. Raised in a middle-class, second-generation Chinese-
American family in Boston, Ron never spoke Chinese or even
knew that his father was a Buddhist. An interior designer,
Ron was living a predictable life in New York City when,
scanning a friend's bookshelf, he pulled out a slim volume on
feng shui, the traditional Chinese technique for bringing people and objects into harmony with the *chi* (energy) in their

home environment. He was intrigued by the idea that the placement of rooms and furniture could affect people's lives, and from that day on, synchronicities seemed to pull him in that professional direction. A neighbor called, asking him to decorate her new apartment; she was open to trying out feng shui. They had so much fun doing it that she voiced the words in his mind: "Maybe you should make a business out of this!"

Well, if I'm going to do it for other people, I have to do it for myself, Ron thought. First he moved his desk into the corner of his living room that symbolized wealth and power. That night he had a powerful dream and woke up knowing not only that feng shui would be his life's work, but the logo and name of his business: Space Alignment.

Two days later, a call from a stranger in Long Island resulted in a string of feng shui clients. Ron began advertising and lecturing, and his career took off. It all seemed to providentially fit together: Ron's Chinese name, his soft-spoken, owlishly wise appearance, and the ancient philosophy from the land of his ancestors.

But lies underlay parts of Ron's life, and a year later, his expanding world collapsed in on itself. In one weekend, three pivotal events happened. On Friday night, he had a car accident when the transmission cracked on the way to a speaking engagement in Connecticut. On Saturday night, his brother called Ron to announce that he and his wife had just had a beautiful baby boy. And on Sunday, his roommate told him he was moving out.

The three events held messages that hit Ron hard. The car accident symbolized that he was moving too fast with his feng shui work: the loss of his car literally stopped him in his tracks. His brother's news forced him to acknowledge a fact he could no longer deny: he was gay, and would never have that kind of traditional family life himself. And his roommate's departure meant that his perilous financial situation—he was heavily in debt—could turn catastrophic.

All this threw Ron into a deep depression—and into the personal work that began to reveal to him what he had been denying. He became relentless in his pursuit of the truth. He refused to take shortcuts or pretend: he was determined to do the work and do it properly. He joined Debtors Anonymous, went to healers, underwent therapy, had acupuncture. He started to uncover the unconscious connection in his mind between sex and money. In both his overspending and his denial of his sexual orientation, he had been avoiding responsibility and not being true to himself. In being totally honest about his sexual preference, his financial confusion cleared up. Soon after he told his mother he was gay, new work started coming his way. And only a few hours before he would have filed bankruptcy papers, he met another gay man, a businessman, who showed him a legitimate way to avoid the bankruptcy.

Today, both Ron's business and his love life are thriving. When he lectures on feng shui, the audience is held in rapt attention by the gentle authority and ease he conveys through his voice and movements. He is a living expression of the philosophy that he teaches.

Ron believes that none of it would have happened without feng shui. "Feng shui is about looking at the truth, and once you acknowledge the truth in your life, it opens all these doors. Now I expect things to flow smoothly all the time. My timing is right, I feel a lot of energy, and things happen very easily."

When we operate from honesty, we are committed to seeking, telling, and honoring the truth. That gives us a great sense of personal power. Integrity focuses our energy: we're not fragmented, not trying to pull discordant pieces together. We move into flow because that honesty and coherence aligns us with the underlying orderliness of the Universe.

3. COURAGE

Courage does not require rappelling across rocky cliffs but rather, day in and day out, overcoming our fears by stepping outside our personal comfort zone, following our intuition, and making ourselves available to the larger plan. It means we transcend our limited self-definitions to be open to new information and stretch beyond the way we've always done things in the past. It means we listen within and sometimes turn left when everyone else seems to be going right. It allows us to risk ridicule to create something new, or to risk rejection when we are being true to our sense of what's right.

Dan Muse, the city attorney of Denver, remembers a personal risk he took as a teenager that had a profound effect on his sense of self. Finishing work at 4:00 A.M. at a hamburger restaurant, he felt an urge to walk the five miles home instead of catching his usual ride—a potentially perilous journey through the heart of the inner city of Columbus, Ohio. As he walked, he pushed through his fear and felt a tremendous sense of calmness. "I knew I wasn't alone," he recalls. "I knew I was guided and I knew I was protected and that the fact it was four o'clock in the morning would not in any way impede my safety."

Today, Dan is known as someone who's not afraid to take on the toughest of challenges, such as his decision as the city attorney to file a lawsuit for cleanup costs against the forty-two largest industrial polluters in Colorado. By taking a strong stand, Dan was able to hammer out a settlement in which the companies paid 80 percent of the costs—much higher than average. Says Dan, who projects intensity and purpose while speaking softly and thoughtfully, "I'm not afraid to push the corners of the envelope, and that is the real strength and power that guides my life. I can tread where others are afraid to go, and it comes out just fine."

What gives him courage, he says, is a sense that his pur-

pose in life is "to grow. To have a more profound understanding of life's cycle. And hopefully to be involved in an effort to advance us beyond what we are now. The great
challenge for me in my work is to deal with my tendency to
be judgmental and my tendency to hold grudges. Fear is certainly a challenge, too. When I'm stuck in those places, I'm
disconnected from the power source and my life does not
move as harmoniously. I have to handle those three issues to
be all that I can be."

His inner voice guides him. It takes him into risky situations—but assures him all will be well. By trusting and acting
on that voice, Dan finds life unfolding for him in harmonious
ways. When he was going through a difficult divorce, his
inner voice instructed him to stop working for his biggest
client, who had been pressuring him to do things that ethi-
cally were "vexatious to my spirit." He stopped working for
the client. "And I struggled. There were times when I didn't
know whether I was going to be able to pay my overhead or
my rent. But every time I got to the point where I ran out of
money, somebody would come in with work for me." A year
later, a new Denver mayor was elected who asked Dan to become the city attorney. Had Dan not had the courage to stop
doing legal work for his biggest client, he wouldn't have been
able to wind up his pending court cases in time to take the
position. "Letting go of this client opened the door for me to
be in one of the most rewarding jobs of my whole life," he
says.

Dan's experience shows how courage empowers us to
take risks with confidence, to stand for what is right, and to
play full out. As we learn to trust our deeper wisdom, we find
ourselves being strengthened by the power of flow. Because in
that flow we see obstacles drop away and our way smoothed
before us, we have more faith in the process, which enables
us to risk even more the next time. This creates more flow,
which precipitates more synchronicity.

4. PASSION

Flow is engendered by passion—passion for life, for knowledge, for a cause, for a relationship, for truth. Passion means caring deeply about something beyond ourselves. It means engaging with it at intense levels. It means letting go of self-protective caution to involve ourselves wholeheartedly with what we love.

Think of what you care most about in life. That is your passion. By exploring it, probing deeply into it, we reach layers of truth about it and ourselves. Pursuing passion with dedication may take hard work, yet it also seems effortless because it is so satisfying. It is our bliss. We become one with it—and that unity, that transcendence, leads us into flow.

As flow expands in our lives, the range of what we care passionately about expands too. Our ardor for a specific object or relationship opens us up to a larger picture. When we live at high levels of flow, we have an intense desire to be active and engaged in the course of events, to participate with the world in ways that matter. And we have an intense drive to know truth, to answer the basic questions of existence: why we're here, what we're supposed to be doing, what it all means. Not satisfied with surface explanations, we use every moment as an opportunity to break through to something new, to learn. We fully engage with what comes our way.

David Fuess exemplifies this attribute. He has a passion for the truth. The first thing you notice about him are his eyes, which are startling in their clarity and lack of defenses. "I've always put myself in challenging situations because I realized early on that I was pretty much of a white, middle-class guy, and if I didn't put myself out there in unusual experiences, I was never going to learn anything about life." As a twelve-year-old on a class trip in Europe, where his family lived, he followed his teacher's instructions and sat for five minutes in the spot where St. Francis of Assisi used to

meditate. When he got up, he says, "I knew there was another reality." He's never stopped looking for those deeper
layers of truth, and his passion has carried him far. He's med-
itated in the pyramids of Egypt, climbed sacred mountains in
Tibet, sat in the presence of holy men and women in India,
been initiated into a mystical society in Bali.

Even more important, it's taken him deep within. "Soci-
etal training does not teach you to be true to yourself. So
you've got to constantly ask yourself, 'Am I being hypnotized?' We're all hypnotized to one degree or another—by
TV, by radio, by ideas, by relationships, by the routines of
our jobs. You just get comfortable and you stay where you
are. Whereas what we're here on the planet to do is to
progress. If you're not in contact with your true self, if you're
not in contact with the Divine, then you haven't fulfilled your
mission."

In his passion for truth, he has sought to remove fear
from himself no matter what it takes. The process began
when he visited Dachau as a teenager and, horrified, im-
mersed himself in reading about the Nazis. "I saw that fear
was a blocking agent in people's consciousness, and that you
had to understand fear in order to get by it." To face his
physical fears, he has white-water rafted and explored remote
nooks of the world. Mentally, he actively explores fear when
it arises instead of pushing it back down under his conscious
awareness. Emotionally, he feels his pain, such as the deep
anger and grieving he went through recently when he and his
girlfriend of five years broke up. "When I'm feeling just
awful, I surrender to that feeling."

Today, as an acupuncturist and polarity therapist in
Carmel, California, removing fear is the cornerstone of the
classes he teaches to health practitioners in the United States,
England, and Australia. "When you're fearful, your whole
body and your whole being goes into constriction on all different levels. Your solar plexus, your guts, your heart, your
throat, your face, your lungs, your back, your legs all tighten

up—and all of this blocks the flow of energy. As you come out of constriction, you increase your natural flow in relation to nature or God, or whatever word you want to use. You're more likely to make the right decision and be where you should be at the right time and the right place."

He was in that right place on a recent day driving down the highway to Los Angeles. Suddenly, he stepped on the accelerator, passed the car of the friends he was traveling with, and kept speeding down the road at eighty mph. Five minutes later, he came upon a crashed car that had flames licking out from under the hood. He and his friends screeched to a halt and saw a man walking dazed through a field, a woman slumped in the front seat, and a baby crying in the backseat. As his friends grabbed the man and the baby, David—who had trained as an emergency medical technician—struggled to free the unconscious woman. The heat was intense and she was deadweight, but he succeeded in pulling her away from the car moments before it was fully engulfed in flames "I didn't have a conscious reason for speeding up," says David. "I found out what it was about when I got there."

That's being in flow, where passion moves us with unerring accuracy to our next step.

5. IMMEDIACY

Living in flow means living fully in the present. We don't hang out in the past rehashing old issues. We don't hang out in the future trying to second-guess how things will turn out. We settle all of our attention on each interaction, whether it's washing a dish, making love, attending a meeting, or reading to a child. We are fully engaged in whatever we are doing, and time seems rich and full and resonant and still, all at once. This state of awareness is called *immediacy*.

Focusing on the past is like driving a car with a giant rearview mirror that almost totally obscures the windshield:

we can't see where we are because we're too busy looking at where we've been. Anticipating the future, we aren't thinking about what we're doing now—and then when we get to the future, we won't be there, either, because our mind has already skipped ahead to the time beyond that.

Immediacy doesn't mean that we don't plan for the future or learn from the past. But we don't dwell in those places: we just visit them upon occasion. We know that our potential for joy, for learning, for excitement, is in the moment.

Paulette and Michael Sun bring a gentle but dynamic state of relaxed intensity into their interactions. Paulette has large, serene eyes with deep smile wrinkles around them; Michael, with a compact frame and blond hair, has stillness in his body and aliveness in his eyes. They listen closely, not just to you but to each other, as though they were married last week instead of twenty years ago. Michael, a former minister, and Paulette, a sociologist, had for years run training programs in communication and personal development for businesses and churches. Now, through synchronicities involving chance conversations and encounters, they're partners in Illuminations, a chain of candle stores based in Kauai, Hawaii.

It's their ability to be in the moment that opens them to such a wide range of possibilities. The way they have learned to do that is by removing the "clutter" from their minds and emotions. Says Michael, "What works against being in the flow with life is being cluttered with concerns or worries or outcomes. If we can create more mental and emotional space—even though that sounds so jargony—then there is room for wonder." Out of that wonder comes a feeling of connection to the whole, which leads to the experience of flow and to increased synchronicity.

Removing that clutter has meant tying up the loose ends from the past. For Paulette, that meant being frank with her two grown children about the mistakes she had made raising them. "I had been looking back and was filled with regret about who I had been as a mother with them, and at some point it came to me that if I continued to focus on what I didn't do back then, I wasn't going to be with them today."

Paulette and Michael know they're not in the moment when they feel distant and start judging the person they're talking to—either negatively or positively—or when they evaluate what they're saying in terms of its impact on the other person. "When you're really being with someone, you are not even aware you exist in a sense," says Michael. "The questions you ask them actually come out of that person, so there is almost no thought involved."

Being that present, they say, requires them to be willing to make mistakes, to give up on being attached to particular results. For Paulette, being in the present also means either finishing up items on her To Do list or crossing them off, and saying everything that needs to be said. "If you walk away from a conversation and are still having a conversation in your head, but not with that person, turn back around and have the conversation. Say things that you might not ordinarily say." This, she says, allows you to move on with a clear mind.

When the Suns are in the moment, responsive to the flow of life about them, they know instinctively when and how to act. Michael was once at a men's wilderness retreat, sitting with the group around a campfire at night after a day of risky exercises. As they passed around a "talking stick" and spoke in turn, they started telling jokes that became raunchy. Everyone was trying to outdo everyone else, and the pitch got frenetic. Michael didn't judge or participate or over-react; instead, he waited for the right moment to arrive. Then he spoke up: "I think it is time now to give equal value to silence." He held the stick for ten minutes. A profound quiet came over the group—and then came an outpouring of honest sharing. Had Michael stepped in earlier, it would have been judgmental; had he stepped in later, it would have been painful. It was his sure sense of immediacy that allowed him to move when the timing was exactly right.

Immediacy engages us in flow, where we are alive and vital. And with our heightened awareness, we notice and enjoy synchronicity.

6. OPENNESS

Being ready and willing and available to a wide range of possibility makes the power of flow abundant in our daily life. When we are open, we waste little energy in warding things off; we do not erect walls between ourselves and the world. Instead, we embrace whatever develops, for we know that everything we experience has value. Events unfold naturally and effortlessly because, without preconceptions or judgments, without fear or anger, we are willing to do whatever a situation requires.

Developing this openness requires that we know ourselves well, that we understand what makes us fearful and closes us down, so that we can then move past those reactions. It requires coming from our heart with other people, having compassion for them, and accepting the fact that they, too, are doing the best they can at each moment—which allows them to feel open and free as well.

This openness comes about through an ongoing commitment to our own growth. For Staci Boden, this process started early. She was only four when her parents divorced, and the differences between them for many subsequent years bifurcated her life—until she found out how to harmonize their approaches to life within herself.

Her mother is a politically radical lesbian psychotherapist who demonstrated to Staci the importance of courage and being true to herself. In raising Staci, she provided an atmosphere of loving support that allowed Staci to see herself as capable of making tough choices and living by them.

Staci's father, a lawyer, drove flashy cars and dated beautiful women, until he became interested in spiritual matters when she was eleven. At fourteen, she went with him on a tour of holy sites in Europe. Staci had planned to go shopping while he prayed with his spiritual teacher, but instead she found herself watching everything, wide-eyed. Every place they went, things flowed smoothly and easily and magic seemed to happen. At one point, at Chalice Well in Glastonbury, England, she was with a group praying for an end to the local drought. Just as her father's teacher said, "Oh God, shower us with your blessings," Staci felt rain sprinkling her face—from a sky without a single rain cloud.

Even though she didn't agree with all her father's views, the trip gave her an expanded view of the potential of life. If prayers could summon rain, what else was possible? Back home, she wanted to do something to change the world for the better, so she organized an antinuclear group in her high school, which expanded to sixteen more schools. In college, she majored in sociology and women's studies; her commitment to feminism was further reaffirmed when a friend was raped. Staci joined a campus safety patrol, which increased her confidence in her own resilience and strength. She met Alex, and after graduation they married and moved to San Francisco, where Staci decided to go to law school to become a professional mediator—a profession that she thought would provide her with an income while allowing her to do some good.

Then came the event that abruptly changed her direction: she earned a D in a contracts course, her first D ever. She had to make a decision that would shape the rest of her life: Should she push through her intrinsic dislike of legalistic thinking and, for the sake of practicality, commit to learning law, or should she go out into the unknown? She didn't run from the decision, she faced it squarely. As she wrestled with her choices, she got a synchronistic call from a friend, who had been living in a teepee and studying Buddhism. Afterward, Staci, in tears, said to her mother, "I don't want to live in a teepee or study Buddhism, but I want to be able to make choices like that." She decided to follow her heart, and quit law school the next day. She was terrified, and at the same time felt a deep trust that she was doing the right thing. She was open to all possibilities.

Thus began the flow of synchronicities for Staci. She came across a course catalog for a master's degree program in women's spirituality. Classes had already started, but she talked to school officials, who were so moved by her story that she was admitted anyway. She found a part-time job a few blocks from her home—and the co-owner turned out to be studying in the same program. She discovered a spiritual path she loved—shamanism, that incorporated her mother's feminism and her father's spirituality while still enhancing Staci's individualism. And to her delight, she became pregnant and had a daughter.

Now flow is simply the way Staci lives life; she is open and available, and she expects to be provided synchronistically with what she needs for growth. "I'm learning to trust the Universe, to come from my heart, to move out of an either/or world into an *and* world in which there is room for everything."

As Staci's experiences demonstrate, openness engages flow, for it connects us freely and fully to others and to what is happening around and within us. From that connection comes the potential for synchronicity, which gives us further assurance that we're on the right track.

7. RECEPTIVITY

Being in flow means that we are ready to take our part in the unfolding of events. We listen to our inner voice for messages, we observe all that happens around us—especially synchronicity—and we then move in harmony with the moment.

But we don't attempt to control the outcome of those events. Instead, we hold open the space in which potentiality exists. Like a dancer poised in the still moment at the start of a movement, we can go in any direction the music suggests.

This receptivity puts us in touch with the place of silence and connection from which the power of flow springs. From that deep quiet comes a sure sense of being an integral, intimate part of the movement of larger events that we may only dimly comprehend on a conscious level. If we listen, the answers will come—and synchronicity is often the way they present themselves.

When Anne Barden was thirty-three, she knew who she was: the wife of a loving husband, the mother of four beautiful children. But she felt as though there was some someone locked up deep inside her, someone other than the pleasant, smiling facade she presented to the world. One day her husband bought her *The Art of Loving* by Eric Fromm ("I think he wanted me to be a better lover," she says, laughing). When she put down that seminal work of psychology, she had a word for what she was feeling: loneliness.

She joined a local Bible-study group so she could better lead children's classes at her church. One day, sitting on her sofa, a phrase flew off the page and hit her in the heart: "By the power of the Holy Spirit, may your hidden self grow strong." She threw herself into the Scriptures, and four months later, "I asked Jesus to come into my life."

For Anne, that was a big risk: her husband and children thought she was crazy. But to her, it felt intuitively right. Slowly, she started to come into a feeling of receiving unconditional love from Jesus, and that caused her even more conflict. She was full of loathing for herself, dating back to her days as a sad, fat child. When she had a spare moment, she would sit on the sofa and talk in her mind to Jesus. She felt guided to eat less, exercise more, and stop smoking.

As Anne's receptivity to Jesus increased, she found herself moving from a sense of herself as separate and alone to a feeling of unity with him. The peace and serenity she received when she prayed made her feel stronger, more sure of herself. What she needed to stimulate her growth came her way.

She had long been troubled with depression, and after an emotionally disastrous trip to Europe, found herself thinking, *God, if this is all there is to life, I want out of it*. Immediately afterward, she ran into a woman at the movies who asked her to work as a volunteer at a recovery center for alcoholics. That was the beginning of Anne's career as a counselor. The means of her healing came when a pastor's wife, during a prayer session, had a "word of knowledge"—a vision—of Anne as a baby being molested. Anne assumed it was her father, who drank heavily. Working with a therapist years later, she had a vivid dream: she saw herself looking down at herself as a baby being molested on a changing table—but the man wasn't her father. Then Anne's sister called. She had had a similar dream three days before in which she, too, saw herself abused by a man—the same man. During a church healing ceremony later, Anne felt the depression lift from her.

Receptivity to a higher power developed in Anne a new strength. She resigned from a position as the first woman on the pastoral staff of her church when she realized the appointment was only for appearance. She has learned to say no to a demanding relative, to a verbally abusive boss.

Today, Anne projects vitality: her eyes crinkle with humor and confidence. Anne feels guided by Jesus, and listens to her inner voice, which provides messages from him that are always borne out by events. She feels that Jesus watches over her and guides her—even rebukes her when she needs it.

Receptivity moves us deeper into flow, for when we willingly give ourselves to life, God, the Universe, the planet, or even an ideal, we discover we are not alone. Our sense of awe, wonder, reverence, and peace is a constant reminder that we are protected and connected, and we do whatever we can to serve the Greatness that fills our days.

8. POSITIVITY

In positivity, we seek out the value in every situation, at every turn, emphasize it, and work actively with it. That's not to say that we are Pollyannas or blind to the negative potential of a situation; through experience, we've learned that in the positive side lies the potential for movement. We believe everything happens for a reason, and that perfection is found in each moment. As a result, we don't shrink from difficult people or situations or challenges—we move toward them.

Being positive means that in analyzing a problem, we are not fault-finders but fact-finders. We don't waste time complaining or criticizing or resenting when things get rough: we either improve a bad situation, stay with it for the valuable lessons we're learning, or leave it. Rather than finding fault in those people around us, we find how to understand and learn from those we meet.

Marilyn Laverty epitomizes this frame of mind. An accountant by training, she's a coordinator of training and development at the University of Colorado in Boulder. Working with different departments, she helps people communicate better and see the value of one another's unique contributions and skills. "I have a service mentality—it's 'What can I do for you? How can I help you and support you?' "

Things happen easily around Marilyn. Instead of having to call three people to arrange a short meeting on a topic, she runs into them all at once, and they decide the matter right then. When she needs to talk to someone, they're likely to call her first. She says of the synchronicity in her life, "It's like Ping-Pong balls. You've got to keep serving them, and they come back at you. If you put yourself in the middle, some balls will come toward you, they just will. And part of serving the balls is knowing who you are and what you're about." For her, that has meant undertaking therapy, participating in personal growth seminars, and reading exhaustively on psychology and metaphysics.

Marilyn always searches for the positive in her experiences. As an employee at a financial institution, she completed a complex merger project, but her boss wouldn't promote her or give her a raise. Instead of complaining, she struck a deal with him in which the company paid several years of her tuition for communication and leadership programs. When the bottom fell out of the real estate market in Denver and she and her husband slipped into financial disaster, she taught herself about financial management and pulled them out of debt. Then she designed and presented a successful workshop to help people reorganize their financial lives.

When, after ten years of marriage, she and her husband realized they were going in different directions, she didn't attribute blame. "I'm an extrovert who loves change and personal growth, he's an introvert who enjoys routine and doesn't believe in therapy, and neither one of us really wanted to change." They ended the marriage amicably. A year ago, she began dating a man who shares her passion for restoring old houses, hiking, and self-knowledge.

The advantage of Marilyn's positive approach to life is that it automatically defines her experiences in a way that allows her to take even "bad" developments and turn them into valuable lessons. Positivity diminishes or eliminates fears we might have about negative outcomes: since everything is a learning experience, nothing can go wrong. This in turn frees us emotionally and mentally to make a contribution to the greater good. Free of cynicism, sarcasm, and harsh judgments, we are buoyed by our enthusiasm, which allows us and those around us to experience flow at exhilarating levels.

9. TRUST

One thing can switch the experience of flow on and off in an instant: trust in flow itself.

We may use other words. We may call it trust in ourselves, or trust in God, or trust in the Tao, or trust in a larger plan, or just plain trust. But the dynamic is the same: trust enables us to proceed with absolute certainty into the unknown. We believe that what we do will not fail, because, ultimately, everything works for the greater good. If we are doing what we are supposed to be doing we cannot go wrong—because the value lies in the process, not in a specific outcome. Indeed, we trust that even an outcome we might dread could be the opportunity for a lesson that will catapult us forward toward clarity and serenity.

Although trust in this larger sense is different in scale than trusting another person, it does have some of the same dynamics. When we first meet someone we like—a friend, a future partner—even though we don't know that person, we take a leap of faith and decide to trust him. Over time, as we learn that we can rely on him, our trust grows. By trusting flow, we make that same leap of faith on a much greater scale. As time goes on, we see our days becoming richer and more purposeful, and our trust grows.

Lloyd Tupper has mastered trust. He has the patrician face and bearing of a CEO, but the twinkling whimsy of a leprechaun. He looks as if he were born to money and power, but he fell from grace in those moneyed regions and, through an entirely different kind of grace, came back into them again.

The key to trust, he says, is the realization that we don't have to make things happen. "As you get more in touch with yourself, you realize that you are not orchestrating the movement, you did not write the symphony, you are not conducting the symphony—you are just part of the movement. You

are playing the oboe." That knowledge, he says, eases anxiety. "Something is bringing it all together, and it has its own
timetable, and the movement will unfold. Your role is just to
show up, be willing, and do what you can. And don't make it
happen. Keep your hand off the baton."

An unusual attitude in financial circles, yes, but Lloyd
keeps being asked back to high-level merger talks because,
around him, things have a way of coming together. He "holds
the space," as the saying goes. When he's there, tempers don't
fly and tensions don't rise. His serenity is contagious—and
conducive to business.

It was not always so. In his mid-twenties, he met a businessman who took to him like a father: Ray Kroc, the
founder of McDonald's. But Lloyd had a falling out with
Kroc's then-wife, which created a chasm between the two
men. Kroc's lawyers took Lloyd to court, and wiped him out
financially.

It destroyed Lloyd's faith in humanity. "It broke me
down into smithereens. There was nothing left of my ability
to function in any capacity that I had known prior. I had to
give up. I had to surrender."

At his lowest point, he went to the Church of Saint Jude
and prayed to be delivered from the impossible situation he
was in. Later that day, his sister, with whom he had never
gotten along, withdrew her entire savings to enable him to reverse a judgment and retain some of his property. It made
him realize that life was all about the heart, and he decided to
enter the ministry. "I realized that when I had absolutely
nothing, there was nothing for me but God. And that I had to
respond to that call."

Three or four years later, after Kroc divorced, Lloyd's
heart softened and he made plans to attempt to see Kroc
again, after a business trip to Canada. On the trip, Lloyd sat
in first class on the plane, the only empty seat beside him. In
walked Kroc. They both cried—and talked for the entire
flight.

The chain of events gave Lloyd a deep trust in the underlying harmony of life. Today, he feels little need to push his way through anything. In fact, if he's speaking to nine hundred people and sees one person in the audience he instantly knows will be important in his life, he does not make an effort after the meeting to cross the room to meet the person. "We're supposed to come together, and we will. That has been my greatest lesson. You just have to let things be and not do anything about them. That is probably the greatest discipline in the world, because our whole thing is about making it happen. The point is to be present and trust the process."

For Lloyd, trust comes from *Not my will, but Thine be done.* "I myself can do no thing, but the Father within me does all things. We are all worthy—worthy to be instruments of some greater power or presence."

As Lloyd demonstrates, giving up our need to control events and force outcomes makes us available to the full power of flow. It can move through us and help us accomplish things even greater than we had planned.

TRUST, THE TOGGLE SWITCH OF FLOW

In the wink of an eye, trust moves us in and out of flow.

✦ When we trust, we are open and available to whatever is before us. *When we don't trust, we're distant and withdrawn.*

✦ When we trust, we align ourselves with an underlying reality. *When we don't trust, we feel an over-*

whelming need to control everything and everyone around us.

✦ When we trust, we hear the voice within and follow it without hesitation. *When we don't trust, our fears drown the voice out.*

✦ When we trust, we are flexible in our approaches, because we know that a better solution than ours might emerge. *When we don't trust, we become rigid and insist on doing it our way.*

✦ When we trust, we tell the truth to and about our-selves, knowing that a greater good will result. *When we don't trust, we lie to protect ourselves.*

✦ When we trust, we give with an open heart. *When we lack trust, we're greedy and fearful of scarcity.*

✦ When we trust, we're willing to risk everything. *When we lack trust, we turn our back on possibili-ties.*

✦ When we trust, we are positive and see the value and potential in all things. *When we lack trust, we are negative, cynical, and suspicious.*

✦ When we trust, we're full of gratitude for all life brings. *When we don't trust, we're filled with resent-ment for all that's gone wrong.*

✦ When we trust, synchronicity abounds. *When we don't trust, life is a struggle.*

Flow Exercise

Use the steps below to come to a deeper understanding of how one, several, or all of the attributes are currently operat-ing in your life.

- ✦ Commitment
- ✦ Honesty
- ✦ Courage
- ✦ Passion
- ✦ Immediacy
- ✦ Openness
- ✦ Receptivity
- ✦ Positivity
- ✦ Trust

Choose an attribute to work on. Take a piece of paper and a pen. Use your "unconscious hand," the one you don't usually write with and *very* slowly, letter by letter, write the name of the attribute five times and slowly say it out loud as you write it. *Do not print.* Pause for a few seconds between each word. Be aware of any thoughts, images, memories, voices, sounds, sensations, or emotions, and let them move through you like a breeze through a chain-link fence.

Quietly explore and savor your experience for a few moments, then say aloud, "I am _____." (Examples: "I am committed," or "I am honest.") Notice how the words sound and how your voice sounds. Again, be aware of any thoughts, images, memories, voices, sounds, sensations, or emotions, and simply let them move through you. Paying close attention to your experience, repeat the phrase several times until it sounds and feels natural and familiar.

Finally, put that attribute into context by saying, "I am _____," and then give an example from your life. ("I am committed to my family." "I have courage when I tell my spouse the truth." "I am passionate about my ideals.") See what immediately comes to mind with the attribute.

Experimenting with these statements can show you where your attribute is already in place and where you may need to make adjustments in your life.

YOUR OWN ATTRIBUTE PROFILE

It always helps to know the truth about where you're start-ing: which attributes are already strong within you and which need to be more developed. On the following scale, mark an X at the point on each line that represents how far you have come in reaching each of the attributes in the right-hand column. Connect the points to form your own attribute profile. Consider what your profile shows you. If some attrib-utes are low, don't be discouraged—even the most advanced flowmasters had to start somewhere.

As you work through the techniques later in the book, your profile will change. Check back later to see the progress you have made.

Hesitant . . . . COMMITTED
Fearful. . . . . COURAGEOUS
Dishonest. . . . . HONEST
Indifferent. . . . . PASSIONATE
Lost in time . . . . IMMEDIATE
Shut down. . . . . RECEPTIVE
Closed . . . . OPEN
Negative. . . . . POSITIVE
Suspicious . . . . TRUSTING

The nine attributes are not something we're born with. We develop them over time in response to the situations in our lives, for each attribute involves conscious decisions based on our beliefs and values. The attributes often develop in a sys-tematic manner, and, in the next chapter, we'll examine the stages we go through to make flow a constant presence and powerful resource in our lives.

5 THE PROCESS OF TRANSFORMATION

We've just seen how we can create lives for ourselves rich in meaning and magic, lives shaped and confirmed by synchronicity. The flowmasters you've read about so far all moved into flow by making conscious decisions to change themselves and their lives. In increasing their inner freedom and outer vitality, they went through—and are still going through—predictable stages of growth. These are the same stages you are now going through or may go through soon.

The first stage is focused on knowing ourselves. In the second stage, we focus on interacting with others. In the third stage, we come into accord with the greater whole. Let's examine these more closely.

Stage One: Knowing ourselves. Our lives are greatly shaped by influences outside us, such as our country, our culture, our religion, our job, our family, friends, and colleagues. "I am an American," "I am a mother," "I am a store owner," we might say, and with those words come automatic expectations and assumptions, from ourselves and from others. Our families have perhaps the greatest expectations of all: we must be a dutiful child, a loving spouse, an involved and caring parent, a supportive sibling. For many of us, these roles shape our daily experiences. It's often hard to tell whether expectations emanate more strongly from us or others, so intertwined are they.

The reward is that we feel useful and appreciated and part of a group. But the price may be our authenticity. Quite often, we're so attentive to everyone else's expectations that we lose the sense of who we really are. We lose awareness of our own passions. We find we're always looking outside ourselves for approval. We are constantly judging and evaluating ourselves and others. From this place, we may not perceive synchronicity because we are busy monitoring our thoughts, feelings, and behaviors, which puts us far from an open, expansive mode.

Breaking out of this pattern requires a greater understanding of what makes us happy and sad, what gives us purpose and joy. This process can begin when we are young, especially if encouraged by our family. Usually, though, we blaze our own way, perhaps refusing to follow the career or path desired for us by others. It might happen later in life, if we're trying to figure out exactly why we aren't happy. Sometimes it takes a trauma such as the end of a marriage or job to shake us to our core. We realize that what we thought was true about ourselves and our world isn't. So what is?

These questions push us to the next step in this stage. We engage in a process of self-awareness: we find out what makes us tick. We delve into ourselves to see what's there, both good and bad. We examine different paths, different philosophies, different ways of life. We try on new ideas for size: some we keep, some we throw away. As we go along we're learning to develop an internal point of reference rather than an external one. We're finding out exactly what it means to be true to ourselves.

A key to this stage is choice. We learn that we can choose to meet the expectations of others, or not. We can choose to keep our old roles, or not. We can choose to get upset for the usual reasons, or not. We see how our habitual patterns keep us bound, and we begin to loosen the grip of the way things have always been.

We remake ourselves from the inside out. We take chances we've never considered before. We speak out where before we were silent; we change hairstyles; we register for a course or workshop. We discover that when people speak from the heart, differences of personality, gender, race, class, and education fall away. We learn how our opinions limit us as well as define us.

Stage Two: Connecting with others. Gradually, the "me" drops out of our personal equation, and "you" takes its place. We aren't seeking happiness from others because we already have it within, and so what matters most to us is the other person's well-being. In the process, we discover what inner obstacles hold us back from loving and giving fully, and we undertake action to remove those. Increasingly, we give unconditionally from our hearts, without holding back or expecting anything in return.

Our circle of caring expands beyond our family and friends. We volunteer to help out, lead local drives, organize people to improve a situation, teach what we know, share what we have. Generosity becomes our nature. Synchronicities both large and small grace our days, for we are open, passionate, and receptive.

Ultimately, "us" is what matters. We feel no distance or difference between others and ourselves. Our daily interactions are a dance of synergy that leaves everyone better for the experience.

Synchronicity kicks in. The people and things we need to learn from appear as if on schedule: the money to take a trip comes out of nowhere, a friend takes us to a life-changing lecture. The underlying order of life surfaces. We are coming into the power of flow.

Stage Three: Oneness with the greater whole. As we develop self-awareness and engage in serving others, we enter into an even broader spectrum of experience: we are part of the underlying order. We feel connected to something larger than ourselves, which seems to be moving and shaping our lives in ways we increasingly perceive.

The key to this stage is trust: trust in ourselves, trust in God, or underlying reality, or cosmic consciousness—whatever we may call it. We learn that when we're operating out of our true self, risk is energizing; increasingly, we're ready to take a deep breath and follow our hearts. As we experience this greater whole, old notions of who we are, as defined by our roles, gently fall away, and contributing to the whole becomes our purpose, the focus of our energy. Our lives may change drastically to accomplish this. Or they may look the same, but they'll be different underneath: we'll see our children and our jobs with different eyes.

In this stage, synchronicity is our daily companion. We experience our essential self—that deepest part of ourselves—and flow becomes the nature of who we are. On an ongoing basis we experience the timeless space we tap into in meditation and prayer, the euphoria some experience as runner's high, when physical, mental, and emotional energies are balanced. Our connection to the whole is strong and steady, yet beyond words and concepts. We struggle trying to talk about it. We rely on metaphors of things we know, like water, to help us get the point across. But in flow, we are free, spontaneous, joyful, open. Life is full of potential. We instinctively help others, without preconditions or preconceptions, and there is no difference between them and us. We do not give our possessions to them, for we are one: they already possess them. It is in this stage that we find particularly powerful experiences of synchronicity, for we are receptive, positive, and patient.

Although this three-part process has a direction of growth—from self-awareness to awareness of others to awareness of the greater whole—our movement is not always linear. We can, at different times in a day, or even an hour, move back and forth between those stages. One moment we might feel serene and open while working in our garden—Stage Three—and the next minute we might be worrying about what the neighbors think of our scraggly grass—Stage One.

But our efforts toward progress make a difference. In the beginning, anxieties about the neighbor's opinion might crowd out our pleasure at being in the garden. Later, we might be so engrossed in the feeling of the moist, rich dirt between our fingers and the sunlight warming our shoulders that the thought of the neighbors' opinion is quickly followed by thoughts of warm connectedness. As we move from Stage One to Two to Three, each stage builds on and incorporates the other. We never stop learning any one stage, and in fact, our learning about self-awareness becomes immeasurably richer in the later stages.

To understand this process better, let's examine the lives of three particular flowmasters. Sunny Schlenger is a vivacious organizational consultant who lives in the suburbs of northern New Jersey. John Beal is a down-to-earth Vietnam vet who lives in a semi-industrial area of Seattle. Soft-spoken Janet Landis is a mother of six who lives in central Denver. Each of their paths is unique—as is yours—and through their stories you'll see how individual, yet universal, the process of coming into flow is.

As you read through these stages in their lives, consider how you would answer these questions: How do I think of myself? How do I know who I am? Where did my ideas of myself come from? What matters most to me? When am I happy, joyful, or fulfilled? Am I true to myself in relation to others? How can I better serve others in my life? How am I contributing to the good of the greater whole?

SUNNY SCHLENGER:
FROM COMPULSION TO TRUST

Sunny Schlenger's home office is small but meticulously organized, with books and spiral notebooks perfectly aligned on shelves, file cabinets lining one wall, and seashells, stones, and nursery school art from her children adorning a shelf near the door. It doesn't look like a meditation cave on a mountaintop, but it's her equivalent. It's the place in which Sunny found her inner self and turned her life around.

When she moved to the house in 1979, she had no clear idea of who she was beyond being her husband's wife. She had married him eight years earlier, at age twenty, seeing him as everything she wanted to be and wasn't—successful, creative, talented. Now their finances were strained by the fact that she no longer wanted the psychological counseling career for which she had trained. The jobs she took—dog groomer, telemarketer—were partly rebellions against her husband, who would say, "Why don't you get a normal job?"

"It sounds right, but I just can't make myself do it. It doesn't feel right," she'd answer. Inside, she'd agonize. "Why can't I be like everybody else?" As frustrating as her days were, she didn't expect much more. Her upbringing had taught her that reality was struggle and more struggle. Life was about coping, and you kept your focus straight ahead and did what you had to do.

She had always coped with her internal confusion by organizing everything around her, from the kitchen drawers to her husband's schedule: knowing where everything was gave her a sense of safety. In irritation, her husband said to her one day, "Why don't you peddle your neurosis to some-

body else?" His words rang a bell. She remembered a clip-
ping she had come across about a woman who organized
other people's lives for a living. Intrigued, she discussed the
idea with a neighbor, who referred her to a friend who
needed help organizing his financial records because his marriage was ending. With those synchronicities, Sunny's life as a
professional organizer began. She started in people's homes,
for $3 an hour, organizing files, accounting systems, sched-
ules, then moved to small offices, and then into the corporate
world. She wrote a book, *How To Be Organized in Spite of
Yourself*. She worked hard and with excitement, for she had
found her place in the scheme of things. Her expertise gave
her credibility. Small in stature, with short blond hair, she
was warm, interested, practical, and creative.

Happiness, however, continued to elude her. Though
her psychology background had given her a level of insight
into herself, she kept running into invisible barriers in land-
ing that really big job. Her marriage held as much pain as
pleasure, and differences with her husband intensified with
the birth of their daughter, Lauren, in 1984 and son, A.J., in
1986. She began searching for answers to her unease, which
led her to read Shirley MacLaine's *Out On a Limb*. She
doubted and questioned all its contents, but as she closed the
book, she was surprised by a feeling of coming home.

Out of curiosity, she went to see a psychic, who pre-
dicted that her son would in the future be surrounded by
books. Sunny thought it hilarious and unlikely. Even at age
two, her son wanted nothing to do with books, so how in the
world would he ever get to be a lawyer or professor or librarian? A few days later, she heard a crash and ran upstairs. Her
son was sitting on the floor, surrounded by books he had just
pulled off a shelf. She was first amazed and astonished, and
then exhilarated. In that luminous second, a new world of
metaphorical understanding opened up to her. Life didn't
have to be literal: it held all kinds of interpretations and pos-

sibilities. It showed her she didn't always have the answers, which meant she could start to let go of her need to always know what came next.

Sunny was moving into greater self-awareness. Motivated by her nagging sense of discontent, she was expanding the limits of possibility, taking the first tentative steps away from the need for control that had brought her through life to that point.

Then another experience opened the door even wider. On a Caribbean vacation with her husband, a horse she was riding took off, racing across the sand. This scenario had been a childhood fantasy; she felt totally in the moment, ecstatically alive. It made her realize she wanted more peak experiences in her life.

She decided to plunge into a major project: designing "The Happiness Seminar" for her business clients, who often complained their lives felt out of balance. She went into her office, closed the door, and over the next five years spent much of her free time there reading self-help and spiritual books, doing self-improvement exercises. It dawned on her only slowly that what she was really doing was rediscovering herself.

She read books such as *Creative Visualization* by Shakti Gawain; *A Journey Through Your Childhood,* by Christopher Biffle, which put her back in touch with the joys of her early life; and *Living a Beautiful Life* by Alexandra Stoddard, about creating beauty. She uncovered unconscious beliefs that had been holding her back: she thought that she was only entitled to achieve so much and no more, and that joy and pain were meted out in equal measure. Understanding those beliefs at last, she realized they were those of her parents, and that she could choose not to have them. She also found another invaluable resource: like-minded friends, who introduced her to a massage therapist, a personal trainer, and more books.

As exciting as these explorations were, they were also

painful. There was a war raging inside her between her practical side, which was critical and suspicious of everything she was reading, and her intuitive side, which gave her a strong feeling of being on the right track. She questioned everything she did, every reaction she had—was it right? wrong? good? bad? yes? no? should? shouldn't? At times it felt as though she was being pulled to pieces. Yet beneath the turmoil was stillness that she touched in meditation, in reflective silence, which gave her strength to continue. She increasingly found herself making decisions based on trust, faith, and intuition. The decisions were often rewarded by synchronicity.

The contradiction Sunny experienced is common as we come into greater self-awareness. Even if we're unhappy with our present circumstances, change holds its own terrors. *What if I'm even more unhappy afterward? What if the people I love reject a different me? Once I start this course, can I back out of it? What if I change too much? What if I don't change enough?*

When it's more than our minds can handle, all we can do is take a deep breath and keep going: on faith alone. In taking that risk, we feel a new aliveness. Fear drops away and we find ourselves thinking and doing things we had never conceived of before, things that astonish us. They just feel right.

For Sunny, that time came when she was reading *Creating Money* by Sanaya Roman and Duane Packer. She was amazed to find herself thinking that the esoteric information in it seemed, well, not all that strange. She surprised herself even more by signing up for the authors' weekend seminar in San Francisco—her first personal growth seminar. She thought, *I don't know why I'm doing this!* But she felt compelled.

There, she learned of energy centers in the body and learned to tap into them through guided meditation. She found that tuning in to inner messages couldn't be forced; she had to relax, stop making an effort, and allow it to happen.

That discovery had ripple effects through the rest of her life; she didn't always have to force outcomes.

When she returned home, she felt she had the self-knowledge to remake her marriage into one that brought her happiness. But after a year of unresolvable crises, she and her husband separated. Sunny accepted that after twenty-five years together, they both had to move on in different directions. Single parenthood and being without a partner had its terrors, but at this point in her life, Sunny was acting on a different basis: she was being true to herself. Although the divorce was painful, she saw it as a new beginning, and she now trusted that her life would expand, not contract.

Today, Sunny operates on trust, feels supported by the Universe, and listens closely to her inner voice, which never lets her down. She sees the bigger picture, hears the greater truth, and feels part of a larger whole. She no longer needs to control and organize everyone around her. She no longer needs reasons for everything in order to feel control: now she's comfortable with ambiguity, undaunted by paradox, enchanted with mystery. But she still organizes, she's still punctual, she still does her homework before visiting a client. Being compulsively organized is part of her personality and probably always will be, but now she has a sense of humor about it, and she's more relaxed.

She takes risks in negotiating with clients—partly because, during a past life regression, she found in herself a persistent pattern of backing away from a goal when she was overcome with fear. That insight gave her the courage to push herself, which resulted in a long-term, lucrative contract with a multinational company restructuring its workforce.

Sunny no longer teaches goal-setting the same way. "I disagree with the concept of planning things out now to cover every possible contingency," she says. "You shouldn't have to control every stage of the process. If we realize we only know part of the picture, then we're more open to other information coming in—through synchronicity, through our inner knowing."

She's now far closer to her children, and even to her former husband, than when she was acting the role of dutiful wife and mother. "I think it's a relief to them because I'm not trying to turn them into somebody they're not—and it's a relief to me," she says.

Her children have learned to respect her advice, because her inner voice has an uncanny way of being right. Once Sunny dragged A.J. to the store to buy a birthday gift for his sister. "It's really important to be generous, not just because it's what you do, but because whatever you put out, comes back," Sunny told him. "Yeah, right—as if someone's going to give me money!" he protested. The next morning, valentines arrived in the mail for the children from Sunny's mother, who, for the first time, had enclosed a check. A.J.'s check was exactly twice what he had spent on his sister.

A new ease has entered Sunny's relationship with her former husband, because she became able to appreciate him for what he was instead of judging him for what he was not. She's happy that he's found another woman, someone who suits him much better than she did. Sunny hasn't yet started dating again, but she surprises herself by how little she worries about it: she knows that when the time is right, she'll meet the man she's supposed to be with.

Synchronicity, a concept she first encountered reading *The Celestine Prophecy* at the time of her divorce, is an everyday experience. She pays attention to what resonates, what seems to have meaning, and listens to what it's saying. Sometimes it will be just a little lift, sometimes it's more significant, and sometimes it's, "My God, this is a message!"

At one point, she experienced an amazing cluster of synchronicities in the space of one week. She arrived at a friend's home just moments after a houseguest there died of AIDS. Viewing his body, she was surprised she felt no horror.

Then, in her own backyard, she found a dead bird, and picked it up gently and buried it, which a few years ago she would have been too squeamish to do. Most astonishing, she rounded a corner at her consulting job to see on a stranger's desk photos of Lauren and A.J. It took her a shocked second to realize that it was the desk of her ex-husband's girlfriend— with whom, in fact, he was moving in with that very week-end. Sunny had no idea the woman—whose last name, coincidentally, was Sunshine—worked there. A second later, she appeared. Their conversation ended with a hug and the woman's profuse thanks for the gracious way Sunny was handling the divorce.

Afterward, Sunny's head reeled as she tried to make sense of it all. What had surprised her most at the office was the peace of mind she felt. The cluster of events showed her that although in the past she had never been good at endings, she was now strong enough to look death in the face—death of a person, a bird, a marriage—and move on with firm steps.

It was confirmation of the path she has been on. "I feel wonderful living this way—and it's not that I'm always happy, and it's not that things are always working. But I have this incredible trust that if something's not working, it's be-cause there's something I need to improve or do differently or that I need to be in a holding pattern. I trust the process, whatever that may be.

"I feel like I'm going to keep reinventing myself, that where I am now is only a step on the way. I've come through the major part, which was breaking through the resistance to this way of life. So now it's really exciting, because I don't have a clue about what's going to happen. Operating without a clue is not something I ever thought I would do. For some reason I don't have any doubt that I'm going to be fine."

About her spiritual beliefs, she says, "I think of God, I think of guides, I think of angels. I think it's like a team— whoever needs to get the job done does. I used to pride my-self on being an individual, and now I pride myself on being part of this team. It's just a question of, 'Well, just tell me where to get in line.' I've found my place."

Sunny's path reflects her intellectual orientation to the world: she collects information, largely through reading, checks if it feels right and will take her to where she wants to go, and then integrates it or discards it. She is on a quest: she is transforming her life.

JOHN BEAL:
FROM NEAR-DEATH TO ABUNDANT ENERGY

John Beal follows the physical action approach to flow: through the sweat of his labors and the power of his commitment, he's transformed a piece of the environment, and himself.

As is often true, his journey to flow began with a crisis that made him grasp what he truly valued in life. "You have three, maybe twelve months to live," the doctors told John in 1980 after his third heart attack. The words hit hard: John, a Vietnam veteran with a square face, shaggy-dog gray hair, and thick black-rimmed glasses, wasn't ready to die. Not that his life was enviable: he suffered post-traumatic stress disorder, and his moods ranged from dark despair to furniture-smashing anger. He had trouble keeping his sales job, and his marriage to his high school sweetheart was rocky.

The doctor's words forced him into a painful process of becoming self-aware. He withdrew inside himself to deal with his despair and sought solitude in the wooded areas near the factories and small homes in his neighborhood in Seattle. He spent long hours among the trees, trying to find the meaning in his life, often heading to a large pond that reminded him of places in Vietnam where friends had died in his arms.

Then one day he arrived to find heavy machinery cutting the trees and filling in the pond—and there wasn't a thing he could do about it. Furious and heartsick, his attention fell on a stream that ran through a ravine near his home. Once, he had been told by an old-timer, it had been so thick with spawning salmon you could walk across their backs. Now it was a smelly rivulet running through an illegal garbage dump. He looked at that stream and it hurt. It reflected himself—almost dead. On a gut level, he identified with it.

He refused to let it die. This was John's turning point. Suddenly, he had a purpose, a mission. Working by himself, without a word to anyone, he started hauling away trash—tires, stoves, boots—eighteen tons of it the first year. He worked to exhaustion, came home wet with muscle and chest pains—and he was happy. For the first time in decades, he had a feeling of accomplishment.

The stream became his teacher. It taught him that he had value, that caring, his perseverance, even his anger, was making a difference in the world. As he hauled garbage, he felt the toxins of self-hatred clearing out of his system. As he planted trees, he was giving fresh hope to himself.

His wife, Lana, a serene woman with quiet strength, encouraged him; in fact, virtually pushed him out the door. "I don't care if you never work another day in your life," she told him. "I want you to live." She insisted they could get by on his $400 disability check and her earnings as a waitress. Others weren't so supportive: "Why don't you go get a job?" neighbors would jeer. "You're out of your mind, it's a ditch!" said one environmental official. "It's been dead for forty or fifty years."

But John at this point was so inner-directed and determined that he didn't care what anyone thought or said, or did or didn't do. Opposition fueled his anger—and the anger fueled his commitment. When he finished hauling garbage from the stream, he would drive to a nearby river and catch fish crawdads, snails, even ants, then bring them back to the stream to rebuild its ecosystem. Three days later, he'd find the fish dead, the crawdads belly up, the snails crawled out of their shells. Disheartened, he looked for a reason to continue; he prayed to God for a sign. It came the day he tried to remove a 300-pound boulder that fell on top of him and pushed him under the waters of the stream. Gasping under the stone, he said, "Lord, if you really want me to do this, you will give me the strength and the power to get this rock off my chest." The boulder moved. John got up and walked away.

He kept observing the stream, and after reading some books, John came to realize life couldn't survive in it because fertilizers and chemicals, rainwater runoff, were cutting off the water's oxygen. He labored over the problem for months. He looked everwhere for an answer, and it presented itself through hard work, dreams, and synchronicity. While planting bushes by the stream, he put down a 2 x 4 board to bridge it. Then, he saw with amazement that all the oil and pollutants were gathering at the wood. A lightbulb went on in his head, and he devised a "boom"—a barrier of sticks and seeds that breaks up pollution and pushes it to the side of the stream. It allowed everything downstream to be oxygenated, and the stream came back to life.

The booms, however, had an unexpected effect: the soil near them became saturated with toxins. John was facing heavy costs out of his own pocket for soil removal and decontamination when he noticed that plants in that area were thriving, plants that didn't grow well elsewhere—buttercups, clover, fescue, rye. In a dream, the meaning became clear: the plants were cleaning up the pollutants. A university laboratory confirmed that the plants were converting toxins from inorganic matter back to organic. By planting them thickly, John solved the problem.

A second dream helped John handle an even tougher challenge: heavy metals had sunk out of the reach of the booms to the bottom third of the stream, particularly cyanide, lead, zinc, and chromium dumped by an upstream electroplate manufacturer. In his dream, he saw a magnet pulling in metals. He experimented with many possible solutions until one day he found a battery someone had thrown into the stream; on it was red coloration where heavy metal had collected. After eight more months of trial and error, he found that a submerged 26.2-volt battery most effectively drew the metals out of the water.

From this process, John learned flexibility and perseverance: he was always trying things out, and if they didn't work, he kept moving on and trying other things. His experiences in Vietnam became an asset: when he ran into opposition or careless polluters, he was fearless. His attitude was, "What are they going to do to me that I haven't already been through?"

John moved from the first process of transformation, self-awareness, into the second, connecting with and serving others. As his work became more public, people began coming to help him out—college students, neighbors—five hundred volunteers in all. A young boy with AIDS spent his last six months planting trees alongside John. A city official he'd banged heads with gave him $200 at Christmas. A Vietnam veteran who hadn't spoken a word in years worked alongside John for five hours and broke down, crying, screaming, venting his anger and frustration. John suggested, "Start with the little creek running through your backyard. Start reconnecting yourself to the earth, and you'll see that everything you did wrong in Vietnam can be turned around by doing something positive right here, right now." The man followed the advice, started speaking, found work, and got a girlfriend.

Animals also came to John for healing and for solace in death. On the battlefields of Vietnam, John's buddies would stumble to him as they were dying; now, possums with heads bashed in by traps came whimpering to him. Dogs hit by cars crawled to his feet. As he was walking through downtown Seattle, an ailing seagull fell at his feet.

The synchronicities in his life got almost uncannily strong. When he was at his dirtiest and sweatiest and most tired, he would meet the person he had been wanting to meet for ten years or someone would give him a donation or valuable advice. Once, laboriously putting down chips for a path, John was approached by the bishop of a church whose construction had damaged part of his project area. The bishop apologized and offered to help John however he could—beginning with the loan of a Cub Scout troop to put down the chips.

Sometimes John received sudden inner messages, even in the middle of the night, to go to one part of the stream—and in that place he'd find someone violating it by dumping barrels of waste products or an old refrigerator. One Sunday morning, on a "hunch," he and Lana drove to the stream and found six rough-looking men dressed in army fatigues, dodging behind trees, trampling the underbrush, and shooting toxic paint pellets at each other. "Get out of here!" John shouted at them. "We're turning this area into a field classroom for kids, and you're destroying the plants." The men argued, but not for long—John is built like a tank, and his determination is just as steely.

Slowly, the stream gained back its life force. In 1991, the Army Corps of Engineers found, to the amazement of all involved, that the stream's pollutant level had dropped by a third in two years; the combined oils and by-products were reduced to half. Three years ago, for the first time, salmon returned to spawn.

John's work was instrumental in getting the county a $390,000 grant to buy a 15-acre tract surrounding his stream, take out an old sewage treatment facility, and re-create a wetland, a marsh, a small pond, and viewing platforms. But what should have been a victory turned into tragedy: instead of allowing John and his volunteers to carefully remove the trees and animals, the county bulldozed the treatment facility and leveled most of the wooded area to the ground. Gone were fifteen years of careful, painstaking work building an ecosystem. At one point, weeping, John sat in front of the bulldozers and succeeded in stopping them from destroying trees close to the stream.

In desperation about his next step, he contacted someone who knew the granddaughter of the last medicine man of the Native American tribe that had once inhabited the area. She walked the property and came to him with tears in her eyes. "This is the place where the tribe used to come every year for a great festival, and there is great joy here," she said. She told him she heard voices belonging to a family that had long ago tended the land. "They are still here because you are here, and they support what you are doing. They will be your eyes and your ears. They want you to know that what just happened here was terrible, but it is a flash of time. In twenty, fifty years, what you are doing is going to be seen everywhere as a very positive thing. The land, the stream, will all come back. They said that they're not worried, and that if they're not, then, John, you shouldn't be worried."

That was the information, the long view, that John needed. It gave him renewed determination—along with seeing what happened when he had withdrawn his energy from the project. He had been spending less and less time at the stream and more time on administration and phone work. He had sometimes ignored the little voice that told him trouble was afoot. One day he noticed that the volunteers and the press had gone away and the phone had stopped ringing.

So he went back to the stream for four or five hours, every day, cleaning it out and planting. The activity picked up again.

What is it all about for him? Commitment to something beyond himself—the river, the ecosystem, the planet—and ultimately, God. "The more I've spent in the way of time, the more 'it' has come to me. And 'it' to me is God. It is a situation where quite literally and figuratively, this is a mission from God and He has kept me alive to get it completed and done." The anger that once ate him alive has abated, rechanneled into action. "Now, I can get things to happen without being the biggest and baddest and angriest dude in the room."

John fully accesses Stage Three—he is self-aware, aware of others, and focused on the greater whole. This takes a literal turn: his concern has widened from his little stream to the 55 square miles of the Hamm Creek watershed to the entire river. Last year, he organized the Green-Duwamish Waterhead Alliance, a group of over 250 agencies and citizen groups.

Sixteen years after receiving a medical diagnosis of imminent death, his health is robust. Says John, "In healing the earth, you heal yourself. By not polluting, you heal yourself. By being aware of what is going on around you, you heal yourself."

He has a deep inner peace, a knowingness. He's not only saving the river, he's saving himself. And he's well on the way to saving at least a piece of the world: his booms are being used in Russia, India, the Philippines. He is a man brimming with purpose and energy.

JANET LANDIS: FROM ISOLATION TO CONNECTION

For Janet Landis, the word *synchronicity* itself propelled her forward. Janet first heard it in a telephone conversation with a friend. "Synchronicity?" she asked. "That's an interesting word. Did you make it up?"

The friend explained the way it worked, and that was all Janet needed. It immediately struck a chord. Within days, her use of synchronicity brought her into a new way of life. A few months later, her world shifted; she discovered her calling. With it, flow became her everyday experience.

A former nurse, Janet lives with her husband and the three youngest of her six children in a restored Victorian house. Adopted as an infant, Janet had been raised in a home in which outside appearances mattered and in which she was expected to smile all the time, no matter how she felt. Though she played by those rules, she was painfully alone and distant from others.

Following a traditional path, she went from high school to nursing school, married a friend's brother, and was eight months pregnant when she graduated. Two more children followed in the next six years. She considered leaving her husband after two years of marriage, but relented in response to his pleas and stayed five more. After their eventual divorce, she fell in love again, married, and had three more children.

Motivated partly by the pain of being rejected by her birth mother, Janet had always sought answers; she had read Gibran's *The Prophet* as part of her search, and also underwent primal therapy. She'd seen various therapists from time to time, but didn't get serious about that process until her early forties, when she experienced confusion and depression with another unplanned pregnancy. Over the next six years, in weekly sessions, she probed the ways she had denied her true feelings to meet the expectations of others. Most of her life, she came to realize, she had been disconnected from herself and therefore never felt truly connected to others. Slowly she gained a clearer understanding of what she needed and wanted in life. When her youngest daughter reached school age, Janet returned to school herself, taking a smorgasbord of college courses that filled her with excitement.

At this point, Janet had reached basic understandings about herself and her relations with others and was in a mode of steady inner growth. Her burgeoning feelings of connection were accelerated by the phone call about synchronicity. Immediately afterward, she started noting meaningful coincidences in her life. At the library, glancing at a rack of books for sale, she was drawn to one sitting by itself on top. It fit in exactly with conversations she'd been having with her daughters. An instructor mistakenly deleted her from his class roll, which turned out for the best because he played loud rock music during class, which she would not have enjoyed. Each time one of those things happened, she found herself smiling and enjoying it in a way she would not have before. "I'm not sure the details of my life have changed, but certainly the richness with which I experience it has," she says now.

Intrigued by the way her inner needs were being met by circumstances, she continued paying more attention to what was going on inside and began trusting her intuition. When a strange thought came up, instead of setting it aside, she paid attention to it, often with fortuitous results. She began to trust her inner urges. Her experiences with synchronicity and her intuition were giving her what she'd never had: a feeling of connection to a deeper, truer layer of reality.

These discoveries dovetailed with another area of her life. She was chair of a committee at her church on race relations. The committee was preparing an educational program, but kept running into blocks in determining an approach. A news item on National Public Radio galvanized Janet's thinking. DNA researchers had found a way to determine whether a fetus would develop into a dwarf or a normal-sized person. They wanted to withhold this information from the dwarf community, thinking that dwarfs would have dwarf fetuses aborted. When they did share the information, though, it was the normal children the dwarf community wanted aborted.

This stunned Janet. To her committee, she exclaimed, "Don't you see what it means? We all want to be with similar people."

In the silence that followed, Janet thought, *Holy cow, that probably was a risk I shouldn't have taken. They probably think I am the worst bigot in the world.* Yet she had had to say it, because for her it was critical to get to the heart of the matter—and that seemed to be a piece of the puzzle. Trusting the process, she was telling her truth to others.

Her words acted like a fresh wind blowing through the door. The committee members realized that, in trying to approach the topic of race relations by looking at what was wrong with other people "out there" instead of at what was going on within themselves, they were heading in the wrong direction. With new excitement, they reframed their questions and called psychologists and communication experts for insights.

Janet began to understand something profound about discrimination. She saw that she judged others to be less capable in order to feel better about herself. By believing them to be less than herself, she made herself feel better. Ultimately, she saw, it all started with the fact that she didn't feel good about herself. The revelation shocked her: she was, after all, living by choice in an integrated area. But she realized that, though she had always thought she put great effort into connecting with other people, on a deeper level she had put even more effort into keeping herself separate and safe.

Something shifted inside her. At her daughter's school, watching a Halloween parade, on impulse she walked over to a grandfatherly African-American man and said, "Oh, isn't this fun to watch them?" The words were something she might have said before, but the feeling she had caught her by surprise. She wasn't speaking to the man through a wall or barrier. And he felt it, too—she could see it in his eyes, as he responded to her warmly. She had never before realized how protected she had kept herself.

At church, everything had fallen into place beautifully for the committee's program on race relations. When Janet stood up to talk before the congregation, she felt calm and powerful. "I am a racist," she began, her voice clear and unwavering. You could have heard a pin drop. For the next fifteen minutes, Janet talked from her heart of how her need to keep herself separate and safe kept her from experiencing connection with others, and how segregation and discrimination emanated from there. Her audience was visibly moved, some to tears. At the end, an African-American woman stood up and said, "That is what we need to hear. We know how we feel, and we've needed to hear how white people feel."

Janet had found her destiny. She was in Stage Three, experiencing flow as she never had before. In the year since then, many opportunities and synchronicities have come her way. She has happened across books that crystallized her thinking, and met people who share her commitment to getting at the deeper dynamics of discrimination. She is invited to meetings and asked to serve on committees. At home, she is more frank and open with her husband and children.

"After all these years of trying to get connected to myself and others, it's happened," says Janet. "And it just keeps expanding. The flow keeps happening. It's a force that is like the essence of spirituality, a force of Will that is saying, 'Here you are, this is what you need to be doing.'

"My speech at the church was successful because I spoke from my own viewpoint. And to be in touch with who I am allows me to just say who I am and not have to worry about who other people are. Not that that doesn't affect me. But that's not where I have any control. I don't need to have any control anymore. Controlling other people was a way of vicariously controlling myself, and I needed to have controls on myself because I was not OK with who I was or where I was or what I was. I was afraid of my own angry impulses. As I've gotten in touch with who I am, I can let go of a lot of that stuff. And how anyone responds to me is up to them. All I need to do is put out what I have learned. And if people can hear it, then they can hear it."

As Janet speaks, she is alive, warm, excited, sincere. She has presence, and you want to get to know her better.

"It's as though the flow, this essence, is the groundwater, and we are the springs coming to the surface," she says. "Even though we all seem individual, we are all connected underneath. And in the connection comes the synchronicity."

YOUR PATH FOR THE CHOOSING

Sunny, John, and Janet show us clearly how the power of flow unfolds. Their unique paths demonstrate some of flow's many forms: Sunny's approach was primarily intellectual and played out in the business world; John's approach was primarily physical and played out in nature; Janet's approach was primarily psychological and played out in a religious and community setting. Approaches to flow are as unique as the individuals using them. There is not a singular way to access the power of flow, and many approaches work equally well.

We also can live life rich in the experience of flow; it requires first that we make the decision to do so. When we make a commitment to swim with the current, not against it, that current carries us along swiftly and surely—sometimes tumultuously—to aliveness, joy, and harmony.

Flow Exercise

Sit down with your journal, with a paper and pen, or at the computer. Close your eyes, and take three deep breaths. Ask yourself, "Who am I?" As an answer comes up, look at it, let it go, and ask the question again, "Who am I?" Write down your responses. Keep asking this question, allowing it to take you deeper and deeper within yourself.

6 USING THE TECHNIQUES EFFECTIVELY

We enter into flow through choice and action. The fourteen practical techniques in the next five chapters are designed to guide you in that process. By using them, you will bring about a transformation in your experience of the world.

Remember the definition: *Flow is the natural, effortless unfolding of our lives in a way that leads us toward harmony and wholeness.* Flow is already in our lives this very moment, for it is simply the nature of reality. For us to unleash its vast power only involves removing any blocks that stop us from experiencing it in its fullness. These blocks are what constrict, contain or limit us, such as self-doubt, fear, judgment, mindlessness, grasping attachment, inertia, and resentment.

The flowmasters demonstrate that we can and do remove these blocks in ourselves. We can choose to adopt the beliefs, values, and behaviors that enhance our attributes of commitment, honesty, courage, passion, immediacy, openness, receptivity, positivity, and trust. We do that moment by moment by making decisions that lead us toward inner freedom and fulfillment. And when we commit ourselves to flow and act on it, we find ourselves supported by fortuitous events and synchronicity as we go about our daily lives.

In this chapter, to lay the groundwork for the techniques, you will:

+ Determine how you want to proceed through the techniques.

+ Create a supportive learning environment customized to your own needs.

+ Launch yourself on your journey with four basic flow skills: visualization, affirmation, journaling, and talk with like-minded others.

PROCEEDING THROUGH THE TECHNIQUES

The fourteen techniques are designed to move you more deeply into flow by presenting steps and exercises that allow you to become aware and accepting of yourself, to gain inner clarity, and to undertake action for the good of yourself, others, and the greater whole. They include:

Self-Knowledge

#1   Be Aware

#2   Accept Yourself and Others

#3   Express Who You Really Are

Inner Action

#4   Create Silence

#5   Follow Your Intuition

#6   Practice Mindfulness

Outer Action

#7   Do 100% of What You Know to Do—and Trust

#8   Finish Things and Move On

#9   Take Risks

#10   Break with Your Old Reality

Connecting with Others

#11   Appreciate Yourself

#12   Express Gratitude

#13   Give of Yourself

#14   Divination

Each technique includes a discussion based on input from flowmasters, survey respondents, and focus group participants, plus specific exercises for you to use to implement the discussion in your life. To go deeper into each subject, you will find additional books listed in the reference section at the end of the book.

You have many options in how to proceed with the techniques, among which are the following:

Comprehensive and Steady. Take the techniques slowly, starting from the beginning. Read a little every day. Do the exercises thoroughly. Write in your journal. Only go on to the next one when you feel you are complete with a technique—don't read ahead or be concerned with the next step. This approach will produce solid learning and results. If you're just beginning to explore yourself at deeper levels, this may be the best approach for you.

Comprehensive and Fast. Read the techniques from beginning to end. Then go back to the beginning and work your way straight through them, skimming over those skills you already have and slowing down to develop ones that need work. This may work best for you if you've already been involved in self-development.

Selective and Responsive to the Moment. What issue in your life at the moment is most pressing? Which of the techniques speaks to it most strongly? Read through the techniques, and find the one, two, or three that address what you're going through. Focus on learning those. Or select a long-running personal issue or goal and find techniques that address it.

Selective and a Risk. Look through the techniques for the one that appeals to you the least or challenges you the most. Examine yourself closely to see why this is so. And then consider doing it first. It may be the quickest route to immediate progress.

Selective and Serendipitous. Sit still, breathe deeply, and do what you do to align yourself with the Universe—getting calm inside, praying, meditating. Then close your eyes and, following your intuition, open the last part of the book to the page that feels right and put your finger somewhere on the page. Open your eyes—and do exactly what the flow exercise there says to do. If your finger lands on the discussion part of a technique, read it carefully, apply it to your life, and do the exercise that follows. You may find this approach effective if you already have high levels of synchronicity in your life.

As you consider the various approaches, remember that commitment—the first of the flowmaster attributes—is of critical importance. Whatever route you choose, your progress is assured if you do the exercises on a regular, ongoing basis—daily if possible—review your steps weekly.

As you proceed, you will find that you are learning

those techniques not just in the book but in your daily life. The Universe will present you with the exact situations you need to accelerate your learning in each particular area.

The **flow exercises** are designed in a range of styles. Some are visualizations that can be done in a few minutes. Others are comprehensive courses of action that require planning, talking, prioritizing, and evaluating, which could take much longer. Don't be worried that you must do every single exercise to experience flow: Use your judgment and tailor the work to your process—this is your journey.

One note on Technique 14, Divination. Divination is an option that is presented because some people have found it useful, but it is not for everyone. If you like the concept, read the chapter; if you don't, skip it.

As you go through the techniques, be patient with yourself. Change sometimes happens so slowly that we don't even notice it. If you were to change just one percent, do you think you would notice it? Would others? But remember that only one percent per week is considerable change over a year, and very noticeable. Anyone who has been on a diet knows how disheartening it can be to stand on the scales each day and even each week. Then when someone we have not seen for three months comments on how great we look, we gain another perspective from which to view the transformation of our body.

Change results in living a part of your life differently. This may stretch you in ways you have not considered: simple tasks may seem complex, comfortable interactions may seem strained. You may find yourself in conflict, either within yourself or with others. Don't worry: this loss of comfort is key to your transformation. A static body does not change and therefore is not transformed, but a body in flux can take another form, can be another way, and is transformed.

Flow is about lifelong learning, and this book is the next step on that path. No flowmaster we interviewed has mastered all the skills covered in the techniques—in fact, many of them are focusing on a particular skill again for the third or fourth time. The process resembles an upward spiral: the same theme emerges again and again, yet each time appears at a higher, more expanded level. With each level, the power of flow becomes steadier, stronger, and more pervasive through your life.

CUSTOMIZING YOUR LEARNING ENVIRONMENT

The techniques are about building skills to remove the obstacles that block the experience of flow from your life. Learning is key to this process. Learning permeates your life, whether you're selecting a phone company or a partner, handling a tough situation at work or a two-year-old's tantrums, evaluating a political candidate or a different approach to life. Some learning processes are common to most people; others are acquired through family, culture, an educational system.

By understanding how you learn and seeing effective approaches, you can customize your process so that you can learn the techniques faster, more thoroughly, and at deep levels of comprehension.

We'll be focusing on four areas in this part of the chapter:

✦ How to make the most of your visual, auditory, and kinesthetic modes of taking in information

✦ How to make practical use of the environment as a mirror

✦ How to advance through the steps in each technique

✦ How to use your daily life as a learning tool for flow

YOUR MODE OF TAKING IN INFORMATION

At any given point in time, out of the flood of stimuli that surrounds us—shapes, colors, sounds, smells, textures—studies show that our minds can take in only seven bits of information, plus or minus two. We tend to use one of these modes—visual, auditory, or kinesthetic—to determine what to focus on and to take in information. Note the words *tend to:* we all operate in all modes to some degree, but at any particular time we're usually depending more on one.

The mode we primarily use has a strong impact on how we learn, so by knowing how we operate, we can consciously speed up the learning curve.

The modes are:

Visual: Do you find yourself saying things like, "I just don't get the picture," or "I see what you mean," or "It's not clear to me"? In describing someone, do you use words like bright, dim, clear, colorful? If so, then you may look at the world visually—which is the mode of about two-thirds of Americans. Sunny Schlenger, for example, takes in information visually, and the clue is such sentences as: "If we realize we only know *part of the picture,* then we're more open to other information coming in."

Auditory: Do you hear yourself saying "I hear what you're getting at," or "That rings true to me," or "That sounds right"? Do you describe someone in terms of their loud car or soft-pitched voice? Then you use the auditory mode to take in information. About a sixth of Americans fall into this category. Ron Chin is in an auditory mode when he speaks of "being *in tune with* universal forces."

Kinesthetic: Do you "grasp the situation," "get hold of an idea" or "have a feeling" that something is so? Do you describe things as gripping, tender, grating, hot or cold, soft-

or hard-hearted? Then you take in information kinestheti-cally, along with a sixth of Americans. John Beal, for exam-ple, is primarily kinesthetic, and he "hits the road" to investigate the men playing war games near the stream he has rescued.

FLOW QUIZ
WHAT IS YOUR MODE?

Circle the words that you are most likely to use in your conversations with others:

bright	loud	grind
clear	sound	handle
look	speak	touch
view	tune	pressure
dark	crash	soft
colorful	harmony	ground
flash	hear	smooth
picture	noisy	push
see	listen	fallen
visions	music	vibrate

Totals: _____   _____   _____

If you have more words circled in the first column, you are primarily visual. If you circled more words in the second, you are primarily auditory; in the third, primarily kinesthetic. Also look at the balance between and among the modes. You operate most effectively when you are flexible enough to be able to use each of them at the right time, so notice where you might focus and stretch yourself to use them all fully.

As you read through the fourteen techniques, you can set up your learning environment to take advantage of your particular mode:

✦ If you're primarily visual, make pictures or charts or diagrams for yourself.

✦ If your favorite mode is auditory, keep noise to a minimum so that your channel is free.

✦ If you are kinesthetic, sit in a comfortable chair. Notice the sensations in your body as you read; notice which information alerts you and which makes you feel drowsy.

You can also use your primary mode to create a nurturing environment for yourself. If you are feeling unsteady, are having a bad day, or are dealing with an emotional topic, you can move to your own space to retreat from pressure. Your safe environment may be a physical location such as your home or office, an internal space resulting from meditation and prayer or from being with a compassionate friend, or a neutral place like the library or the park. To find that place, consider your mode:

✦ If you're visual, pick a place of beauty such as a garden.

✦ If you're auditory, find a background sound like a fountain or waterfall that's soothing.

✦ If you're kinesthetic, find a warm place in the sun where you can sprawl out and relax.

You can also actively work to expand the modes you operate in comfortably, which will open up a new world of sensation and discovery for you and greatly enhance how you learn.

Flow Exercise:
Expanding Your Modes

Try this exercise in three places: your home, a familiar place such as work or a mall, and a place you've never been before.

1. Start with the mode you're most comfortable with. For three minutes, focus all of your attention on taking in information that way. If you're visual, take in everything with your eyes; if you're auditory, listen for sounds (you may have to close your eyes to do so); if you're kinesthetic, explore the sensations in and on your body.

2. Move to a second mode, and spend three minutes there.

3. Move to the last mode, for three minutes.

4. Reflect on what you've learned. What do you know now that you didn't know before?

The better you get at this, the more you'll be able to switch to the mode that is most useful: a visual mode for an art exhibit, an auditory mode for the symphony, kinesthetic for splashing around a lake. Practice using words from all three modes in your conversations.

THE MIRROR GAME AND HOW TO PLAY IT

Flow gives you a sure sense of the connection between your inner world and the outer world—and you can use this dynamic in the most practical of ways in your learning process.

Think of the outer environment as a mirror of your inner environment. When you see something on the outside, such as an event or situation, look inside yourself for the reflection, the parallel, the connection.

If you don't like what you see, change it within yourself—and this will change your experience of the environment as well.

The mirror game is valuable because it is often easier to see something outside us than inside us. Let's see how this can work with the way in which you handle conflict. Your conflict style has an impact on the way you learn—especially when you are dealing with new ideas that may be at odds with your current beliefs and practices. This can create dissonance within you, which, though uncomfortable, is the way you change yourself for the better. The chances are high that you deal with internal conflicts the same way you manage conflicts with people in your life that you care about.

Think how you handle disagreements with your significant other, your child, your parent, your sibling, or a friend:

+ If you tend to deal straightforwardly and with positive regard for your loved one, you will likely treat yourself directly and kindly when you have an inner conflict.

+ If you usually avoid discussing a hot issue with another person, then you probably avoid resolution with yourself, especially when it involves what you feel to be a risk.

+ If you judge and condemn those who differ with you, then you may also find fault with yourself, which creates additional stress.

+ If you compromise in the sense that both you and your loved one give up what you want and settle for a lesser solution with which neither of you is truly happy, then in your own problem-solving you probably do not persevere to find creative options that meet or exceed your objectives.

If you look at conflict as a normal part of life to be managed the same way you manage your time and money, if you seek the greater good, if you pursue options with others which are at least as good as where you started out and usually better, then your conflict style will greatly enhance your learning—and your life.

ADVANCING THROUGH THE TECHNIQUES STEP BY STEP

Education researchers have found that there are six basic steps to learning, which most often occur one after the other in a logical fashion. If you know these steps and are certain to include each of them in your learning process, you will get the greatest benefit from the fourteen techniques and accompanying exercises.

The six steps we go through in learning are:

✦ Knowledge
✦ Comprehension
✦ Analysis
✦ Synthesis
✦ Application
✦ Evaluation

You'll find as you go consciously through these steps of learning that you encounter variations on this process. The steps may follow this order one time and an entirely different order the next time. Each step is independent of the others and yet dependent upon them: seldom, however, does understanding develop without each of the steps. The time it takes for you to perform each one may also vary: one step may take only a moment of reflection, and another may require a longer time to mull over.

As you go through each technique, do the following:

1. KNOWLEDGE: Take in the new information about the technique.

Read the information closely. You might have any of a number of responses. You may find that what you are reading confirms long-held beliefs. You may find that it is contradictory to your present thinking. Or it may be uncomfortable just because it is new. Absorb the new information and stretch yourself by including it in your perspective. You often learn best when you see something with fresh eyes: to see the technique clearly, you may have to take off the particular glasses through which you currently look. Don a new pair that are less colored by your past experience, your culture, your decisions, your ideas about your future hopes or plans.

2. COMPREHENSION: Interpret the new information based on what you already know or do.

How does the new information compare with what you already know and do? Think of a situation recently when this new information or approach might have been useful. Play out in your mind how events would have unfolded if you'd had the new information, comparing that scenario to the actual events.

3. ANALYSIS: Break this new information into smaller components in your mind and examine those.

Split the technique down into its smallest possible components. Think through each individual piece and apply it to a situation. Keep your mind open and able to see in a new way. Sit with the outcome without judging its rightness or wrongness—just look at the result that is produced. Seek out its value.

4. SYNTHESIS: Reassemble those components into a new version of the technique that is useful to you.

Keep the parts that work. Combine them in any way you want. You have now customized that technique and adapted it to your own use.

5. *APPLICATION: Try out the new version in your life.*

Now it's time to risk. Use your new technique, your customized way of expressing yourself, in your daily life. Apply it to a situation that is not earth-shattering. Notice how everything feels. Give it time, for this step is also about persevering. When we are comfortable, we often are not growing.

6. *EVALUATION: Observe whether it works: keep it, modify it, or reject it.*

Does your new technique improve the quality of your life? Does it bring you closer to where you want to be? Does it move you into flow? This evaluation process is about seeing what works for you, what transforms your life.

In this learning process there are no mistakes, just opportunities to learn. You will find that consequences arise that are not exactly as you anticipated—and those consequences may include synchronicities. Keep an eye out for them, for it is in attending to these unintended consequences that learning often takes place.

INQUIRY: USE YOUR DAILY LIFE AS A FLOW TOOL

When you go about with an inquiring mind, consciously investigating what happens in your life, you'll be able to turn both ordinary and exceptional circumstances into valuable learning tools. You'll bring into conscious awareness habits that might be holding you back, which will enable you to choose to fresher, better ways of behaving.

The seven steps below are ways to inquire into a situation you find yourself in. This process is highly interactive: it requires you to converse. You can do this by working internally and carrying on discussions with yourself, perhaps in your journal; by talking with a like-minded friend; or by finding a discussion group.

1. Be a fact-finder. Observe yourself at several levels. What exactly did you do or say in a particular situation? What were the circumstances that brought up this response in you? Were you authentic or were you putting on an act? What was the process you went through? What result did you produce? How did you leave the others with whom you interacted? This step is not about fault-finding, and it is not about making yourself or others either right or wrong. It is about looking objectively at an event and describing it from as many perspectives as you can.

2. Reflect on the process and on the result. Compare the facts you found with what you meant to accomplish. Were you successful at what you set out to do? Did you produce the result you intended? Were you considerate of those with whom you interacted? What worked well? What would you add or change if the same situation were to occur again? What lessons do you see in the process? Was your investment worth the return?

3. Mull over the information. After bringing your full attention to the fact-finding and the reflecting, go on doing what you ordinarily do. As thoughts surface during the day, watch them go by, much as you casually glance up when a car drives by your window. Unless there is something particularly noteworthy, you just register the car and return to whatever you were doing. When something noteworthy does pass by the window of your mind, ponder it briefly and objectively, then let it go. After some time, focus again directly on the event or interaction and review the facts, adding any new insights that have surfaced during this mulling period. Particularly fruitful times for this step are after prayer, meditation, a period of silence, or a night of sleep.

4. See the mirror. Look for any part of positive or negative interaction with another person that reflects back what is going on inside you. Did you react to the other person as though you were five and they were your mother or father? Is the fault or strength that you found in the other person the same fault or strength that lies in you? It is often easier to see another's fault than to see your own, to appreciate another's strengths than it is to appreciate your own. By using the mirror process we talked about on p. 108, you learn more about the hidden side of yourself. When you hear yourself judging another, make the same judgment about yourself and see if it also describes some facet of yourself.

5. See yourself in the future. Project this same scenario into a future situation. What would you do the same and what would you do differently? How do you feel when you resolve the future scenario with your new-found knowledge? Call upon your strengths to meet the new challenge and to shore up your weaknesses. If the outcome of your future scenario does not suit you, play it through again and again, modifying it until it does.

6. Review similar situations. If other past experiences are similar, review what happened with those. Are there recurring themes and responses? What are the differences in how you operated? What are the differences in the results produced? Replay those memories and change them to include any new perspectives or processes. See if you feel any differently about the people involved or the outcome.

7. Evaluate your learning. Be clear about what you have learned and what value this has for you. If in first analysis there seems to be none, look for the long-term gain. There are no failures in the process of inquiry, only opportunities for learning.

FLOW AIDS: FOUR BASIC SKILLS

Throughout the techniques, there are four basic skills you can use to accelerate your progress: visualization, affirmation, journaling, and working with like-minded others. Because these skills are so effective, not just in the techniques but in your life, we'll go through them one by one.

VISUALIZATION

Creating a visualization involves making an internal image of the result you want to obtain. Visualizations are extremely powerful because they put your unconscious mind to work for you even as your conscious mind is going about your everyday life. As you work with each technique, construct a visualization for it: for example, see yourself being intuitive, finishing projects, feeling full of gratitude, overflowing with generosity.

A visualization involves the following steps:

1. Begin with silence. Sit quietly, close your eyes, and breathe deeply. Feel the air as it enters your nostrils, travels through your chest, pauses, turns, and begins its return trip, passing lightly out your nostrils. Do this five to ten times, until you are deeply relaxed.

2. Form an image in your mind that depicts your focus for the exercise. The image may be a snapshot or a moving picture. Experiment with the image until you find the visualization that creates the feeling you want, such as soft, gentle, dynamic, intense, or relaxed. This image is your creation, so spend time with it until you get it exactly as you want it.

◆ Holding the image before you, try intensifying its colors, changing it to black and white, expanding the parameters so that it is larger than life, shrinking it so that it is small and manageable.

✦ Move the image to the left or right, up or down.

✦ Listen for sounds connected to your picture or add them, then intensify or reduce them. Give your image a musical score.

✦ See the texture of the image, and change that.

3. Experience your visualization in all its dimensions, textures, colors, sounds. See it, hear it, feel it. Put it in a file folder in your memory so you can bring the image easily to mind when you need it.

Flow Exercise:
Visualizing Yourself in Flow

Form a visualization of yourself fully in the power of flow. To make it clearer, focus on a specific area of your life in which you would like to experience more synchronicity and fortuitous events, such as family, career, romance, spiritual life, finances, or travel.

1. After becoming silent by doing the breathing described above, construct a picture of what it would look like to be fully in flow in that part of your life. Is it a snapshot or a moving image? If a moving image, see yourself in a variety of situations eased by flow. Hear what you say and others say to you. Feel it in your body and emotions.

2. Adjust the visualization until it is exactly as you want it. Intensify or change the colors, make it smaller or larger, move it around in your mind's eye, listen for sounds or provide them.

3. Stay with the visualization, feeling it permeate every cell in your body. Then go about your day.

AFFIRMATIONS

Affirmations are positive statements you make to yourself, which consciously program the unconscious part of your mind and set the stage for self-fulfilling prophecy. They can be extremely powerful in producing desired results. Repeating an affirmation throughout the day can help you feel more in control, more able to deal with the difficulties of life. Say it at set times: in the morning, as you drive down a particular street, when your wristwatch goes off on the hour, when certain commercials come on the TV. As you go through the techniques, design affirmations for each one—and then proceed as though what you are affirming is already accomplished, is already true.

+ Word affirmative statements as though the action you are affirming has already taken place: *I am healthy, happy, and aware* rather than *I want to be healthy, happy, and aware.*

+ Word affirmative statements in the positive: *I have changed* rather than *I am no longer stuck.*

+ Word affirmative statements so that your inner critic agrees with you. If you find inner resistance, a little voice saying "Oh, yeah?" reword your affirmation so that you and your critic are aligned on the result.

Flow Exercise:
Composing an Affirmation for Flow

Return to that same area of your life in which you visualized having more flow, and design an affirmation. Some possibilities:

I am confident and happy dealing with clients at work.
Money comes to me easily from many sources.
My teenager and I have a deep, loving relationship.

For increased effect, combine affirmations with visualizations. In your mind, as you affirm yourself and your actions, see others watching you and hear what they have to say. Add colors, sounds, textures, tastes to your affirmation so you have a full experience to guide you to the power of flow. Incorporate your affirmation into your daily life on a regular basis.

JOURNAL WRITING

Bringing your thoughts, ideas, emotions, and wishes into the concrete world through journal writing makes them real and tangible, giving you more conscious control over your life. It allows you to step back from your thoughts and emotions and take an unattached, objective view of what's going on inside you.

Obtain a journal. It can be as simple as a yellow legal pad, as elegant as an embossed diary, or as high-tech as a file on your computer screen. Once a day or every other day, use it to record your journey into flow. Record your Flow Exercises in it. Write about what is happening to you internally: what insights, synchronicities, fortuitous events did you experience today? What came up that was germane to the technique you're learning? What are your thoughts, feelings, hopes, fears about it?

Journaling can clear your thoughts and prepare you for action. (Action plans and To Do lists are variations on journal writings, for they are also ways to work externally on your thoughts.) It's not necessary to spend hours at a time on your journal. Even a few minutes every day, done day after day, will have a measurable impact. In *The Artist's Way,* Julia Cameron suggests spending a few minutes every morning quickly filling three pages of a yellow legal pad with whatever comes into your mind, without censoring or judging your writing.

On a regular basis, at a specific time, put down on

paper your thoughts about the major issues in your life. To work with a specific issue, start off with stream of consciousness writing. Make no attempt to organize the words or even spell them correctly. When you've finished, read it over and think about it. Either then or at your next session, rework the piece and get it just right so that it clearly expresses your thoughts and feelings. Once a week, review your journal to reflect on your steps toward flow and plan your next ones.

Flow Exercise: Journaling into Flow

1. Returning to the area of flow you focused on previously, write in your journal your thoughts, ideas, fears, and wishes about it. Fill two or three pages, without self-censoring or striving for perfection.

2. Perform the visualization from the previous exercise for several minutes. Stop. Write your thoughts and feelings.

3. Say the affirmation from the previous exercise several times, until you feel it solidify inside you. Stop. Write your thoughts and feelings.

4. Reflect on this process: What have you learned about yourself? Make adjustments if necessary to make the visualization and the affirmation more compelling.

TALK WITH LIKE-MINDED OTHERS

A like-minded person—someone who shares your interest in personal expansion and growth—can be of invaluable help to you on your path by being your sounding board, support system, and source of inspiration. And you can do the same for that person, which will further accelerate your progress. This "flow partner" might be a friend, a spouse, a relative, a coworker, someone you meet at a workshop or on the Internet. (The web site for this book has a place for people in search of flow partners: http://www.FlowPower.com.) Their path may not be identical to yours—perhaps they are reading another book or following a different spiritual practice—but if they are happy to share their learning with you and support you in your path, that is fine. Agree to work together, and set up ground rules. One might be that everything said is confidential, another might be that neither of you will "buy into the other's issues." This means that just because one has a bad experience with a particular person, thing, or place, the other will not assume the same would happen to them. Agree upon the times you meet in person and when you are available by phone. It is important that you can reach each other both at those wonderful times of brilliant insight and to ponder the latest upset.

Once every week or two, meet with your flow partner to go over your short- and long-term plans, voice your commitment to the process, and review your journal. Practice good listening skills, both on yourself—hear what you have to say—and on your partner. This includes taking in nonverbal as well as verbal messages: be alert to your partner's posture, tonal quality, eye movements. Listen carefully: When people are expressing true commitment, their voices have a deeper, quieter tonal quality, while a "good idea" that they haven't committed to fully is spoken more quickly in a higher tone. Share at deepest levels, for this is what makes the process work effectively for both of you.

Flow Exercise:
Levels of Communication

To experience what it means to communicate at various levels, sit across from your flow partner. Take turns with each step below, each speaking for 30 seconds while the other listens.

1. Chatter: Exchange greetings and light talk that is impersonal in nature.

2. Data: Give information, such as facts and figures about something.

3. Opinion: Tell your partner what you think about a current issue or event.

4. Feelings: Share an emotion you're feeling.

5. Nonverbal: Look at each other without speaking.

Now share your thoughts and feelings during each of the steps. When did you feel most connected? Least connected? What did you learn about yourself?

PRACTICAL ADVICE FOR THE TECHNIQUES

Use a beginner's mind. As you go through the techniques and exercises, take risks by setting aside your own ideas and proceeding as if you had no idea which way to go or what comes next. This is the beginner's mind of Zen, and from there you can move in any and all directions. Act as though the technique you're learning is the only way, the right way, the truth. Then see what result is produced in your life. This does not foreclose options: If it isn't what you want, you can always go back to your previous ways.

Be focused. Concentrate your activity on one part of your life, such as home or work or inner growth. As a technique becomes integrated there, watch for it to show up in other parts of your life as well. If you are working on acceptance, when you become more accepting with members of your family, you may find yourself being more accepting of coworkers—and they of you. As you become more receptive to acknowledgment from your boss, you may find yourself more able to receive a friend's sincere thanks without twinges of self-consciousness.

Be patient. As you teach yourself the techniques and apply them to your life, you will transform yourself. Your changes may be so dramatic that they will be immediately gratifying. More often than not, though, they happen slowly and surely. Make your goal to be changing just one percent a week for a year.

Remember that flow is a lifelong process. It takes time, energy, and commitment—but no one who experiences the harmony and power of flow ever wishes to return to a life of struggle.

Flow Exercise: Make a Commitment

Do something concrete to signify to yourself and the greater whole that you are on the path of flow. Be creative. Have fun. Some possibilities:

✦ Create your own ceremony. Light a candle, read a poem, say a prayer.

✦ Draw a line on the ground. Step over it.

✦ Get together with a flow partner. Shake hands on your commitment.

✦ Write out a contract to and from yourself.

✦ Climb to the top of a mountain.

✦ Plant a flower that represents the qualities you want in your life.

Now that you understand your learning process better, know the four basic skills, and have made a commitment, you are ready to proceed on your journey through the techniques. You cannot fail, for the power of flow is yours for the undertaking.

7 KNOW YOURSELF

Knowing yourself is the first step—and the foundation—of the journey into flow. Before you can advance very far, you must be aware of who you are, where you are, and where you want to go. Although this sounds easy, all too often we live unconsciously, unaware of the beliefs that drive us, the opportunities that surround us, and the effect of our behavior on others. If we're unaware, we can be bogged down, derailed by powerful emotions and unknown drives. We lumber through life when we could be doing figure eights on Rollerblades. We struggle when we could be in the ease of flow.

The techniques in this chapter develop self-awareness and self-acceptance, then press us to express ourselves fully in our relations with ourselves and others. The techniques are:

1. Be Aware
2. Accept Yourself and Others
3. Express Who You Really Are

Awareness is the beginning, and it is a skill that we develop and keep on developing until it permeates all aspects of our lives. Opportunities to increase our awareness are present in every moment, and they keep coming around again. We might spend a great deal of time and effort working through some area of our lives, think it is behind us, and find ourselves again addressing the same issues, but at a more intense and more fruitful level.

Once aware of how we believe, think, and act, we move into accepting the place where we are now, which means accepting ourselves with all our strengths and limitations. Only then do we use the present as a place of beginnings rather than a place of self-recrimination. Then we consciously mold our lives, expressing ourselves with authenticity and power in the way we work, play, interact, love, and connect with others.

As we seek the forms of self-expression that feel right, and as we risk being ourselves instead of acting like everyone else, we find what gives us passion. From the excitement this generates, our commitment grows to ourselves, to others, and to the greater whole, and we find things falling into place in our life. We are in tune with our deepest selves—and from there, synchronicity bubbles forth.

BE AWARE

What lies behind us and what lies before us are tiny matters compared to what lies within us.

Oliver Wendell Holmes

Do you have a situation in your life that, no matter what you do, always hits you broadside? That seems to knock whatever synchronicity and flow you have out of your days? It might be a testy relationship with your mother or teenager, or bills piling up, or your jealousy when your spouse gets attention instead of you. Maybe it's your fear of speaking in public, or your ambivalence about getting married, or deadline pressure at work. When you're in those states of frustration and fear, everything seems hopelessly tangled together. You find yourself getting upset the same old way, saying the same destructive things to yourself or another, and feeling angry and guilty afterward.

Congratulations! You, too, are on planet Earth. There's not a flowmaster we interviewed who hasn't dealt with such issues—and who isn't still dealing with them in some way. Unhooking ourselves from triggers and pain is a large part of what is involved in experiencing more flow in our lives. When we're out of sorts with ourselves, it's hard to be in tune with others, not to mention with underlying reality. So although the process of awareness isn't always easy, it is what leads us into more joy and clarity. The more we know ourselves, the more quickly we can pull ourselves out of those states and come again into the power of flow.

Self-awareness is the first step. You must first get a grip on exactly what you're doing in an emotionally charged, mentally frustrating situation. Awareness in itself changes you: reflecting on the process, watching it happen from a detached perspective, causes change to happen on an uncon-

scious level. Developing awareness can be an individual in-
trospective process or an interactive group or seminar
process. It can involve interpreting dreams, attending work-
shops, reading books, consulting with therapists.

As you consciously undergo the process of self-
awareness, talking things through with another person can
give you greater clarity. If it is someone you care about, it can
also strengthen the bonds between you. Sunny Schlenger took
her twelve-year-old daughter, Lauren, to a synchronicity
focus group meeting in which core beliefs were being discussed. During the meeting, Sunny found she had problems
grasping what it was all about, much to her chagrin. Back at
home, Lauren drew her mother a diagram that had been presented and explained it to her. "But why did I react the way I
did?" wondered Sunny. Using the diagram, they traced her
embarrassment back to a fourth-grade teacher who used to
humiliate her. "That's it!" said Sunny. "I think I should know
things, and I don't feel worthy unless I do." She started crying—an indication of hitting upon a hidden core belief. "I
feel the same way when Daddy asks me to make up my mind
real fast and I don't know what I want," said Lauren softly.
Together, they learned more than if each had worked alone.

DELVING INTO CORE BELIEFS

We each have values that drive our behavior, and those values
are based on core beliefs that often remain unconscious and
unexamined. Coming into greater awareness means gaining
insight into those beliefs and making choices to keep them or
to put them aside and develop different ones. The process is
well worth the effort, for the most direct way to change your
behavior is to change your core beliefs.

The first step is to understand how your belief system is
constructed. Think of an onion. The innermost layers, the
core, are your *core beliefs*. These are the pieces of informa-

tion you hold most dearly and most preciously protect. They include who you see yourself as being—your core identity—and what you know most surely to be the ways of the world. They include your deepest ideas about God, about society, about yourself. There are few words for them: you just *know.*

The next layer of the onion is your *attitudes* about those core beliefs. Attitudes are evaluations: whether something is good or bad, first or last, most or least. You have many more attitudes than you have core beliefs, and they are more responsive to change because they are less integral to the way you define yourself. Experience and information can change attitudes.

BELIEF SYSTEM

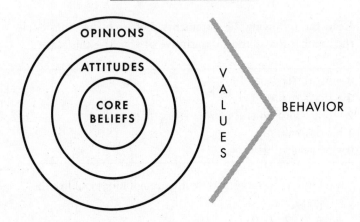

The outside onion layer is your *opinions,* those bits of information that you share readily with others and that seem much more important to you than to anyone else—because everyone has so many opinions of their own. Opinions are the most easily changed of these three elements. Typically you have at least one opinion about everything, and often several, depending upon the circumstances in which you find your-self.

This belief system produces your *personal values:* what makes a difference to you, what you would take a stand for, what you would put time, money, and energy into. Values motivate your *behavior,* the way you act day in and day out. Your values shape your commitment, your courage, your honesty, your receptivity, all your flowmaster attributes. And they are totally of your own design.

The following quiz and exercises will help you identify the values that are paramount in your life and allow you to trace those values back to the core beliefs that create them.

Flow Exercise: Values Quiz

Read the following 24 statements. For each question, circle the number that is most descriptive of you. Use this scale:

---

4 = DEFINITELY TRUE

3 = MOSTLY TRUE

2 = UNDECIDED WHETHER STATEMENT IS TRUE OR FALSE

1 = MOSTLY FALSE

0 = DEFINITELY FALSE

---

1. I intend to retire early with enough money to live the good life.
    4   3   2   1   0

2. I believe that I am loved by and connected to a higher power or larger reality.
    4   3   2   1   0

3. I enjoy now, or have enjoyed in the past, a close relationship with one or both of my parents.
    4   3   2   1   0

4. I enjoy and appreciate beauty and beautiful objects, events, or things.
   4   3   2   1   0

5. I enjoy creating projects of my own.
   4   3   2   1   0

6. I feel that a rich life contains many friends and much friendship.
   4   3   2   1   0

7. I feel that life is a positive experience.
   4   3   2   1   0

8. I enjoy both giving and going to parties.
   4   3   2   1   0

9. I would choose to take a class in art, drawing or sculpture over a class in math.
   4   3   2   1   0

10. I think holidays should be spent with family and close relatives.
    4   3   2   1   0

11. I like fine things and have expensive tastes.
    4   3   2   1   0

12. I think decorating an apartment or house is a fun thing to do.
    4   3   2   1   0

13. I expect to earn more money than the average person on the street.
    4   3   2   1   0

14. I take pleasure in buying special gifts for members of my family.
    4   3   2   1   0

15. I have a personally meaningful relationship with God/the Universe/underlying reality.
    4   3   2   1   0

16.　Had I the talent, I would write, draw, or create art of some kind.
4　3　2　1　0

17.　I have a close friend I talk with about almost everything.
4　3　2　1　0

18.　I enjoy owning good music, literature, and artwork.
4　3　2　1　0

19.　I think it is good and fun to make something out of nothing.
4　3　2　1　0

20.　I agree with the phrase "money can't buy happiness, but it sure makes life much more comfortable."
4　3　2　1　0

21.　I think that spending time with my family is both necessary and enjoyable.
4　3　2　1　0

22.　I feel fulfilled and satisfied with life.
4　3　2　1　0

23.　I would give up sleep in order to spend time with good friends.
4　3　2　1　0

24.　When I see a new building or house, I think first about how it looks and then how it will be used.
4　3　2　1　0

SCORING: On the tally sheet opposite, enter the number you circled for each statement next to the number for that statement. (Notice they are not all sequential.) Then total your score for each value.

VALUES

MONEY	SPIRITUAL	FAMILY	BEAUTY	CREATIVE	SOCIAL
1 ____	2 ____	3 ____	4 ____	5 ____	6 ____
11 ____	7 ____	10 ____	9 ____	12 ____	8 ____
13 ____	15 ____	14 ____	18 ____	16 ____	17 ____
20 ____	22 ____	21 ____	24 ____	19 ____	23 ____

Totals

____	____	____	____	____	____

This tally sheet gives you a snapshot of your current values. There are no right answers, just *your* answers. Think about the relationships among your scores on the different values. Which numbers were higher? Lower? Do the scores reflect your existing ideas of what you consider important?

Flow Exercises:
Understanding Your Core Beliefs

TRACING VALUES BACK TO THE CORE

You can use knowledge of your values to work your way into your core beliefs. From there you can make changes that you would like. This exercise is most easily done with a flow partner.

1. Choose a value you'd like to examine—perhaps one that surfaced in a difficult situation, such as Sunny's.

2. Ask yourself what your opinions about it are. Opinions are characterized by a fluid outpouring of words and little emotion.

3. Ask yourself what your attitude about it is. Attitudes are a more intense discussion since they involve an investment in something or someone. Discussing them, you might have a feeling of being "right" about the topic.

4. Ask yourself what your beliefs about it are. Beliefs are usually stumbled upon as you talk about an issue or topic. They are difficult to talk about, and sometimes they are impossible to find words for. They are precious to us because they *are* us.

5. Explore whether you choose to keep those beliefs or change them.

CORE TRANSFORMATION®

Core Transformation is a simple and effective process to melt away core beliefs that limit us and block the power of flow. Designed by Connirae Andreas of NLP Comprehensive in Boulder, Colorado, it works in a surprising way: It uses your limitations to provide you with a direct route to an experience of the love, peace, and oneness that lie at your core.

Core Transformation is based on the idea that our personal obstacles all have a positive purpose. The positive purpose we discover doesn't always make sense to our logical minds, because it is based on emotional logic, not mental logic. By becoming aware of the deepest purpose, we gain clarity and self-acceptance, and the core belief and the behavior we don't want can effortlessly melt away. Shannon, for example, had been trying to conceive a child for two years, and in doing Core Transformation she discovered that a part of her wanted freedom and felt uncertain about being tied down with a child. One month later, she was pregnant.

The following exercise is a shortened version of the ten-step process detailed in Andreas's book, *Core Transformation: Reaching the Wellspring Within.*

Find a quiet place where you won't be bothered for 15 to 30 minutes. Have a pen and paper handy. You can read these steps yourself or have someone read them to you.

1. Ask yourself, *What stops me from being what I want to be?* Think of a time when you had a feeling you didn't want to have, perhaps because you were behaving in a way you didn't like. Notice where that feeling is located. Where do you feel it most strongly? Where does it "live"?

2. Welcome that feeling or image as a part of you that is a long-lost friend. Be gentle and loving toward it. Then ask the question, *What do you want?* Await its answer. It may come as words, a feeling, a picture, a twinge in your body. When you get it, write it down. Don't try to figure out the answer; let it come from inside you. You'll have a sense of it emerging. Remember, there's no right or wrong answer, and it doesn't have to make sense—in fact, if it doesn't make sense, it's a sign you're on the right track, responding out of emotional logic, not out of mental logic.

3. Invite that part of you to step into having what it wants—for instance, it may want to feel satisfied or accepted. Let your inner part fill with that feeling. Ask, *What do you want, through having this feeling fully and completely, that is even more important?* Await the answer. Write it down. Then invite the part to step into the new feeling, becoming permeated with it. Ask again, *What do you want, through having this feeling fully and completely, that is even more important?* Keep gong until you reach a state that feels deeply peaceful and loving and quiet. When you get to whatever your

inner part most deeply wants, the core state, you'll find it profoundly moving, and there won't be anywhere else to try to get to.

4. Next you'll let the core state transform each of the "wants" that your inner part has from step 3. Use your notes as a guide. First, allow your inner part to experience the core state deeply. Let that feeling of love, peace, or oneness radiate through each of the wants on your list. Start with the last want, and go backward to the first. Invite your inner part to experience how already having the core state transforms each. You don't need to understand exactly what is changing; just enjoy it as it radiates through each. When your inner part arrives at the beginning—that feeling you didn't like—notice how different it feels now. Take a moment to let the core state fill your whole body. As you go about your day, you may be surprised that this process has transformed more than just the issue you began with.

AVENUES TO SELF-AWARENESS

SELF-REFLECTION

By watching your own actions and listening to your own conversations, both internal and external, you can uncover the beliefs that are underneath what you say, do, feel, and think. In order to perceive those beliefs and thoughts, you must be having them, but not entangled in them. You must maintain a delicate balance between inner observer and participant. To gain insight into yourself and practice this skill, do the exercise below.

PSYCHOTHERAPY

Undertaking therapy is one tried and true way you can sys-
tematically undertake the process of self-awareness, particularly if you feel blocked or frustrated in one area of endeavor.
A psychologist, social worker, or counselor can be pivotal in
helping you make sense of the patterns in your life and heal
old wounds. Find someone who works with an approach that
appeals to you. Jungian and transpersonal psychologists are
more likely to have a worldview that acknowledges spiritual
drives than a Freudian psychoanalyst will; cognitive therapists, who focus on changing destructive thinking patterns,
behavioral therapists, and body-centered therapists can produce results in short periods of time. Even more important
than technique is chemistry: don't hesitate to interview therapists until you find one who seems wise, compassionate, and
trustworthy. When you find someone you click with, give it
everything you've got. Don't hold back in the goal of making
your life all it can be.

DREAMS

Your dreams are a rich source of self-awareness. By noticing
them, giving them value, and exploring them, you can find
startling clarity and insight in images that seem at first non-
sensical. Jung believed dreams work on three levels to move
us toward wholeness: they show us parts of ourselves we
don't want to acknowledge; they link us to underlying arche-
typal patterns that drive us; and they point to future possibilities.

The language of your dreams is uniquely your own. To
interpret it, try retelling it, substituting other words for the
objects in the dream. A dream of yourself with a baby in a
carriage at the bottom of a long steep staircase might be interpreted as "I have something precious and fragile, enclosed
in a certain form, that I have to take on what seems a hard

and upward journey." Suddenly, your real feelings about that pet project you're pushing at work become clear.

Metaphors and similes can expand the possible meaning. A dream of seeing your deceased body may refer to the end of an aspect of your life, not to literal death. The birth of a male child may be about your getting in touch with your masculinity, or it may be about starting a new business that is sports-oriented. Or you can consider every part of a dream as some part or attribute of yourself, relating it back to you explicitly. A dream about your mother is a dream about your maternal aspect; a dream about a path is about your chosen direction in life; a dream about a flower is about your spiritual unfoldment. Follow whatever interpretation comes intuitively forward and gives meaning to you.

Flow Exercises: Becoming Aware

SELF-REFLECTION

Sit comfortably in a quiet place, very early in the morning, before the activity of the day presses upon you. Allow yourself a generous amount of time and space. Breathe slowly into the depths of your lungs, move your attention gently around your body, stretching it and relaxing it. Then sit in a comfortable posture that is alert and open, your hands lightly on your lap and your feet flat on the floor.

Imagine you have a television screen or window immediately in front of you. As your thoughts come up, see them on that screen or through that window. You will be somewhat detached or distanced from them. When a thought or feeling or sensation arises, notice it. Remark on it as though you are watching a television program you are not too interested in. Do not think about it or respond to it or engage in it in any way. Ask: *What does this accomplish? What does it get me? How does it work? What is behind it?* When the answer comes up, observe it in the same way, and ask the questions again. Continue this observe-and-ask process until there are no more answers, or until a different thought appears in your window.

If stress or tension develops, gently take a few more deep breaths and focus on tensing and relaxing first your arms and legs and then your whole body. Spend a moment appreciating what you have learned about your deepest self, and gently move on to the activities of the day.

WORKING WITH YOUR DREAMS

Dreams, like synchronicity, respond to attention: if you want them, they will come; if you use them, they will be more frequent and vivid. Use the following steps to enhance your dreams as a tool toward self-awareness.

1. Think of something in your life or behavior you'd like to know more about. Write it in your journal.

2. Spend a few minutes reflecting on it. Write down your thoughts.

3. Ask your unconscious to provide you with a dream that you will be aware of upon awakening.

4. Set your alarm for an hour before you usually arise. Put a pen and your journal within reach of your bed.

5. When the alarm goes off, without getting out of bed, start writing in your journal what you dreamed and what images are in your mind. Draw pictures if you'd like.

6. Read what you wrote. Continue writing any thoughts and interpretations you might have of it.

7. Accept the gift of the dream. Give thanks.

8. Go about your day, keeping your eyes and ears open for further information about the topic that comes to you

in the form of synchronicity and fortuitous events. Look at what happens metaphorically: if it were a dream, how would you interpret it?

9. For more information on your question, follow the same steps for several more nights.

ACCEPT YOURSELF AND OTHERS

Accepting yourself means being okay with who you are, exactly as you are right now. It means seeing the value in how you've lived your life. It means acknowledging that you've always done the best you could in any particular circumstance. It means treating yourself as tenderly as you would a small, innocent child.

It also means accepting other people as they are instead of trying to change them. It is understanding that when people don't act as you'd like, they're still doing what's right for their own growth even if they're taking a more difficult path. It is trusting that when things don't go your way, they're still in the larger picture, going the way they're meant to go.

Acceptance does not mean that you ignore your limitations or that you don't change your life for the better, as you see it. But it does mean you stop blaming yourself and finding fault with yourself, dragging down your spirits.

When we accept ourselves and others, we find ourselves greatly energized. It gives us a place from which to start. Instead of berating ourselves for what we are not, we are building our futures on what we are. It makes our energy available for moving forward—and enhances flow in our lives.

Don't be surprised to see synchronicity bringing things to your attention that you need to accept. If you're angry about something in yourself and want to avoid thinking about it, you'll see it mirrored all around you. If you can't accept what someone else did to you, you're likely to keep running into that person or someone like him or her. By facing what is necessary, you move ultimately into greater freedom.

Some of the ideas may be new or unusual to you. Try them for a period of time and see what result they produce. If you like them, keep them, and if you don't, put them aside.

SEE EVERYTHING THAT HAPPENS
AS A LESSON

By understanding that there is a purpose to each and every event, that there are no mistakes, we move into acceptance, because then everything is an opportunity for growth and learning. There is value in everything that comes our way, both good and bad. Understanding this will illuminate your life in new and intriguing ways, and will help you learn from the experiences in your life.

Flow Exercise: Life Lessons

What lessons have you learned in your life, and what value have you found in events? You can spend a few minutes or a few hours on this exercise. To get more value, go into it deeply and work on it over several days.

1. Draw three vertical columns on a sheet of paper. In the left-hand column, list the major events and turning points of your life. Include times of insight, crisis, and joy.

2. In the middle column, list what you learned from each one. Ask yourself: *What did this teach me? What did it lead to? How has it made me a better person?*

3. In the right-hand column, look at each event in terms of flow and synchronicity: *What coincidences happened? How did one thing lead to another? When did it seem I was being directed a certain way?*

4. Now stand back and look at it. What kinds of patterns emerge? What are the major lessons you've been dealing with? Ask yourself, *What can I do consciously to enhance my learning?*

ACKNOWLEDGE THAT YOU'VE ALWAYS DONE YOUR BEST

Look back at a time you wish you had done something different. Were you doing the very best you could have at that time, given the situation? Of course you were, because if you had known what to do to make it come out better, you would have. If you'd known how to correct your children's behavior effectively without making them cry, you would have. If you'd known how to break off your relationship without causing pain to yourself or another, you would have. So much of life seems to be about learning how to do things right. But just as you wouldn't punish a six-year-old for not being able to do algebra, don't punish yourself for not knowing then what you know now. This attitude opens up a space for learning, because when something goes wrong, the assumption is that what is missing is not integrity but skill. Human living skills in active listening and relationship building we can learn—when we aren't entangled in self-blame and guilt.

Flow Exercise: Acknowledging Your Personal Best

To deepen in yourself the certainty that you've always done your best, go through the following steps with a flow partner.

1. Sit facing your partner. Describe something you've done that you feel good about. Say sincerely to your partner, "And I did my best."

2. Your partner, after listening closely, will repeat the statement back to you, emphasizing, "And you did your *very* best." Listen deeply. Take it in.

3. Repeat the statement again, adding, "And I did my *very* best." Notice how different it feels. Acknowledge your partner with a nod.

4. Without pausing, exchange roles and repeat the process.

5. Go through the process several more times, choosing things you've done that you second-guess and doubt yourself for.

VALUE YOURSELF

The difference between who you think you ought to be or want to be and who you judge yourself to be is your level of self-esteem. If you see yourself as an excellent student but receive a C in a class, you will likely consider yourself not good enough. If you think having long blond hair and a slim body is the key to finding true love, but you yourself have brown hair and a large frame, you may find yourself inadequate. If you value youth, but your children are no longer teenagers, you'll consider yourself too old for happiness. Now that you understand this equation, you can change it.

Flow Exercise: Self-Esteem

Look carefully at who you think you ought to be or want to be. Visualize this ideal self standing in front of you. As you do this exercise, remember that your ideal self and the objective self you'll be looking at are your companions in self-esteem. But they are your creations. You can re-create them as you wish, at any time you wish. As you look at your ideal self, ask yourself these questions:

1. *Who do I think I should be?*
2. *How much of my ideal self is what someone else values—my spouse, my family, society—and how much of it is what I value?*
3. *Even if I valued my ideal self in the past, do I still?*
4. *Is my ideal self really possible?*

Look at the second part of the equation, how you see yourself. As you ask yourself these questions, view yourself objectively, looking at yourself from the eyes of another person.

1. *What are my strengths and weaknesses?*
2. *What are my blessings?*

Now consider the relationship between the two.

1. Recall your ideal self.
2. Put the picture of your objective self next to the picture of your ideal self.
3. How are they the same? How are they different?
4. Is there any new information that would change your ideal self?

    If your objective self is close to your ideal self, consider adding to the ideal self so that reaching it is a stretch, yet ultimately possible. If your ideal self is so far away as to be impossible to achieve, reconsider the information you used to create it and change it to be attainable.
5. Spend some time with this new ideal self. Project yourself into it and feel it. Hear through its ears the things that people will be saying about it. Look around to see what the world looks like through its eyes.

LOVE YOURSELF

If *love* and *myself* are two words you can't imagine putting together, don't despair: it's a big jump for many of us. And yet we have no problem when it comes to others: we love deeply when it comes to our partners, our babies, or our parents. We open our hearts to our dogs and cats, our flower gardens, our cars, our sports teams, the morning sun.

Because we are connected to all things, loving these people and things is loving yourself. But feeling your own love in a more direct way can transform your sense of yourself and open you to new understandings.

Flow Exercise: Practice Self-Love

Find a quiet place to sit. Close your eyes. Compose yourself and take three deep breaths. Think of someone you love dearly, without reservation: your partner, your child, your grandmother, a friend, your pet. See that person, animal, or thing in front of you, and send it love from the center of your heart. Stay with it, making it stronger and stronger.

Imagine that love curling back to you in a smooth boomerang. Breathe it in. Let it fill you from head to toe. Feel full of light and energy. Stay with it until you feel your body tingling. Then fold your hands together, bring them up to your chest, and thank yourself and the Universe. Sit with this sense of love a while before gently going about your day. Do this for seven days straight, and watch the effect it has on you and your relationships with others.

ACCEPT OTHERS AS THEY ARE

Accept others? With all their faults? We don't have to: we can try to set them straight. But it doesn't take living in the world long to know the futility of that. Instead, try a different approach. Accept others with a full heart.

The key to accepting others lies in accepting yourself. Whether you look at yourself with compassionate or harsh eyes, you'll look at others the same way. Look back at a time when you suddenly snapped at someone. What were you thinking and feeling beforehand? More than likely, you felt put down or demeaned in some way: maybe it was a driver who cut you off in traffic, or careless words a friend said that you took personally. Feeling bad about yourself, you lashed out at another—which, in turn, may have made them feel bad, and made them lash out.

When we're clear about who we are, we no longer see being cut off in traffic as a personal insult or feel that careless words are important. Once you understand how you personally operate, you can see how the other driver might have been confused because the sun was shining in their eyes, or how your friend might have meant something totally different than what you had heard.

Flow Exercise:
Walk in Another's Shoes

This technique is a powerful way to break the habit of blaming others. It involves mentally taking three positions on a matter or in an interchange: 1) your own; 2) the other person's; and 3) an objective observer's.

As you are talking with someone or reconstructing a scene later, put yourself in his shoes. Quite literally see yourself in his clothes, feel his shoes on your feet, his hair around your face. Adopt his point of view, his education, his spiritual beliefs, his family, his fortunes. Now continue the conversation.

After a time, shift again. Mentally stand aside and watch the two of you conversing as though you are watching television. Notice how your perspective expands. Then return to your own shoes. Practice this several times and become flexible in changing positions. In the future, when you don't understand someone, step into their shoes and see what a difference it makes.

ACCEPT THINGS AS THEY ARE

A classic Chinese story tells of a farmer who had an old horse for tilling his fields, until it escaped into the hills. His neighbors sympathized with him over his bad luck, but he replied, "Bad luck? Good luck? Who knows?"

A week later, the horse returned with a herd of wild horses from the hills, and this time his neighbors congratulated him on his good luck. His reply again: "Good luck? Bad luck? Who knows?"

When his son attempted to tame one of the wild horses, he fell off its back and broke his leg. Everyone thought this very bad luck. Not the farmer, whose reaction was, "Bad luck? Good luck? Who knows?" Some weeks later the army marched into the village and conscripted every able-bodied youth they found there. When they saw the farmer's son with his broken leg, they passed him by. Was that good luck? Bad luck? Who knows?

Accepting things as they are gives us a place from which to move forward. Since we cannot be certain what the outcome will be, we don't waste time and energy in criticizing what is happening; instead, we use that energy to figure out what to do next. Our approach is *That was then. This is now. So what now?*

Accepting things as they are means looking at situations, events, and circumstances with clear eyes—not rose- or dark-colored glasses—and withholding judgment. This is not to say we shouldn't try to change the misery caused by injustice, poverty, and environmental degradation. But we don't paint anything in dark colors or demonize the enemy, which creates separation and suffering.

Instead, we accept everything we see as having value in our life, even if it's to teach us what we value. We follow our hearts, do what we have to do—but let the Universe be in charge of judging.

Every day gives you many opportunities to practice this skill. When you're running late and come to a red light, instead of cursing it, take it with equanimity and use it as an opportunity—to breathe more deeply, to view the scenery, to listen mindfully to what's on the radio. Open yourself to the possibility that the red light isn't an irritant but a synchronicity-in-progress: perhaps you'll meet somebody because you're arriving a few minutes later, or you'll avoid an accident that might happen.

Look for flow to ease your way through this process of acceptance, for it comes fully into force when you choose to move toward connectedness and unity.

Flow Exercise: See the Contribution

One way to learn acceptance is to regard everything you encounter as a teacher that leads you to greater understanding. For each person you talk to in the next few days, ask yourself: *What value is this person bringing to me?* For everything that happens to you, ask: *What is the value in this occurrence?* Write down your responses in a small notebook that you carry with you.

EXPRESS WHO YOU REALLY ARE

Our deepest fear is not that we are inadequate. Out deepest fear is that we are powerful beyond measure. It is our light, not our darkness, that most frightens us. We ask ourselves, 'Who am I to be brilliant, gorgeous, talented, fabulous?' Actually, who are you not to be? You are a child of God. Your playing small does not serve the world. There is nothing enlightened about shrinking so that other people won't feel insecure around you. We were born to make manifest the glory of God that is within us. It is not just in some of us; it is in everyone. And as we let our own light shine, we unconsciously give permission to other people to do the same. As we are liberated from our own fear, our presence automatically liberates others.

Nelson Mandela

This technique is about letting your light shine. You have something to give the world that you and you alone can contribute. No one smiles like you, thinks like you, walks like you. No one else can give what you can give. You are a unique part of the whole.

Expression is how you share who you are. It is how other people know who you are. It involves every aspect of your being. It is the clothes you wear, the way you behave, the work you do, the prayers you say, the children you raise, the cars you drive, the truths you pursue, the food you eat, the relationships you maintain, the services you render.

Expression is a means of active discovery, expansion, and growth. It is the way you engage with the world, and if you go about it consciously, it offers limitless opportunities for exploration and learning. The more aware you are of yourself, the more your expression will truly reflect who you are. The more accepting you are of yourself and others, the freer you will feel to express yourself in all your creativity and richness. If awareness and acceptance are the in-breaths, expression is the out-breath.

There are innumerable ways to express yourself. Here are a few to begin the process.

Creativity. The fact that we label an activity as art, designate it as an occupation, and set aside special buildings in which to enjoy it shows how far we've come from our innate creativity. Within you is an artist, a dancer, a singer, a musician, a writer, an interior decorator, a fashion designer, a chef, a carpenter. The key to expressing those parts of yourself is to enjoy what you are doing for its own sake, to learn for the sake of learning, to revel in every step of the process rather than be focused on the product. The result is that you're constantly in touch with and expanding your essence. Take a class, get together with friends to explore, subscribe to a how-to magazine. Take risks—and watch the joy in your life unfold.

Relationships. Being with others is a form of expression that requires and begets mindfulness, creativity, passion. Lovers, family, friends, and coworkers spur you to explore the many sides of yourself and challenge you to be who you really are. Relationships require attention: unless you are careful, you may find yourself falling into old roles, being present in body but not in spirit. But when you are in touch with your own essence and with the essence of others, you can see the similarities and underlying unity that is an element of flow.

Spirituality. Here is to be found unity, harmony, and connection with the greater whole. Spirituality expands your circle of concern and makes you more available to the power of flow. If you have a spiritual approach that nourishes you, then you have only to go deep into that environment. If you don't, start by praying or meditating or asking for guidance. Then go to a bookstore and start thumbing through the religion and philosophy sections. Go to local churches and temples, societies, and meditation centers. Where do you feel most comfortable? What pulls you? Be receptive and open to discovery and synchronicity pointing your way.

Flow Exercises:
Enhance Your Self-Expression

TAKE A SELF-INVENTORY

On a sheet of paper or in your journal, record all the things that define who you are right now in other people's eyes and in your own. Consider all aspects of your life—physical, mental, emotional, spiritual; family, work, play. Include those things you are happy with as well as those things you wish were different.

Go back through the list and put a star by the things that give your heart a lift. Put a dash next to the things that, though they once worked, no longer reflect who you are.

Now write a new sheet that includes only the starred items. Add some new possibilities, perhaps a risk that takes your breath away. This is your checklist for the future.

FOLLOW YOUR BLISS

What makes you smile inside? What gives you a thrill? What opens up horizons before you? What brings peace and harmony to you?

Take a sheet of paper and write down everything you love. Be specific: Periwinkle blue. Hot cider on a fall day. Curling up in bed with a book. The good-tired feeling after a long run. Focus on details and keep your senses in mind: What do you love to look at? Hear? Smell? Taste? Feel? Look especially at your relationships: romantic, family, parental, sibling, friends. Keep going until there are no more things to list.

Check off items you include routinely in your way of expressing yourself. Star a few to start including in your life in the short term and a few to add in the longer term. Continue adding to this list as you become ever more aware of how you express yourself in your personal and private life and in your professional and public life.

STATE YOUR MISSION OR PURPOSE IN LIFE

Getting a clear sense of your purpose in life gives you focus and determination and provides a larger picture in which to frame your everyday decisions and actions.

First, set aside a quiet place and time, at least an hour, when you won't be interrupted. Then consider all the thoughts and ideas you gained from the previous exercises. Mull over your priorities: not just the ones you think about but the ones that you demonstrate in your daily life by how and with whom you spend your time and money.

Now, full of these thoughts and feelings, take pen and paper in hand.

1. Write several short statements about what seem to be the important aspects of your life: for example, your love for your family, your concern for their safety and yours, your motivations at work.

2. Select a word for each statement that reflects its essence, words such as breadwinner, teacher, caring, learning.

3. Assemble these words into a statement of purpose: *My purpose in life is* ____. Or, *My mission in life is* ____. Then modify the statement with other words until it resonates with you. Keep working on it until a deep part of you feels heard; you may feel silent and calm or even moved to tears. Continue working with this statement until you have one that is truly you.

4. Imagine a symbol that to you represents that purpose: a candle, a flower, a book, a painting, the wind, the sunrise, a special color, a twinkle, a chill of excitement, a feeling of peace, a singular note or a song, a word, a mantra, a prayer. Your symbol is very personal, and when you see it, you know it.

5. Determine how to bring this symbol into your everyday life. If it is a candle, have candles in your room and on your desk. If it is a color, accent your house or office with it. Whatever your symbol, keep it near you. Use your symbol when you have decisions to make, especially involving how you express yourself in the world. Consider the options before you, then look at, listen to, or feel your symbol, review your mission statement, and think about your priorities.

6. Gently look back over the last few days. What did you do that was in line with your mission? What are you now doing to further your mission?

7. Write down three actions that you will take in the next day or two that further your mission. Write two more that you will do within the week. And choose one more, a bigger challenge, that you will do by the end of the year.

8. Create affirmations and visualizations for these mission plans.

8 CREATE A SUPPORTIVE INTERNAL ENVIRONMENT

You unleash the power of flow when you create a supportive internal environment that frees you mentally. The three techniques in this chapter are designed to make space for flow to exist by allowing your mind to be disciplined, focused, open, and receptive. Techniques 4, 5, and 6 build that foundation for flow. They are:

4. Create Silence
5. Follow Your Intuition
6. Practice Mindfulness

When you have these skills, you enter into a rich new aliveness—and that aliveness brings you into harmony with the underlying rhythms of the Universe.

CREATE SILENCE

Silence is far more than absence of sound. It is also the absence of activity, the absence of stimulation, the absence of thought. Yet although silence is absence, it is not emptiness. It is full of unlimited potential opening out into all directions. It is inner composure. It is being attuned with your depths. It is being fully and completely in the moment. In silence, your awareness develops, approval grows, mindfulness emanates, intuition flourishes, appreciation blossoms, gratitude wells up, and generosity flows. It is in silence that you make a commitment, embrace honesty, develop openness, establish courage, cultivate passion and positivity, and practice receptivity and trust. It is in silence that your memories, dreams, and creativity emerge. It brings you into the space from which synchronicity emanates and flow abounds.

Silence is defined by stillness of mind, body, and emotions, not by the absence of noise and commotion alone. You can be sitting alone in the woods with only the wind whistling in your ears, but if your mind is racing about how lonely you feel, you won't be in silence. Or you can be jogging through Times Square amid garish X-rated marquees and honking taxis, suffused in silence, feeling joyful and fully in flow.

From silence you can move in any direction. Like the conductor of a symphony, you are alert and aware, poised to begin the movement.

Silence creates the space in which option is available and choice possible. Unfortunately, silence is not highly prized in our culture. Commotion and busyness are sometimes mistaken for aliveness—and that mistake can be precisely what keeps us from knowing ourselves by keeping us from silence.

Silence can be accessed by prayer or meditation. Some

prayers are praises, some are affirmations, some are petitions for help, some are thanksgiving. Meditation is inward attention focused on becoming more aware of your internal states. Some people sit in a meditative posture and pray, others who pray go into meditative states, many combine both.

Whether in prayer or meditation, when you turn your attention inward, compose yourself, and open your heart, you step out of your mundane pattern of existence into a larger picture. And when you become used to doing this on a regular basis, silence becomes easier to tap into throughout the day, without regard to the circumstance.

The key to both prayer and meditation is breathing— something we all take for granted. Yet we can change the way we think and act by simply changing the way we breathe. That might seem too simple to be true, but it works. Breathing can be a pause to allow you to review your choices: when you have a difficult decision to make, take two or three deep breaths; allow yourself to settle into a moment of silence; and then look with new eyes at the choices available. Breathing works as a release from an emotion that has engulfed you: take a couple of deep breaths and feel yourself move out of the middle of the turmoil into a position of observing yourself from the periphery.

The word *deep* is key. For one minute and without changing anything, watch the way you breathe. What part of your abdomen is expanding? Are your shoulders moving? Point to your breath as it comes into your nostrils, following it down to the place where it seems to stop before starting its return trip out. Is the stopping point high, in your chest; midrange, about the bottom of your rib cage or stomach; or low, below your navel? If you breathe shallowly, you expel no stale air, thus retaining higher levels of carbon dioxide in your blood. The job of breathing is to move oxygen into the blood and remove carbon dioxide, and deep breathing does that best.

Higher levels of oxygen affect the brain by lengthening

and slowing its waves, and this then benefits your well-being. When you're in periods of intense mental activity and high stress, fear, or shock, the beta brainwave predominates. Beta, which at its best performs calculations and analysis, at its worst locks you into judging, critiquing, and defending— which can produce more fear and stress.

But by taking a deep breath, you can drop into a lower state, that of alpha. Alpha is the brainwave associated with calm and integrated thinking. In the alpha state, all the parts of your brain work simultaneously and in concert, which makes possible relaxed attention, an openess to additional information, creativity, and flexibility. It is the path to silence.

Flow Exercises: Reaching Alpha State

BREATHING

Do this exercise at the beginning of each of the flow exercises that follow.

Sit erect but in a comfortable position, your gaze falling lightly on the floor a couple of feet in front of you, lips closed, arms relaxed with hands in your lap, fingers slightly entwined, thumbs gently touching.

Breathe deeply, focusing your attention on the outside of the nostril where the breath enters the nose. Feel the light brush of air as it enters and leaves the nostrils; follow the breath as it wends down the back of your nose, through the throat, into the lung cavities, expanding the cavities all the way to the bottom, filling your lower abdomen, pushing it out.

Notice when the breath pauses, turns, and begins its return trip. Follow its path all the way until it passes with a slight swish through the nostril and back out into the air.

Until you become accustomed to filling the lower lobes of your lungs with air, practice lying on the floor holding your hand flat an inch or so away from your navel. As the air fills out this cavity, move your hand away, as though showing your belly how to fill up.

Distending your lower abdomen may be unfamiliar: "Shoulders up, chest out, and breathe" is the old military axiom, but "Shoulders relaxed, chest relaxed, stomach moving in and out" is the axiom of deep breathing. Practice until it is a familiar way to breathe. Although you can learn this breathing exercise in a few minutes, doing it as a matter of course takes effort and attention over time. Your payoff of greater mental clarity, lessened stress, and improved health makes it worth it.

To further your development of silence, when you are breathing deeply, work with the thoughts that come up. This builds silence in your mind. As your breath starts to come into your nostrils, label it in your mind "incoming breath" using a slight, gentle voice. After it turns and before it starts out again, label it "outgoing breath." When you hear a sound, label it "sound" without investigating it or determining its sources or purpose. When a thought arises, label it "thought," again without investigation or judgment. Then again turn your mind to its task of following your breath. This labeling helps you gain distance from your thoughts.

You can use this breath exercise at any point in the day to come into silence. You can use it to get in touch with your intuition. You can use it to focus on mindfulness. This breath is the first step to waking up to a richer aliveness than you've known before.

BODY TOUR

This process stills the body. It is deeply relaxing, and drops you into alpha state. While lying prone on a hard surface, tense each part of your body for a count of ten, then dramatically release the tension. As you release, say silently to that part of your body, "Becoming heavy, sinking into the bed (or floor)." Pause a moment, letting the full effect of the process relax you. Start with the extremities: First toes, then feet, then ankles, then calves, then thighs, then legs; move on to fingers, then to the head. Finally, tense up your whole body, hold it, and release it, sinking once again into the surface. Lie quietly for a few moments, relishing the silence within your body. Then assume a meditative posture, allowing whatever feelings you have to float like bubbles to the surface and break up. Continue this process until no more feelings surface for several breath counts of four.

REPETITIVE MOTION

Observing nature. Calm your mind by looking at waves lapping on a beach, clouds drifting across the sky, fire crackling in a fireplace, wildflowers swaying in a meadow, fish swimming in a tank. Scientists term these *fractal patterns:* the movements repeat themselves in a way that is always the same and yet always different. They engage the mind while simultaneously relaxing it.

Physical movement. Movement can bring you into a fuller experience of yourself. Intense physical exercise produces an outpouring of endorphins, creating a state of expansion and peacefulness (the "runner's high"). Yoga slows the mind with gentle stretching interspersed with periods of rest. Tai Chi, improvised dance, and Sufi dancing can also bring you into mental stillness. Also effective is walking meditation—walking slowly and deliberately back and forth in a small area as you focus on the movements in your body, on the touch of your heel, foot, and toe as you move forward, on the lengthening and contracting of the muscles as you pick up your foot.

SILENCE BY OTHER MEANS

Quiet time for receptivity. Set aside time in the evening. Take a shower, have some food. Then put on some gentle music you love and look at an object that has a spiritual meaning for you. Close your eyes and be receptive. Open up to being given to. Do this twenty minutes or thirty minutes at a time on a regular basis. On weekends, do it in nature or in a church, creating the same experience in different environments.

Music. The mindfulness of sound stills your thoughts and movement. Listen intently to beautiful symphonies, or lilting music such as that of Kitaro, melodious jazz, choral music, Gregorian chants, or intonations of Tibetan monks.

Retreats, sacred places, and holy people. Go on a silent retreat on a weekend or, if your responsibilities allow it, for a week or two. An intense, prolonged period of silence will stay with you in profound ways and allow you to drop into that state later when you need it. Visit a place that is sacred—a church, a temple, a mountain, a place of pilgrimage, a religious historic site. Being in the presence of someone who is holy—a spiritual leader such as Mother Teresa, a healer, a teacher—can give you an experience of the vastness of silence.

PRAYER: THE EMBRACE OF PEACE

Prayer is a way of creating silence by opening your heart and communicating directly with the greater whole. You may have your own words for that process—talking with God, praising the Lord, addressing a Higher Power, touching Spirit, invoking Universal Mind, thanking the Universe—but the dynamic is the same: you open yourself to a power, an energy, a presence that both envelops and elevates you. In its embrace, you come into the deep peacefulness, stillness, and joy of flow.

According to a 1992 Gallup Poll, 90 percent of Americans pray; 75 percent pray every day. Across the country, prayer takes a multitude of forms: a quick prayer for victory on the playing field, a prayer of safety for children, a prayer of thanks for a beautiful sunrise. Across the world, Christians read the Bible or say the rosary, Jews recite the Torah, Muslims bow five times a day to Allah, Hindus chant mantras, and Buddhists prostrate themselves and pray for the happiness of all beings. What matters is not the words or the form, but putting all of yourself into it.

Often praying emerges when we're in a tough spot or a seemingly hopeless situation. "Prayer and love are learned in the hour when prayer has become impossible and your heart has turned to stone," wrote Trappist monk Thomas Merton. Dawn Stobbe of Grand Island, Nebraska, was a devout Catholic, but it wasn't until she was diagnosed with advanced ovarian cancer that her life *became* prayer. Feeling stripped of any kind of control, she laid herself before God and asked Him to help her. She beat 1-in-20 odds to recover.

One thing she prayed for in the early morning hours when she couldn't sleep was "Thy Will be done." In *Healing Words,* Larry Dossey, M.D., writes of experiments that show that nondirected prayers—"Thy Will be done"—were twice as successful as directed prayers such as visualization and asking for specific results, even though both approaches work. Many people have found that when they say "Thy Will be done," their restless mind calms. When you say those words, you hand over your burdens, your sufferings, your hopes, your fears. You just trust—trust in God, trust that everything will turn out as it should. With those words of surrender, when you have given up all attempts at control, the mind stills and silence enters—a silence in which you can feel stillness and caring and a Presence beyond words.

Some say when you pray it's cumulative: Lyndall Demere, a consultant and healer in Carmel, California, says, "I believe that every prayer that you have ever said is still working for you and that every meditation is still in your energy field; it fills your soul and is part of who you are. Over the years that becomes very great. Every year just doing simple prayers and doing simple meditations brings you more and more synchronistic experiences."

Flow Exercise: Prayer Experiences

Develop a daily practice of prayer by setting aside a special period of uninterrupted time. Begin each session in a quiet, comfortable place. Still your mind with deep breathing and a body tour. Afterward, you may want to write your insights and thoughts in your journal.

Special petition. Every morning or night for a week, ask a Higher Power for what you want. Focus on the substance of your desire rather than the form: a means to get easily to your job, say, rather than a new blue Taurus. Make the request in your own special ceremony: light a candle, burn incense, sing a song, pray deeply, whatever feels right to you. Just give it to God: "Thy Will be done." And watch for the response—which may come through the grace of synchronicity.

Repeat the name of God. Still your mind and touch God at ever deeper levels by repeating one of the many names of God throughout your day whenever your mind is idle or anxious. Choose a phrase that resonates with you—*The Lord is my shepherd, Shalom, My Lord and my God, Hail Mary full of grace, Allah be praised, May all beings be happy.* Say the words with attention and meaning. At first it may take effort, but after some time, you'll find the words going on almost by themselves, as soothing as a gentle stream of water running through your fingers.

Make special space for receiving. During your prayers set aside five to fifteen minutes just to receive. Sit quietly with an open heart and mind, gently accepting whatever appears. The gift may be a feeling of warmth, or words, or perhaps silence itself.

MEDITATION: REINING IN THE CHATTER

Meditation stills the mind. It is a process of focusing your attention and calming emotional activity. By meditating, you increase your mental awareness, decrease your physiological tension, and move into an alpha state. This gives you control over your mental life as well as access to the continuing experience of flow itself. Meditation slows down your thoughts so that you can receive information from deeper sources—your intuition, your Higher Self, God, spirit guides, however you perceive it.

"When I first started meditating, they were talking about getting to this glorious place and what a wonderful experience it was," recalls flowmaster Ann Medlock. "I said, 'What if you get there and it is not a wonderful experience? What if it is really lousy?' And they said, 'Well, you would be the first person in five thousand years to discover such a thing.'" What she discovered was "a glimpse of what people talk about in the near-death experience, an incredible light that is totally joyful, wonderful, comforting."

There are hundreds of ways to meditate that have value to those who use them, and many books, tapes, and retreats available through which to learn them. You have your choice of approaches, and when you let synchronicity and intuition be your guide, you will more easily find what suits you and moves you forward. Don't be afraid to experiment. Go to the library or bookstore and browse: Pick up that book that catches your interest, that seems to leap out at you. Is there a class a block away that neatly fits into your lunch break? Try that approach for a while. If you like the type of meditation you're using, find a place that offers it during a weekend retreat and pursue it further. If it doesn't work for you, use that experience as a stepping-stone to another method.

To get you started, here are two of the basic styles of meditation. Each has dozens of variations:

The path of the intellect is the most common. It involves contemplation in which you see, touch, feel, and give language to your experience of an object. It begins, as all paths do, with deep breathing. Count the number of breaths you can follow with no distractions, up to four. If you are distracted by thoughts or sounds or sensations, then start with one again. Continue this breath-counting exercise until you can follow four breaths easily. Then select some object to visualize, usually one of interest but of no significance to you (at the beginning, do not select a flower, cross, or mandala). Examine the object minutely, mentally touching, smelling, hearing, and tasting it. Do this for ten minutes a minimum of five times per week. After two weeks, and when it feels right internally, add five more minutes for the next month. The next month, add an additional five minutes. After three months of this contemplative meditation, decide whether this is the form for you, based on whether it seems right, not whether you are good at it or whether you like it.

The path of emotion, also know as the path of devotion, involves feelings of intense connection, love, and respect for your chosen form of the Divine. Meditation on this path often includes prayers and inspirational readings and is unstructured in form. Begin your session with a breath-counting meditation. Next, tour the body. Call your chosen form of the Divine to mind by saying inspirational words or lovingly gazing at a favorite picture. Hold this connection. If some thought, sensation, or sound draws your attention away, say gently, "This is where I am now," and return to the experience of connection. You may choose to use a certain word or question in this same connected manner. Stay with your experience. If an "aha" insight happens, stay with that experience; don't probe. When it feels like your mediation time is over, end the session gently. Then sit quietly for a few more minutes. Write down any thoughts or experiences in your journal to start your session the next time.

You can use a mantra as the object of focus on either the

path of intellect or the path of emotion. A mantra is a word or series of words that you repeat over and over again. Sometimes the syllables have no meaning, but are a way to focus internal sounds, just as visualization focuses inner sight. Dr. Herbert Benson, author of *The Relaxation Response,* has found that the simple word *one* works well, but that a phrase that has even deeper spiritual meaning for a person—*Our Father Who art in heaven,* for example—works much better.

Flow Exercise: A Basic Meditation

1. Choose the path of meditation that suits you: intellect or emotion.

2. Establish a consistent time of day to meditate. An ideal time is early morning, when the tasks for the day have not yet filled your mind.

3. Set aside a certain amount of time for the effort. Be realistic: don't think in terms of the amount of time you *should* spend, but the amount you *will* spend routinely. If you ease into a meditation practice in five- or ten-minute segments, you are more likely to stay with it than if you jump into hour-long sessions.

4. Keep with it for an extended period of time. Success in meditative practice is dependent on focused and consistent work.

5. Don't examine it to death. Recall the story of the gardener who couldn't understand why his plants were not flourishing: After all, he pulled them up to check on the growth of their roots every day.

Start with this basic meditation. Find a quiet space where you can sit for five to ten minutes in an erect, upright position, either on a straight-backed chair or on a pillow on the floor. This posture will keep you attentive and alert. If you recline, rest your elbows on the flat surface and extend your fingers and arms upright so that there is effort involved in keeping them up; if you should drift or fall asleep, your arm will fall and awaken you. Sit as still as possible, noticing when your body just has to move. Notice and don't move. Momentarily focus all your attention on the uncomfortable physical sensation you feel; investigate its intensity, its location, its color, its temperature. Persevere and shift your attention gently back, thinking, "This is the sensation I feel right now." Five or ten minutes is not a lifetime, although your body may try to convince you otherwise in the beginning.

In this state of silence, you find the space to move in any direction, for you are no longer encumbered with the many conflicting thoughts that produce stress.

FOLLOW YOUR INTUITION

When you learn to turn down the static of your mind and listen to your intuition instead; you will find it moving you swiftly into flow.

Intuition is knowing what you know without knowing how you know it. It comes as gut feeling, as words, as images in a dream, as pictures in your mind. You feel certainty in a way that doesn't lend itself to logical, rational explanation. To some, intuition is the voice of God; to others, it is angels or guides, or the pull of their heart. Some consider it unconscious knowing surfacing into consciousness; some say it is information picked up through the five senses below the level of conscious awareness.

Intuition speaks from silence. You'll find that when you're deeply in flow, intuition and synchronicity engage in a dance together: intuition is often confirmed by synchronicity, and synchronicity can lead you to further intuitive insights. David Spangler, an author, teacher, and former guiding light of Findhorn, a spiritual center in Scotland, says the two have underlying similarities in structure: "Intuition is another form of synchronicity. It's meaningful coincidence operating in a mental domain," he says. "When I intuit something, there's no apparent cause-and-effect relationship between my knowledge and how I got the knowledge. Likewise, synchronicity is precipitated intuition. We know of a connection not inwardly but outwardly, through action and perception: we know it because we see it. In both cases, the pattern carries the same message: we live in a world more intricately and holistically organized than we may ever have previously supposed."

For flowmasters like Ron Chin, the inner voice of intuition is a constant companion. It's the instigation to change jobs, make a phone call, fix a mixed green salad, and even affects the home. Chin says that his highly intuitive clients usually have their furniture and colors arranged in the proper places, and his job as a feng shui consultant is only to validate their choices. People who don't follow their intuition need more direction.

Intuition has four levels: physical, mental, emotional, and spiritual, according to Frances E. Vaughan in *Awakening Intuition:*

+ *Physical intuition* shows up in sensations such as a headache, stomachache, neck pains, or digestive discomfort. It is reflected in such common phrases as "out of touch" and "gut feeling." It is a conscious awareness of bodily sensations—rather than instinct, which is unconscious. When you are attuned to your body, you may respond quickly and directly to cues in certain parts of it. You can develop awareness of cues in the other parts of your body through practice and attention.

+ *Emotional intuition* is relayed through personal feelings, such as shifts in mood and changes in perception. Self-awareness is essential to be comfortable with these messages. Because they have emotional content, you may not follow them if they have triggered some uncomfortable response within you or if you fear looking foolish to others. Knowing your own strengths and weaknesses will help you to distinguish between intuitive information and your own fears and beliefs.

+ *Mental intuition* occurs when a pattern of order emerges that organizes information. Intuitive answers that flash into your mind following an intensive logical and analytical investigation are another form. Mental intuition is often associated with brainstorming, problem-solving, mathematics, and scientific inquiry. Many scientific theories and hypotheses leaped out at scientists in dreams, internal visions, or voices giving them direction. This recognition of patterns is not limited to the visual mode: A musician may hear passages of notes and write them down, as Mozart reported doing.

✦ *Spiritual intuition* is associated with mystical experience. Roberto Assagioli, the founder of Psychosynthesis, philosophy of psychology, declared that pure intuition is "devoid of feeling, and, as a normal function of the human psyche, can be activated simply by eliminating the various obstacles to its unfolding." Indian philosopher Sri Aurobindo said intuition is "a memory of the Truth."

INCREASING YOUR INTUITIVE SKILLS

To create an internal environment that nurtures the gentle budding of intuition, positiveness, receptivity, and trust are your first order of business. The nature of your reality—beliefs, attitudes, opinions, behaviors, and values—forms the environment that impedes or invites intuition into your experience. Look carefully at this environment. Be certain there is space for intuition in it. In order to expand the role of intuition in your life, you need to be aware of your reality and perhaps change some of your assumptions.

To increase your intuition, there's a tried and true basic formula:

Step One: Make it your intention to increase your intuition. When you're in a relaxed or meditative state, start a dialogue with that inner voice. Ask it to make its messages clear to you. Open up your awareness to it: carefully look and listen to see what happens. Create affirmations and visualizations to invoke your intention.

Step Two: Learn how your intuition speaks to you.

Intuition comes in many shapes and forms: a picture, a symbol, a voice, a feeling in your body, dreams. It can be a popular song inside your head whose words are meaningful. Sometimes it is simply a knowing. Medical intuitive Caroline Myss says in *Anatomy of the Spirit* that intuition often makes its presence known "by making us feel uncomfortable, depressed, and anxious—or at the other extreme, drifty and detached, as if we were suddenly cut off from all of our own feelings."

Step Three: Trust it. Don't judge it; don't argue with it or try to convince it otherwise. And don't doubt your ability to hear it: including when it's telling you what you're not eager to hear.

Step Four: Follow its guidance. Yes, it might be running counter to common sense, or at least to the way you're intent on doing something. And it doesn't come with a preview: you may not get the whole picture or story, but will have to wait for events to unfold. If you get an intuitive hit to carry your umbrella out of the house on a sunny day, you have to trust that ultimately it makes sense.

Step Five: Review what you've learned. How did it turn out? If everything fell into place in unexpected ways, if you were the only person on the street who wasn't drenched, or if your umbrella helped you beat off a mad dog, then you're on to intuition. If, on the other hand, it was sunny and uneventful all day, review carefully what the intuitive information was. It is possible that it wasn't intuition but fear, based on the fact that last week you were drenched in a sudden downpour. Examine what it sounded, looked, or felt like—and the next time you get an intuitive hit, explore whether it's the same or different.

INTUITIVE TIPS

Start on the little things. Does someone cross your mind out of the blue? Pick up the phone and give them a call. Do you get a feeling that you should go to the store right now instead of waiting until later? Go, and maybe you'll have a chance to help someone change a tire. Even though you were supposed to bring a salad to the potluck, did something tell you to bring a cake instead? Do it, and don't be surprised to see that someone else had brought a salad instead of the desert they were assigned. In this way, you can build your trust.

Watch for synchronicity to double-check your intuition. If you follow an inner urge and synchronicity results, it's a sign you're on the right track. You can trust that voice in the future.

Use coincidence to play around with intuition. Ray Simon, a Massachusetts writer, is constantly scanning the environment for oddities and coincidences; he runs quick intuitive checks on them and follows where they lead him, often with fortuitous outcomes. For example, he was at a library looking up material on philosopher Alfred North Whitehead. A computer search listed twelve references, the third of which was blank. He pulled up more information on it and found it referred to a book on Sartre, not Whitehead. Obeying his intuition, he went to the shelves to find it. Next to that book was a different one on Sartre, a comic book that laid out his philosophy in a whimsical format. "I needed that information because I write computer manuals, and it's an ongoing battle to stay light," he says. "That book enriched my life and expanded my thinking about what could be done."

Pay attention to your seemingly random thoughts. If a mental picture or feeling comes out of nowhere, give it a second look. Ray Simon's friends consider him intuitive, even psychic, but he says "What they don't realize is that I don't really think or do anything differently than they, except that I watch small things, insignificant patterns nobody else watches, and I pay more attention to random, fleeting thoughts than most people do. Since I basically have the attention span of a chihuahua on a Tilt-A-Whirl, I get plenty of these fleeting thoughts, believe me." If he is asked by a friend about the friend's grandmother, an image of a cedar-paneled room might flash across his mind. Those rooms make him feel claustrophobic, so he might accurately intuit that she was feeling trapped in a nursing home. "I assume, often correctly, that random thoughts bear some *synchronistic* information—for me or someone else," he says.

Don't force it—let it flow. Like synchronicity, intuition can't be controlled or forced or created. By giving it your attention, relaxing into it in a playful way, and being open to what it has to say, you will unleash the power of flow.

Flow Exercises: Welcome Intuition

1. Keep a journal of intuitive hunches and record what happens when you follow through on them. Be alert for all flavors—physical, emotional, mental, spiritual—and practice being receptive in each one.

2. Do you have a question you want answered? Ponder it as you fall asleep, while you ask your inner voice to provide an answer. When you wake up, write down your dreams. Explore them for clues to an answer.

3. Practice, practice, practice. When someone asks you a question or to do something, watch the first response that flashes into your mind. Go with it and see what happens.

4. Improve your powers of concentration to strengthen your intuition. In a meditative position, go into a state of relaxed awareness by counting to four with your breath. Take a tour of your body. Tune into its sensations, but put your relaxed attention on the space *between* things—between your bones, your eyes, your organs, your breath.

172 THE POWER OF *flow*

5. Another concentration exercise: After breathing deeply and touring your body, hold a three-dimensional geometric shape such as a pyramid in your mind's eye. Examine it, but don't allow it to move, change colors, or become one-dimensional—a tall order, as you'll see.

6. Free-associate words by using "thought bubbles." On a piece of paper, draw a circle and put a word inside it that is related to something you want more intuitive information on. Surround that with all the connected words that come to your mind, and draw circles around them. Associate more words within bubbles to those words, and so on.

7. Enlist your unconscious mind to strengthen your intuition. Go into a contemplative state of relaxed awareness by following your breath up to the number four and touring your body. Then, with your eyes closed, see yourself walking down a hallway with many doors. Ask your intuition to give you what you need to increase its voice. Open a door and go in. Take from that room whatever you need to enhance your intuition. Be receptive to whatever you get—you don't have to know exactly what it is or give it a label. Thank the room, and go on to the next room, continuing until you intuitively feel it is time to end the exercise and that your intuition is much stronger.

PRACTICE MINDFULNESS

When you are mindful, you pay attention to the details. A rose is not just a rose: it is the vibrant depths of the color crimson, the whirl of intricate interlaced patterns, the soft texture of velvet. When you focus on the details of your mundane daily life, you open yourself to discovery. You get the most out of every minute because you look with fresh eyes. It's not the same old street you walk down every day, but the anticipation in the face of the child waiting for a hot dog, the brush of wind across your cheek, the aroma of fresh coffee pouring out the door of a restaurant.

Mindfulness puts you in the moment—and when you live fully in the moment you can experience the power of flow. When you are mindful, you are aware, engaged, and nonjudgmental, a state which encourages synchronicity to surface.

Mindfulness is inward: it is being attentive to the twinge in your stomach, knowing when it is hunger and when it is intuition, and acting accordingly. It's also outward: it connects you to others by allowing you to be fully present with them. It gets your mind off yourself and your troubles. Next time you feel bored or out of sorts, look up at the sky: study the shape of the clouds, see how many different colors you can detect, explore the differences from horizon to horizon. As you lower your eyes, notice the difference in your aliveness. When you're with a person you've known for a long time, look at the specifics in his face as he talks: the way the color changes in his cheeks as his emotions change; how the folds around his eyes affect his expression; the way he moves his head to emphasize a point. You'll experience that person as never before.

In her definitive book *Mindfulness,* Harvard psychologist Ellen J. Langer speaks of being flexible and responsive to changes, of operating from what is really in front of you, of building options for yourself—new ways to see, be, listen, learn. Instead of being stuck in the old categories of thinking, you create new categories to better reflect the current situation and context. You find alternatives to the usual way of doing things. You seek new ways and risk the loss of comfortable old ones.

Mindfulness moves you into flow by enlisting your mind to manage your fear. Fear always takes place within a context: The mountain lion safely behind bars in the context of a zoo or circus is a different matter than one prowling your neighborhood. Contexts are learned, many of them during your early years, when your parents might have instilled meanings about people and things to enhance your safety: "Don't talk to strangers, they can hurt you." As you grow older, that original context unconsciously governs your perceptions. You believe all strangers are dangerous, and if you perceive anyone different from you as a stranger, being open to that person is difficult to do. You automatically withdraw to the safety of silence when a stranger strikes up a conversation in the elevator.

By becoming mindful, you enlist your mind to manage your fear. You consider the context more closely—you're an adult on your way to work. You consider the other person as an individual—woman with nice eyes, man looking for directions—rather than a category called "threatening stranger." From there, you can move in any direction—and synchronicity might emerge when you find the man is searching for the exact place you're going or the woman is wearing a necklace that reminds you of your mother, which in turn reminds you that tomorrow is her birthday.

Mindfulness is well described by what it is not: mindlessness. In our society, mindlessness is the rule rather than the exception. It starts innocently enough when you develop habits and routines to make your life simpler to live. Later on, you may find yourself following those routines, even though they have long outlived their usefulness. And you'll be blind to them, even if you're good at self-monitoring your attitudes and behaviors.

At its best, mindlessness is fitting massive amounts of information into categories to make your life more manageable; at its worst, it is relying rigidly on larger categories, such as male and female, to frame your perceptions rather than paying attention to the uniqueness of each individual. At its best, mindlessness works off a single perspective to produce a singular result and may win the battle. At its worst it dogmatically pursues your pictures and loses the war.

Do you want to move into mindfulness? Here are some ways to do it:

Create new categories. Categories are your mental constructs, the distinctions you make between things. Don't take them for granted. Instead, look at the context and the situation. Mentally review your old categories to see if they fit. Be flexible when you create new categories. Brainstorm. Don't limit yourself by trying to figure out the consequences of new categories. Decide on appropriate new categories, but be ready to change them again on a moment's notice. New categories are just as dangerous as old ones unless held lightly.

Open yourself to new information. Be particularly receptive when you think you know what to expect, because that is when you are most inclined to overlook new clues. This is especially true in family situations or with people you have spent a lot of time with. Ask yourself *what* has changed, not *if* anything has changed. Welcome new information, and respond to it with compassion and kindness. This process will keep you interested, present, and connected.

Be aware of more than one perspective. Because of different past experiences, present circumstances, and future expectations, there are at least as many different perspectives as there are people. Remember that others are doing the very best they can and that they probably have good reasons for their actions and opinions, just as you do for yours. Consider how an action may be interpreted positively or negatively. The action you deem spontaneous may be considered impulsive to another. A person who agrees to a plea for help may be seen as compassionate or as weak. A person who has chosen to stick to a certain approach rather than explore a different one may be seen as loyal, or as close-minded.

Focus on the process. If you are totally focused on a desired result, you can become mindless and inflexible and ultimately be less effective. Instead, break the task down into the steps necessary to get to the result. Focus on each individual detail, and apply yourself 100 percent to each. When you focus on detail, you build energy and aliveness. The old adage of counting sheep to go to sleep is based on the notion that your mind will be lulled into mindless boredom by the repetition, but try to sleep when you are looking at the scraggly hair and green eyes of each of those sheep as they jump the hurdle!

And when you focus on a task one step at a time, you allow room for synchronicity and fortuitous events—which may point you toward a different, better outcome.

Mindfulness builds on silence and intuition to create a nurturing environment for flow. It involves being aware of yourself by monitoring both internal and external activity, and accepting both your own way of operating and the ways others operate. Silence provides the space in which you can enlist your mind, and intuition provides information for new categories, perspectives, and actions. This all takes place in the present moment, where you experience the ultimate power of flow.

Flow Exercise: Learning Mindfulness

THE ORANGENESS OF AN ORANGE

This exercise emphasizes being in the moment, open and aware, and challenges you to see, hear, and feel an old, familiar item in a fresh, new way.

Select an orange. Hold it gently in your hand. Feel its weight, its roundness, the roughness of its skin. Place it under a trickle of water and rinse it off completely. Notice the interaction of the water and the orange. Investigate the space between the water and the orange. Holding the orange in one hand, use the other hand to slowly pick up a paper towel, spending a few moments investigating the texture, surface, color, weight, and feel of it. Blot each drop of water that remains on the orange, allowing it to be absorbed into the towel. Notice how the water moves into the fiber of the towel from the surface crevices of the orange.

Now smell the orange. Holding it close to your nose, crease the surface of the orange with your thumbnail, releasing a tingling spray of juice. Hear the spray break loose from the orange and jump into the air. Lick the tiny droplets of juice from your lips. Feel the juice between your fingertips. Continue to peel the orange one careful movement at a time, thoroughly concentrating your senses of smell, touch, sight, sound, and taste on this one activity. Finally, eat the orange.

When you have completed this part of the exercise, using the same careful, attentive, slow, deliberate actions, pick up the peelings, place them in the waste receptacle, and sit quietly, savoring the experience. Then write about your experience in your journal.

Do this exercise each week for a month, using a different object of focus. Some suggestions:

✦ Listen to the sounds of an instrument.

✦ Examine an emotion in your body.

✦ Look at a flower in full bloom.

✦ Visit a coffee shop or cafe.

MINDFULNESS MEDITATION

A powerful tool for developing mindfulness is a type of meditation known as Vipassana, also called insight meditation or mindfulness meditation. It consists of sitting in a meditative position and gently but persistently directing one's attention inward to what is happening moment by moment in one's body, emotions, and thoughts. A number of books give thorough instructions for undertaking this practice on your own, including *Insight Meditation: The Practice of Freedom* by Joseph Goldstein and *Wherever You Go, There You Are: Mindfulness Meditation in Everyday Life* by John Kabat-Zinn (see References for Further Study, p. 252).

Now that you are engaged with yourself and the moment in a new way, it's time to enter into action—and see what happens when you stretch and trust as never before.

9
DIRECT YOUR ACTIONS

This chapter propels you into action—with a difference. Within silence, guided by intuition, aided by mindfulness, you are now grounded in a place of deep connection with the whole. That connection informs your every move.

The four techniques in this chapter focus on *doing* things in your life to increase the power of flow:

7. Do 100% of What You Know to Do—and Trust
8. Finish Things and Move On
9. Take Risks
10. Break with Your Old Reality

As you undertake these techniques, you experience flow as a participatory sport. When you do your part, flow plays back by sending synchronicity and fortuitous events your way.

DO 100% OF WHAT YOU KNOW TO DO—AND TRUST

Looking back on a situation you don't feel good about, do you often think, "I knew exactly what to do. So why didn't I do it?" It could be gaining two pounds at a wedding when you had sworn to skip the cake. It could be getting a grade you didn't like in a class you cared about. It could be letting your child misbehave. You knew at the time in these situations that you were ignoring your calorie count, had seen a few too many movies instead of studying, had been getting lenient about enforcing bedtime.

You may have had several good reasons why you acted as you did. But the focus of this technique is this: Did you do *all of what you knew to do*? If you sell out on yourself by quitting before you do every single thing you know to do, failure may be the first outcome, guilt the second, and losing trust in yourself the third. You may make a comeback—learn from your failures, shoulder your guilt, and struggle to rebuild your lost trust. Or you can bypass the whole difficult process—and consistently *do 100% of what you know to do at that very moment*. This involves:

1. Being aware of what there is to do, which is both an intuitive and an intellectual process.

2. Knowing when you are not doing what there is to do, which is often signaled by sensations in your body.

3. Persisting in doing it, no matter the short-term consequences. Fill up on unbuttered popcorn before the wedding, stay up late to study, face your child's feedback —as writer Og Mandino says, "Walk an extra mile."

Then, when you know in your gut that you have done all that is required, that is, all you know to do at this moment, turn loose. Breathe a sigh of relief, and turn the results of your actions over to the powers that be—whether you call it God, the Universe, a Higher Power, angels, the fates, karma. Consider the matter done and out of your hands; trust that whatever happens will turn out to be for the greater good.

This creates the space for magic and synchronicity. It allows the Universe to do its part. And the results can be different—and better—than you ever conceived. No matter what happens, your conscience is clear because you did your very best. Assess the results in terms of facts rather than faults, and you will be without guilt, blame, or self-recrimination.

Doing everything possible and then letting go is a powerful dynamic that has been scientifically validated in laboratory experiments at Stanford Research Institute. A researcher tried to move a free-hanging weighted magnet by his will alone. Focusing all his attention on it for twenty or thirty minutes, doing everything he knew to do, nothing happened. But at the moment when, totally exhausted, he said to himself, "I give up," the magnet moved dramatically. The researcher found that when he intensely focused on establishing a connectedness and then totally surrendered, the magnet would sometimes move at a force a thousand times stronger than the earth's magnetic field.

Doing 100% of what we know to do looks different to each of us, for it depends on our beliefs and how we operate in the world. When Susan LeTerneau of Denver ended yet another relationship, she vowed she wouldn't accept another date until she figured out what she wanted. She plunged into a year of self-discovery to get to the root of why she hadn't found a lasting love. She discussed her emotional blocks to love with a therapist. She read books about women who love too much and men who don't love enough. She sat in front of a mirror and did affirmations, saying over and over "I love you" so she could become accustomed to hearing what it sounded like, and really mean it about herself. She visualized being deeply absorbed in conversation with someone, leaning in to talk with him.

She made a list of what she wanted in a man—eighty-five items that included everything from height range to in-laws who liked her. She spent months polishing a personal ad. It read, "Have you survived the midlife crisis and found that failure is not the falling down, but the staying down? Will you understand that even though she has learned to grow her own garden, she still appreciates bouquets? Have you learned to understand your parents, forgive your ex, and enjoy your children? Are you ready to fall in love, not just for the next time, but for the last time?"

It drew forty-five responses. On her first date with Larry, she realized that they were leaning in toward each other—and that he fulfilled every item on her list. They were married fourteen months later.

For Lisa Bankoff of Kingston, New York, doing 100% in finding a partner meant asking the Universe for help in letting go of the pain of past relationships so she could move on to what life had to offer. It meant forgiving those who had hurt her, which she did by writing letters to them in her journal. It meant not being anxious, trusting that when the time was right, a relationship would happen. A month after she wrote the letters, she met the love of her life when he saw her across the room at a restaurant and fell head over heels for her at first sight.

When doing your 100%, approach the matter at hand with dedication and perseverance. Use your rational mind and your intuition to assess the best path to your goal: then make your phone calls, set up your systems, say your prayers, do your visualizations. Do intuitive checks along the way: Is there anything more? Does anything need a second look? Act reliably. Keep your word. Put energy into it. And move on. Validate your actions rather than second-guessing them. Be in the moment with your 100%—that is where movement is possible.

You might want to undertake your 100% with a comprehensive, focused program of visualization, such as that detailed by David Spangler in *Everyday Miracles: The Inner Art of Manifestation*. He provides a series of powerful exercises to help you turn the seed of a thought in your mind into physical reality by aligning yourself with underlying reality. The following is an example of one of those exercises.

Flow Exercise: Creating What You Want

Visualize the object of your manifestation. Imagine that it is slowly becoming transparent, and as it does so, you see a light glowing within it. As you watch, this light grows brighter while the actual form grows dimmer, until all you can see is the light itself.

Walk into this light. Stand in it for a while, and let its nature wash over and through you. What does it feel like? What qualities does it evoke in you? What is its energy like? What is its presence like?

Step out of this light and turn around. You are now looking at yourself. Like the object of your manifestation, you, too, are becoming transparent and glowing with an inner light. Step into this light and feel its qualities, its energy, its presence.

When you are satisfied that you have attuned to this presence and have a sense of its nature, turn back to the light glowing from within the object of your manifestation. Remaining in your own essence, walk over to it and into it, blending the two essences together. Feel their light interpenetrating. What is that like? Does it spark any images, thoughts, or feelings?

Spend some time in the midst of this combined essence. Become familiar with what it feels like. When you feel you are finished, close your inner eyes and open your outer ones. The exercise is ended.

INCREASING TRUST

All along the way, as you do your 100%, trust. This will distance you emotionally from the outcome. Realize that ultimately whatever happens is beyond your absolute control, just as everything in life is: many things could happen that would prevent the results you want. Realize that your perspective as one person is necessarily limited, and another outcome that you haven't thought of might actually be much better. Or your hard work might fall flat on its face, and the outcome be the opposite of what you wanted—but in the long run, that could turn out to be for the best. For all these reasons, give up control. Trust that whatever is supposed to happen does happen.

Trust has two advantages. First, it allows learning to take place because it keeps you in the moment, engaged in the process rather than in hopes and fears about the future. Second, it gives you tremendous freedom because you aren't attached to a picture of the results.

To have the joy and peace of mind of doing 100% and trusting, we have to give up operating from control and from attachment to our pictures of what we want. In Western society, control and *attachment* seem necessary to get ahead. From a cause-and-effect standpoint, that may be true. But the power of flow is acausal, and many of those usual ways of thinking do not apply to it.

Attachment in this context does not refer to healthy psychological bonding between a child and its parents. Rather, it refers to those cases in which we clutch tightly to the concept of *mine* and *I want it my way.* By its very nature, this kind of attachment is limiting: it cuts off creativity and possibilities. It makes us anxious, demanding, super-polite, aggravated—whatever we go through to get our way. We feel it physically as tightness in our chest, head, or heart. These types of constrictions dam the flow of creative energy.

From attachment comes judgment, which is necessary to determine if an outcome fits your anticipated picture of it. From judgment comes doubt, then guilt, then blame. This leads to alienation and separation, to lack of respect, to greed, and ultimately to anger and pain. The need to control develops as a way to force an outcome. Lying, manipulation, half-truths, lateness, heavy debt, possessiveness, territoriality, and at its extreme, even fear and violence are products of attachment.

When you are unattached, you have inner freedom. You have no investment in a particular outcome, and so you do what is necessary in the moment. You explore every option and are receptive to all new information. You do all that you know to do, and then trust, because you have no attachment to either the result or how the result is produced.

Flow Exercises:
Examining Your Attachments

PROBING WHAT YOU ARE ATTACHED TO

1. On a piece of paper, record all of your physical attachments—things you can't walk away from without regret, which might include your stereo, cars, shoes, house. What effect does each attachment have on you?

2. Write down your emotional attachments, including people, places, and things. Ask yourself: *Why do I have this attachment? Is it preventing me from experiencing something I don't want to experience?*

3. Write down your mental attachments, particularly your ideas about yourself. Ask yourself: *What about myself do I have to be right about? What points of view about*

myself do I feel I have to defend? What's at stake? Why
does it matter? Who do I really think is me?

4. Look at some of your strongly held opinions and viewpoints. Ask yourself: *Is it possible I'm not right about
this? Is it possible the opposite is true? What if the opposite were true? What difference would it make and
why?*

5. Write down your power and authority attachments,
such as lawyers, police, media, and parents. Ask yourself: *How am I influenced and controlled or manipu-
lated by them and why? What is the origin of that
control? What fear is it related to? Where does the fear
come from?*

FOUR WAYS TO BREAK FREE OF ATTACHMENTS

1. *Do figure eights.* In her book *Cutting the Ties That Bind,*
Phyllis Krystal has a powerful exercise for cutting attachment. As you sit or stand, imagine a circle of golden light
around you, touching the ground, its circumference as far out
as your outstretched arms. Now visualize the object of your
attachment opposite you, inside its own golden ring of light
which touches but doesn't overlap yours. Now see a thin
stream of neon-blue light making a figure eight just inside the
rings: starting at the point where the two circles meet, it first
flows around the opposite circle in a *clockwise* direction,
then crosses over and goes *counterclockwise* behind you in
your ring. See the light moving swiftly around the "8" for
one or two minutes. Then stop. Do this twice a day for two
weeks and you'll find yourself becoming free in your relationship with that object or person. This book also includes detailed visualizations to cut the ties.

2. *Burn it up.* Prepare a fire. On slips of paper, write
down the things that seem to possess you, from which you
can't seem to turn loose. Visualize each item, touch it, feel the

emotion attached to it. With firm composure, wad each slip of paper into a ball and throw it into the fire. Watch as the flames consume it. Visualize the actual object, not the paper, in flames. Keep watching as it turns to black embers, then gray ash. Contemplate not having this item in your life. Breathe deeply and feel any pain of separation and loss for what might have been. Now see the gift of freedom from the grip of desire. Gently go on with your day without any further reflection on the process.

3. *Meditate on your decaying body.* Our greatest attachment is often to being alive, which can fill us with pervasive fears of being harmed. This meditation can do much to free us of that attachment and can help us appreciate each day fully. While meditating, vizualize your dead body. Examine it carefully, detail by detail. Then pull back and see your body from a distance of 10 to 20 feet. Look down on it as it turns black with decay, as animals or worms devour it, leaving only your bones, which slowly turn to dust. Exhale deep breaths and release any fear, tension, pain, suffering, and tears that may come up. Conclude the meditation with a prayer of thanksgiving for having had that exact body. Go gently about your day.

4. *Make it disappear.* See the object of your attachment directly in front of you, at eye level. Examine it thoroughly and mindfully. See its textures, its intensity, its contours, its qualities. Then see the item move away from you. Watch as it becomes more indistinct and distant, as it becomes a speck on the horizon. With the flick of your wrist, turn off the picture in your mind—like the dot that vanishes from the center of the screen when you turn off the television. Quickly go about your day, not reviewing or reliving this exercise. Just be done with it.

FINISH THINGS AND MOVE ON

What promises have you made that you haven't yet kept? What is it that you haven't yet said to someone important to you? What tasks have been hanging around on your To Do list for ages? What closets, drawers, and rooms do you have to organize someday soon? What paperwork do you keep pushing to the back of your desk? What repairs have you been putting off?

Chances are, it won't take you long to think of the answers; in fact, they're probably right there on the tip of your tongue. That's because they're right on the tip of your consciousness—and that's the best reason for pushing completion to the top of your To Do list.

Like unpaid bills that come around month after month, incompletions are a strain. They take up your attention and clutter your space. They keep you from being fully in the present; they anchor you to the past with regrets and guilt, and to the future with fear they will rear their ugly heads. While you may be able consciously to set incompletions aside, they are in your unconscious, clamoring to be done away with. They occupy space on your plate—valuable space you need to experience the fullness and joy of the moment.

Here are some ways to accomplish completion. *Say what you'll do and do what you say.* Think of how many times you've said, when taking leave of someone, "I'll call you" or "Let's do this again." Or the times when you promised to send someone a magazine article or make a phone call to a friend on their behalf. Maybe you meant it, maybe you didn't—but those innocuous words become a major discomfort when you do nothing and then see that person again later. Make a commitment because you will keep it and not because someone wants you to make it. Make your intentions known to those around you and then keep that commitment. Say yes when you mean yes, and no when you mean no.

Skillfully tie up loose ends in your relationships. Complete the lingering relationships that drag you down. Saying final words, you gain your freedom. But don't do it at someone else's expense: Saying "I hate you and never want to see you again" may give you a feeling of power and finality, but the cost is high—you have hurt another person, which gives you more unfinished business to deal with. It's better to think carefully of what you want to say, and then look at your motives. Is what you're saying or doing for the greater good? Are you being compassionate? If the answers are yes, then go ahead. If the answers are no, then wait. Find a moment of silence to reflect on the relationship. Recall the positive times you've had together and the contribution the other person has made to your life. From this space, consider how best to complete the relationship. Perhaps, in this moment, in the peace of your heart, it is already complete.

Maintain an orderly living and working environment. Everyone has different levels of comfort with disorder. But if you spend more than five minutes a day looking for things that are supposed to be somewhere they aren't, it's a sign that you're bogged down by clutter. Messy stacks of papers gnaw at the back of our minds just as used pans piled in a jumble make cooking a chore. External conditions mirror internal conditions, so straightening your room settles internal disorder.

Forgive past wrongs. Grudges corrode the soul. We sometimes think that if we don't forgive someone for what they did to us, we're getting back at them—but the truth is, we're hurting ourselves with that stored bitterness. And our anger keeps us a hostage to the person who has hurt us. "When we forgive, we set a prisoner free and then discover the prisoner was us," writes Lewis B. Smedes in *Forgive and Forget: Healing the Hurt We Don't Deserve*. Forgiving another person may be a slow, gradual process. "If you manage forgiveness in fits and starts, if you forgive today, hate again tomorrow, and have to forgive again the day after, you are a forgiver," writes Smedes. In this process, you give yourself a new beginning.

Live each day as though it were your last. Complete discussions with people in your life each time you are with them as though you will not see them again. Tell those you love of your affection for them. Start actions and interactions that are authentic and integral to your essence. Be committed to them. Do them 100 %. Complete them. Celebrate them.

Flow Exercises: Undertaking Completion

1. *Trim your To Do list.* Take a pen to your To Do list, and be ruthlessly honest with yourself. Are you ever going to finish that project? If so, take one small step in that direction. If not, then pronounce it complete in your mind, and cross it off your list. Do the same to those well-meaning creative projects around the house or office that nip at your conscience and pull your attention away from more fruitful efforts.

2. *Throw out excess items.* Each day, throw out five items—just five. That's five old magazines, five miscellaneous bottles from your bathroom shelves, five odds and ends from the catch-all drawer in the kitchen. You may like the feeling so much that you'll double the number.

3. *Practice a forgiveness visualization.* What color is forgiveness? Let your unconscious consider this and supply the color. See it or hear the word. Create an image of yourself and let that color begin to glow somewhere in that body. As it gets stronger, let it spread until you see yourself glowing with that color. Notice if it has a tingle or a vibration or a sound or music. Let the color expand to other people that you want to forgive and let it spread until they glow as well.

TAKE RISKS

When you look at your life, you'll see that there's no place in which risk and expansion are not possible. Look to where you hold back. What makes you feel unsettled, uncertain? Where do you close down? Where do you feel adamant? What is it that you know you must do, for the sake of your growth and happiness, but keep putting off?

Flowmasters know that risk is essential to change. That doesn't mean they're daredevils or thrill-seekers. But day after day they're willing to step outside their personal comfort zones. When they come up against what feels like a self-imposed limitation or a fear that holds them back, they go forward instead of backing away. They brave the discomfort of the unknown and untried. They stretch, and then stretch some more—in mind, body, emotion, spirit.

When we take a deep breath and move into unfamiliar ground, we can enter fully into the present moment. We can operate in trust, and we grow in self-knowledge, expanding into deeper parts of ourselves. We become open and receptive to opportunity in all its forms, which increases synchronicity. And we come into the experience of flow, in all its richness and power.

Risking doesn't mean you plunge head-on into something that terrifies you. That approach may look romantic, but it's often foreboding in practice, and it doesn't necessarily produce lasting results. Psychologists have found that a more effective approach to dismantling a limiting fear is to take it on a piece at a time.

Fear is the rope that ties you down, and when you risk in a skillful, gradual way, you are taking the smallest thread, isolating it from the rest of the strand, and pulling on it until it gives way. Then you move on to the next thread, which is weakened by having its neighbor gone. After a few threads are loosened, the strand itself gives way. The constricting hold of the fear relaxes, and you move on more freely.

If you're shy, unloosening that strand might mean putting on a shirt in a brighter color or wilder style than you usually wear, striking up a conversation with people in a store, or taking a personal growth class where you know you'll be required to share your feelings. If you're in a painful relationship, it might mean reading a book about listening skills, telling your partner your true feelings, or seeking counseling. If you are afraid to be alone with your thoughts, it might mean eating in a restaurant by yourself, driving to work with the radio off, or taking a weekend trip alone to a nearby state park.

For Jan Effenberger, married sixteen years to a verbally abusive professor, risking meant signing up for a music history course. Doing well in the course gave her courage to risk more by going into therapy, which in turn gave her the strength to leave her husband. Risk was paying off, and she made a big leap by taking a two-month leave from her secretarial job. She borrowed money and took her children on a cross-country camping trip. It was more freedom than she had ever known: "To drive across the continent and meet all kinds of people! To stop where we wanted and see what we wanted! Afterward, I felt so powerful, so self-assured. I felt I could handle anything." On that trip she drove into Boulder, Colorado, and immediately felt at home. Through a string of synchronicities, she got a job there a few years later, then quickly met and married the love of her life.

Risk is a destroyer of comfort, which sets the stage for change and growth. "Sleep on a hard bed," goes an old Buddhist saying, which David Fuess takes literally. When he travels in third world countries, he sleeps in local dives rather than five-star international hotels—and meets interesting people who send him on further adventures, which give him more knowledge of himself. As he puts it, "If you get real comfortable, it's less likely you'll make a lot of progress. If you're always seeking pleasure, you're not necessarily in Truth."

Comfort seduces us into repetition, and if we keep doing what we're doing, we keep getting what we're getting. Although that may allow us to develop certain skills, it doesn't lead us to transcend our limitations. It works fine for learning to play the piano, not so well for creating great symphonies.

By doing what's not comfortable, we understand ourselves better and we grow. If the idea of seeing a psychic for the first time attracts you but also makes you nervous, go the low-risk route of a psychic fair at the local mall. Pay $25 and sit across from a woman who looks like your Aunt Maude. You've stretched: you've put yourself in that chair. What she says may change your life, or it may be totally off base. Either way, when you get up, you will have learned something about yourself: you took the chance, and now you can decide whether you want to walk farther down that path or not.

Risk comes in many sizes, colors, shapes. One person's risk is another person's yawn—but in another area of life, those reactions may be reversed. Your friend's casual jaunt to Macchu Picchu may strike you with wonder: your ability to give to your partner with no holds barred may leave your friend awestruck.

Look at your life. What both beckons and scares you? When you examine your physical, mental, emotional, and spiritual arenas, where do you feel uncomfortable about upsetting the routine? That may be the place to start. If you make a New Year's resolution again and again without following through, that's another place to begin.

Be aware that when you choose your risk, your mind might get very noisy. You might find all kinds of objections and anxieties rearing up. Just go ahead with what you're doing. These anxieties are proof that you're on the right track, for the function of the mind is to protect you and keep you safe, even if that means safely stuck in the old ways.

Risk is not about harm, either to yourself or to others. If you are challenged by the thought of attending college in a distant city, but the change in location will put your family in financial peril, the risk requires careful planning. If you want to be more truthful in your life, but telling a good friend about her unpleasant personal habits would send her into a tailspin, then tell your truth elsewhere.

Be mindful of yourself as well: it might work best to intersperse periods of risk with periods of introspection. Aikido teacher Henry Smith says, "You don't always have to be in that state of being on the edge. After a certain outpouring of energy you become full and then you can just be in the moon and receive. And then once you've filled up with that, it is time to go out and take an action, perhaps. There is power in both ways, and one seems to trigger the other."

When you risk, be mindful beforehand, so you can move freely as the process requires. Persevere, keeping in mind the payoff: personal growth, increased self-knowledge, touching your own essence.

Flow Exercise: Take a Risk

1. Consider the physical, mental, emotional, and spiritual arenas in which you work and play. Think about your interactions with friends, colleagues, teachers, and even with yourself. Ponder your levels of comfort and poke into your corners of fear.

2. Make a list in your journal of the first ten places to risk that come to your mind: asking for a raise, learning to sing, changing a destructive habit.

3. Prioritize them from the most to least challenging.

4. Start with #10, the risk on the bottom of the list. Think of the ways you can go about taking that risk and the resources available to help you. Talk over the various scenarios with a like-minded friend or your flow partner.

5. Select one of the risks. Develop a set of plans: begin with the desired outcome, include the process, and set up the dates and "deliverables": When you do what, how you will do it, and how you will know when it is done.

6. Commit yourself to the beginning, middle, and end of this risk. Now that you have taken a stand, take the step. Do it.

7. When you are done, evaluate it with a friend or your flow partner. Then move on to risk #9—and so on, up the list.

The following options are some ways you can risk and stretch in different parts of your life.

THE PHYSICAL ARENA

✦ Commit yourself to an exercise routine for a specific duration.

✦ Undertake a physically challenging experience, such as hiking in new terrain, bicycling to another town, or learning advanced yoga routines.

✦ Learn a new sport and play it on a set schedule, preferably with friends who are also committed.

THE MENTAL ARENA

✦ Learn about a subject that has piqued your interest. Get books on it, find an expert to talk to, participate in a class or club.

✦ Immerse yourself in a new culture, in a foreign location or in your own town. Consider a culture of the other gender or a different generation. Spend time there: talk the talk, eat the food, learn what makes people tick.

✦ Break a longstanding habit or redesign a routine. Vary your route to work, the food you eat, the movies you see, the way you relate to someone.

THE EMOTIONAL ARENA

✦ Tell family members or friends how much they mean to you.

✦ Expand a relationship to a new level: ask a colleague to dinner, confide in your sister more, be vulnerable with someone you've kept your distance from.

✦ Be honest with yourself about something within you that's hard to face. Accept it in love.

✦ Forgive someone.

THE SPIRITUAL ARENA

✦ Increase the intensity or level of your spiritual practice.

✦ Study the commonalities among religions and spiritual approaches with books, tapes, and discussions. Investigate the basis of a friend's belief that differs from yours, and attend a religious or spiritual function with him.

✦ Go on silent retreat, with a group or on your own, at a retreat house, monastery, convent, or in a natural setting such as a woods or the beach.

BREAK WITH YOUR OLD REALITY

What hurts us, blesses us. . . .

Rumi

It is the nature of being alive that, sooner or later, we encounter a devastating crisis involving ourselves or someone dear to us: an unexpected death, an illness or accident, financial disaster, betrayal, assault, unemployment, divorce. It can be precisely what we fear most deeply. It can crush our world and end our day-to-day life as we've known it.

This is a break with our reality of life as we have been living it. It destroys our worldview and our operating assumptions. Our beliefs didn't protect us—so what can?

But a break with reality can be the most impactful thing that happens to us—because it can lead us directly into flow. For many flowmasters, including John Beal, Ann Medlock, and Lloyd Tupper, their lives in flow began when their old reality changed.

These breaks create a tremendous opening for transformation. They put us in touch with our true selves, our essence. Our old facade is stripped away, and we're open and vulnerable. We may access part of ourselves we've never experienced before, and allow others to touch us too. We are driven to look under the surface; we probe intensely the existence of a higher power and the purpose of our own existence. Synchronicity surfaces, giving us reassurance and direction. We learn of the strength and perseverance we have within ourselves. And then we construct new understandings, new beliefs, a new reality.

This technique is about making use of breaks with reality as the tremendous opportunities they are: exploring not only how to heal your wounds, but how to transcend your woundedness. When you can see dissolution as a gift, you can resurface into a new way of life, triumphant and enriched by what you have been through.

A break with reality can also result from experiences of transcendence, such as near-death episodes and mystical experiences. The challenge then is to reintegrate those numinous insights into workaday reality. Some people deliberately set out to shake up their comfortable worldview so they can reach deeper levels of reality. This often takes the form of a spiritual or personal quest. No one returns unchanged from a stint in the Peace Corps or a trip to India. Henry Smith, an Aikido teacher and the founder of the intercultural dance company Solaris, did a four-day vision quest without food or water in the desert. "Pray to the Thunders," he had been advised by a Lakota Sioux elder, and, in 100-degree heat, he did. In the far distance, he saw purple clouds forming. As he prayed and chanted, the clouds came close and a drop of water fell on him. "That drop, that little drop, cut through so much," he recalls. Three bolts of lightning hit the ground within ten feet of him. He gained an entirely new sense of what it meant to be in harmony with the Universe, and returned home to find flow heightened in his personal and professional life.

RECONSTRUCTING YOUR LIFE

As you move through a challenging time of life, you can access many caring people and groups to hold your hand and help you put the pieces back together in a way that moves you forward. These supports can help you learn from your experience and see the possibilities for a different, better future.

THERAPY

Therapists hail from a wide variety of disciplines and approaches. The most important factor, however, is the rapport and respect you have for a particular counselor. Don't hesitate to interview a therapist, to ask for his credentials, and to move on to another if the first person is not a good fit for you. Give synchronicity a chance: See if things fall together to push you toward a particular approach or person.

Solution-focused therapy deals with the solving of problems, rather than the emotional reactions to those problems. Behavioral therapy is a structured way to change one's dysfunctional or destructive behavior. Psychoanalysis is highly analytical and works on the pain in one's life caused by the repression of underlying conflicts and issues. Body-centered psychotherapy uses the body as a way of accessing the subconscious. It is not concerned with the content of a problem, but rather its effect on a person in present time. Cognitive therapy focuses on the content of beliefs, attitudes, and opinions, and is considered highly effective as an agent of change.

GROUPS AND ORGANIZATIONS

Twelve-step programs such as Alcoholics Anonymous, Narcotics Anonymous, and Gamblers Anonymous have proven success records. Based on the acknowledgment of addiction, surrender of the problem to a Higher Power, and the loving support of others in the same circumstances, these programs have a profound effect on many lives. Participation is free of charge, and local chapters can be found in your phone book or newspaper.

Self-help and support groups exist for virtually any imaginable issue and can be located through local mental health centers and hospitals. Finding others in the same situation as yourself can be tremendously supportive and life-enhancing: a Stanford University study found that women with breast cancer who were part of a support group lived twice as long as those who weren't. If no group exists in your area that meets your needs, consider starting your own. For information, contact the American Self-Help Clearinghouse, Northwest Covenant Medical Center, Denville, NJ 07834 (201-625-7101).

PHYSICAL APPROACHES

Do not neglect your body during times of turmoil and change. It is inextricably linked to your mind and emotions, and treating it well will accelerate your process of self-renewal. An ongoing exercise program such as aerobics, running, weight-lifting, or yoga will reinvigorate you and supply stamina to counter stress. A massage therapist or body-worker can help you experience greater energy and clarity. Approaches include massage techniques such as Swedish and shiatsu, in which the body is kneaded and stroked to increase muscle and joint suppleness and flexibility; and energy balancing techniques such as polarity, Jin Shin Jyutsu, and acupuncture, which involve gently stimulating selected points on the body with hands or needles to enhance the flow of energy. With any physical approach, follow a rule of thumb: How do you feel and look when you leave a treatment or workout? Are your eyes bright and your cheeks glowing? Do you have more energy? Then it is worth doing again.

RETHINKING YOUR WORLD

Part of what makes a break with reality so difficult is that it strikes at the core of our beliefs, at that place where we need few words because we simply know something to be true. That loss of old beliefs can give us a dreadfully unsettled, shaky feeling or make sleeping through the night impossible, as our minds race on and on, seeking answers and a way out. But just as the mind can fill us with anguish, so can it fill us with peace—if we use it creatively. The following approaches are ways to focus your mind and direct it toward your re-emergence.

REFRAME THE SITUATION

You can get emotional distance from your situation by re-framing it—seeing it in the context of a larger picture. Try out some of the following reframes and see if they cast new light on your process. If they don't work, keep on turning over your situation, looking at it from all angles, until you find something that makes you feel better.

+ *What are the lessons?* Since life is about learning, what are you being taught by these circumstances? Look back over your life: Is this a recurring lesson? What forms has it taken?

+ *What is the value?* How is your crisis going to change you? Are you becoming a stronger, better, wiser person? Is your crisis showing you things you never realized about your life? What skills and information are you learning?

+ *How did you set this up for your growth?* In the book *Life Between Life,* some patients of Dr. Joel Whitton reported that when they were in altered states, they saw themselves, after death in one life, meeting with light-filled beings in order to plan out their next life—including illnesses, deaths, and trials that they needed to undergo to gain wisdom and strength. The intricate planning involved coordinating their times on Earth with other people they loved or wanted to repay a debt to. Even as a metaphor, this is apt: You are the screen-writer scripting your own life. Think of writing your next act, complete with scenes and roles.

+ *How are you being spared from an even worse situation?* Look at what you *do* have, whether it's loving friends and family, working physical organs, financial means, good care, your health. Consider how many people do not have those things, and feel gratitude.

✦ *Will you be able to do good for others as a result of this situation?* Many people, including the founders of national anti–drunk-driving, child-support enforcement, and cancer advocacy groups, recovered from tragedy by organizing efforts to help others in the same situation. This might be what your life is all about. Or perhaps your crisis situation will make you wiser and more able to help those near to you.

LEARN OPTIMISM

Martin Seligman in his book *Learned Optimism* reports that you can begin to view an experience positively by changing viewpoints on its circumstances. He advises regarding difficulties as temporary rather than permanent; as impersonal rather than personal; as specific rather than generalized through your life. If you get terminated from your job, you will recover more quickly if you regard it as a temporary pause between jobs rather than a long-term problem due to corporate downsizing rather than your own failings, and as something that affects only one part of your life rather than as an indication of deficiencies in your character. Try this way of thinking in terms of your current issue:

✦ Examine how your situation is a temporary stage of your life.

✦ Examine the things beyond your immediate control that made it happen.

✦ Examine the parts of your life that it has no bearing on.

Flow Exercises: Resurfacing

1. *Resolve inner conflicts.* This brief but powerful process helps you find harmony when you feel you're being pulled two ways. It can help you decide on a course of action when you're torn by two choices. First, sit quietly. Place your hands in front of you, palms up, far apart from each other. In one hand, put one viewpoint, and in the other hand put the other. Now, across the distance between hands, have the viewpoints talk to each other about their differences. As they talk back and forth and as it is comfortable, slowly move your hands and viewpoints together, continuing the dialogue. When your hands touch, fold them together, bring them to your chest, and imagine taking them into your heart.

2. *Grieving visualization.* If you are dealing with the death of a loved one, locate that person in your mind's eye. If she is far away and indistinct, which is often the case, mentally move her up close and adjust the colors until they're strong and clear. Now how do you feel? Move her to the left and to the right. Now how do you feel? Move her away in the distance. Switch the picture to black and white. Put a picture frame around her. Now how do you feel? Mentally hang the picture in a place where you can go to see it only when and if you wish. How do you feel?

3. *Slide show.* To gain perspective and emotional distance, mentally step back from the situation to see it as a black-and-white slide show. Underscore it with your favorite music.

10 CONNECT WITH YOURSELF AND OTHERS

I used to have a two-word spiritual vocabulary: Yes and Thanks. Lately I've added two more: God Bless. And that seems to cover just about everything.

Ann Medlock

These words of flowmaster Ann Medlock reflect appreciation, gratitude, and generosity: three techniques that generate the power of flow. When we appreciate the gift we are given, when we are grateful to the giver and then give in turn with a full heart, the power of flow puts joy and ease into our lives. The techniques included in this chapter are:

11. Appreciate Yourself
12. Express Gratitude
13. Give of Yourself

You'll learn to appreciate and nourish your body, mind, emotions, and spirit; receive everything that comes your way as a gift; and be full of gratitude. When you commit acts of kindness and generosity from that overflow of appreciation and gratitude, you'll find that helping others is your way of expressing yourself and synchronicity is your constant companion.

Appreciation, gratitude, and generosity are states of being from which we act. It is one thing to give a donation because we ought to do it, and it is quite another to share what we have because we are deeply connected to others and what is ours is theirs already.

When these three states of being permeate your life, you will experience not only being deeply in flow yourself, but be able to be a vehicle that effortlessly furthers flow for others. As the flowmasters demonstrate, when we master flow, we smooth the way for those around us: our appreciation, gratitude, and generosity overflow to create an environment of perfect timing and flawless serendipity for those we come in contact with. And that is the real gift to which we say *Yes*.

APPRECIATE YOURSELF

Appreciation charges the ordinary, unexamined parts of our lives with significance and puts them in a place of honor. Think how you feel when your boss or your partner appreciates something you did and lets you know it. Appreciation creates openings for communication and interchange.

Appreciation starts with ourselves, by accepting ourselves exactly as we are and showing our appreciation by taking care of our own well-being. From there, appreciating others is a natural, spontaneous outgrowth. You might be blessed with good health, a creative mind, a wondrous spirit, fulfilling possessions, and a joyful life. Then appreciating yourself is easy. But even if you have poor health, a restless mind, few possessions, and an uninspired life, these things are yours nevertheless.

Looking back to technique #2, acceptance, embrace what you have, exactly as it is. Take it compassionately in your arms and hold it. Bring it close to you and pull it into your heart. Appreciate it exactly as it is—not as it will be or as you would like it to be or as others think it should be, just as it is in this moment. With that, you close the door on anxiety and resentment, and open the door to love and joy.

Show appreciation for yourself—your body, your mind, your emotions, your spirit—by acts of kindness, both routine and random.

APPRECIATE YOUR BODY

Your body is precious and unique. No one else has one like it or ever will. When you look at the myriad genetic factors, the chance of your getting the body you have is one in a billion

billion. Some go even further with the odds: The Buddha is said to have said that obtaining a "precious human body" is as rare as a turtle swimming on the floor of the ocean, surfacing once every hundred years, and emerging at the exact spot necessary to put its neck through a lone ring floating on the surface of the ocean.

There is no right body for you—there is only *your* body for you. This body is the only one you will have in this lifetime. It is the right one because it is yours. It hangs around wherever you are, it goes wherever you go. If you overfeed it, underexercise it, or deprive it of sleep, it will be hurt. If you ignore it, it will be hurt. But your body will never ignore you: it will respond to whatever treatment you give it.

Your body has an important role in bringing you into flow, for it's hard for a body that is fatigued or stressed to muster the energy to align itself with underlying reality. High vitality, on the other hand, makes you more available to fill your role in the Universe.

If there is something about your body that you would like to be different, change how you treat your body, and it will respond. Change may not be easy for you, but it is easy for your body, which simply responds to your input.

If you want to change your body, first do a fact-finding tour of it: talk the facts over with those parts of your body that will be affected by the change. Visualize your goal, and carefully construct an experience of it by seeing, hearing, feeling, tasting, touching your ideal in your inner experience. See it as if the change were already accomplished; hear others comment on it; feel the difference. Tell the part of you that is changing how much you appreciate it for getting you this far and ask if it is all right to change. If not, ask why. Constructing a visualization and practicing it daily gives your body a map of where it is going.

Consult books, seminars, and magazines to uncover a path that will take you to your goal. Then mindfully go through whatever process you choose, do 100%, and trust the outcome. If the result matches your goal, celebrate. If it does not match it, cycle through this process again.

There is a vast number of books, seminars, experts, tapes, and merchandisers who have ideas on what your body should look like and are ready to give you instructions on getting there. These instructions may be a useful part of your process, but none will make the change for you. None of these instructions can take into account the myriad circumstances in your past, present, or future that are part of your physical and mental makeup. So choose carefully: check out what resonates, what feels, sounds, and looks right. Give flow and synchronicity its due when exploring these various methodologies.

Eat the right foods. And you know what they are! This is the arena of personal change that is toughest for many of us, since food is linked to emotional as well as physical comfort. And although there are many experts, viewpoints, and alternatives, the basic rules are clear about the need in our diets for more vegetables and whole grains, and less fat, red meat, and sugar. Check with a nutritionist to be sure you provide your body with enough vitamins, minerals, herbs, and amino acids. Be responsive to what your body tells you: there are times and seasons for everything—even for chocolate cake.

Move your body. There's a wide array of movements to sample and include in your everyday life: dance, aerobics, yoga, weight-lifting, swimming, skiing, tennis, hiking, walking. Studies show that walking 30 minutes a day five times a week, or 60 minutes a day three times a week will ensure a minimum level of fitness.

The book *Dr. Dean Ornish's Program for Reversing Heart Disease* outlines a straightforward, effective daily program that includes simple yoga, breathing, and guided meditation. In *The Life We Are Given,* George Leonard and

Michael Murphy present a comprehensive exercise routine that, combined with affirmations, was shown to produce significant personal changes in participants in their program.

Relax and refresh your body. Find ways of delighting yourself. It may be spending extra minutes in your morning shower or having a luxurious candlelit, aromatic bath on a cold winter day. It may be a facial, a new haircut, or not shaving all weekend. It might be a massage—Ron Chin alternates every other week between a male massage therapist who does deep tissue work and a female massage therapist who uses aromatherapy, reflexology, and visualization. Take yourself to a Jin Shin Jyutsu session, touch therapy, a spa. Surprise your body: give it a good belly laugh, a cold shower, a brisk rubdown, a tingling new fragrance.

APPRECIATE YOUR MIND

Your mind, like your body, is unique to you. It is the powerful tool that you use to perceive your world, to grow, to change, to experience life in all its dimensions and variety. Treated gently and used carefully, it cuts through clutter and illusion and brings you to new heights of joy, power, and clarity.

Feed your mind. As with your physical diet, carefully select what moves you toward good health. The computer saying, "garbage in, garbage out," can be just as easily applied to your mind. So avoid giving your mind the equivalent of junk food. Learn new subject matter at your local college or learning institution. Read books or watch television shows that stimulate your thinking and give you a broader perspective on the world and its people. Seek out people who stimulate your thinking.

Exercise your mind. Stretch your mind to its limits by challenging your beliefs, reevaluating them, and adapting them. Look at dichotomies from both points of view: as F. Scott Fitzgerald put it, this involves "the ability to hold two opposed ideas in the mind at the same time." Mindfully differentiate every category that presents itself to your mind, creating new ones. Find options to every action, and compare them to see which works best. Take up an engaging and demanding new hobby, such as playing an instrument or growing an herb garden. Do puzzles and word games to challenge your mind. Meditate to increase your flexibility and adaptability.

Relax and re-create your mind. Seek out silence, space, inner peace, and joy. Watch clouds drift across the sky, feel the warmth of a crackling fire in a fireplace, hear waves crashing on a beach. Turn loose your thoughts for a while each day: let them float by like an interesting but distant parade passing the window of your mind.

APPRECIATE YOUR EMOTIONS

Your emotions deserve your utmost appreciation, for they add texture and richness to the details of your daily living. They give you messages you need to heal, provide opportunities for you to learn, and connect you to others and to your deepest self. Like your body and your mind, they too need to be nurtured, cared for, and re-created.

Nurture your emotions. Feel them when they come up. When you're in the moment, you can have pain or anger or love or peace in all their fullness—then release these emotions and move on to the next moment and its requirements. This doesn't necessarily mean acting on your emotions: when someone rudely cuts you off in traffic and your anger rises, mentally explore your emotional triggers rather than tailgating their car.

The first step is to be aware of the physical cues: feel that knot in your stomach, that burning in your throat. Acknowledge that this is where you are right now and turn your full attention to mindful driving. When you stomp on your emotions and push them underground—Who me? Angry?—they resurface later in disguise: you might snarl at a store clerk or turn it against yourself through illness. In other words, have your anger without your anger having you.

Care for your emotions. Treat them like the blessings they are. Emotions enrich your experiences with joy, sadness, excitement, pain. Don't force them unnecessarily to extremes: watching a brutal film can leave your emotions bruised and raw. When pain or sorrow come up, treat them tenderly like delicate, sweet children.

Exercise your emotions. Do it. Choose an emotion you want more of, such as joy or delight or unconditional love. Then set up a means to tap into it: reading a humorous book, gazing at a picture of someone you love, watching a favorite old film, or listening to special music. When you're feeling that emotion strongly, close your eyes and make it even stronger: turn up the intensity, give it sound, increase the sensations in your body. Revel in it. You'll find that, later on, you'll be able to access this emotion more easily.

APPRECIATE YOUR SPIRIT

Appreciating your spirit means caring for that part of yourself that is ineffable, transcendent, beyond concepts. It speaks to you through the small voice inside that you might call God, conscience, intuition, the higher self, your guardian angel. Unless you follow those inner messages—which demonstrates that you appreciate them—they will become faint and surface less frequently. Internally arguing with them or brushing them aside diminishes them, just as you feel diminished when others argue with you or brush you aside.

Nurture your spirit. Surround your spirit with positive regard, with like-minded people, with silence. Hold it gently like a newly planted flower, shielding it from the winds of criticism and the heat of judgment. Allow it to take root by trusting it and allow it to grow stronger by following it. Then celebrate its blossoming, its unfoldment.

Care for your spirit. Treat your spirit to a steady infusion of inspirational reading, lectures, and music. Soothe it with long nature walks and days on the beach. Elevate it through time spent in the presence of wise ones of any spiritual path. Be with those who love you.

Exercise your spirit. Attend to your underlying beliefs and values. Discuss them with like-minded others. Observe those of differing disciplines, and appreciate their faith. Expand your spiritual path by going beyond your comfort zone: meditate routinely, then go on a retreat for a weekend, then for a week, then for two. Visit the holiest places of your faith and the holy places of other faiths.

Flow Exercises: Appreciating Yourself

Let your body know how much you appreciate what it's done for you. Compose yourself, enter into silence. Starting with your feet and moving upward, send appreciation to each part of your body, each system, each organ. Tell each part how much you appreciate all the hard work it's done for you, in spite of the sugar you've eaten, the liquor you've drunk, the exercise you avoided. Ask each part in turn what it wants to say or wants you to do. Your answer may come as a sensation, a picture, words. Be receptive and respectful of whatever information you receive. When you've completed each part of the process, record your thoughts, feelings, and responses to your body's requests in your journal. Do you now look at your body differently? Do you know any new information? Do you have more ideas about how to appreciate your body?

Embrace the child within. Close your eyes, enter into silence, and ask your small child within to reveal itself to you. Take it in your arms, console it, and shower it with love. Actually wrap your arms around yourself and give that small child a hug. If it appears as a threatening shape, shrink it, change its color and tone of voice, and make peace with it. If you feel a special need, visit a specialist or therapist who is especially attuned to help you heal.

Maintain a routine practice for body, mind, emotions, and spirit. In your journal, write out the daily and weekly routines that you do to show appreciation for your body, mind, emotions, and spirit. Include such things as brushing your teeth, eating, sleeping, working, leisure time activities, and silent time. Leave plenty of space between your listings for changes and further details. As you go through the week, embellish your list, with other things that come to mind that you wish you were doing. Include things you know to do but haven't when those items occur to you—intuitively, or in silence.

At the end of the week, make a new list of all the items that you know to do, whether you are doing them or not. Read through the list and mark one or two that are a stretch, or a risk. Prepare affirmations and visualizations to support your new ways. Take like-minded friends or your flow partner to lunch and discuss the process with them. Whether or not they join in themselves, tell them what you have committed yourself to doing. Ask them to support you by being a check-in point at specific intervals (daily is a great starting point).

Now begin. Do everything you routinely do plus the two new items. Celebrate your success by calling your supporter and by giving special care to yourself in this and other areas. At the end of that first week, select two more new items to begin the next week. Tell your supporter about this choice and your commitment.

Continue this process of adding and maintaining new ways of showing appreciation for your body, your mind, your emotions, and your spirit. As always, do all this with compassion: compassion for yourself, compassion for others, and compassion for life.

EXPRESS GRATITUDE

Everything is a gift. The degree to which we are awake to this truth is the measure of our gratefulness. And gratefulness is the measure of our aliveness.

Brother David Steindl-Rast

Gifts are by definition gratuitous: they are free. Gifts are surprises: even the most mundane gift is unexpected. It is this element of unexpected fulfillment that creates the fullness of gratefulness. Freely given fulfillment is the doorway to joy, and joy is the expression of gratefulness.

Gifts must be given, so there is always a giver. When you realize that something is a gift, there is a bond created between the gift-giver and you, the receiver. That bond is gratefulness. It is a circle: the receiver takes the gift and gives appreciation, the giver takes the appreciation for the gift given. There is an interdependence between the two: they are connected.

As Benedictine monk Brother David Steindl-Rast discusses in *Gratefulness, the Heart of Prayer,* when we are grateful, our intellect, our emotions, and our will work together in harmony. Our intellect identifies the gift, our emotions feel the fullness of surprise, and our will gives thanks from our full hearts. We grow in gratefulness as we receive even more gifts: we see life as full of surprises, and each surprise as a gift. In emotional wonderment we find meaning, in intellectual concentration we find purpose, and those come together in the surprise and freedom that gives rise to gratitude. Meaning is important because it rests the mind, stills the emotion, and elevates the spirit. We find meaning in gifts and synchronicity; we feel joy in the expression of gratefulness and flow.

Sandra Widener of Denver is not sure she believes in a

higher power, yet she finds herself constantly giving thanks for her husband, her daughters, her home, her life. "It's an al-most constant sort of thing—I think about it all the time. I'll open a cabinet and I'll think, 'Yeah, we built this, and I love it.' And the main thing that I end up thinking in these conver-sations with myself is that I don't do nearly enough for other people. The two thoughts are always linked in my head."

The bond of gratefulness is a powerful antidote to alienation and the cynicism and sarcasm it spawns. The won-derment and surprise in gratitude brings up the child in you—the child who once woke up every morning excited about life, who saw everything with fresh eyes. Gratitude re-stores awe and wonder to your days. Brother David writes of his boyhood experience in Nazi-occupied Austria, when he ran into a church and dived under a pew as a bombing raid started. When the explosions stopped, he got up and stepped out into a glorious May morning. "The buildings I had seen less than an hour ago were now smoking mounds of rubble. But that there was anything at all struck me as an over-whelming surprise. My eyes fell on a few square feet of lawn in the midst of all this destruction. It was as if a friend had of-fered me an emerald in the hollow of his hand. Never before or after have I seen grass so surprisingly green." The grass was an awe-inspiring gift in that unlikely moment.

Sunny Schlenger keeps a journal of things she's thankful for. "You know how you feel when someone does something nice for you, that you want to do more for them? I've read that the Universe is the same way. If you're appreciative, it just wants to do more and more and more. I'm not necessar-ily looking at my journal as a way of getting more. It feels so good to be thankful and it keeps the energy flowing."

Many say that giving thanks for synchronicity seems to encourage it to show up. "When things converge in a surpris-ing and hopeful way, as though there is a hand extended to me or a flashlight shining on a path, I call attention to it by saying thanks," says flowmaster Michael Sun. "I think with that you encourage your relationship with the intelligence of the unknown."

And when we want to show gratitude, sometimes synchronicity provides the opportunity. When Beverly Ciokajlo of Detroit was fourteen and the eldest of eight children, she was waiting for a bus in a blizzard on her way to find a job when a church pastor rescued her in his car and found her a job. Forty-six years later, she ran into him again. "It was a dream come true that I could thank him again in person and tell him how important his help was to my life," she says.

Gratefulness is demonstrated by giving blessings, thanks, and praise. Blessings have religious undertones. Giving thanks is often thought of in terms of polite conventions, like saying thank you or writing notes. But a deep personal engagement from receiver to giver is beyond words. Praise is more formal and is a value-driven or moral response.

These actions are important, yet they are only the beginning. The power of gratefulness comes when it is the way we live our lives, when it is where we come from rather than where we are going, when it is a state of being rather than a state of action. And the key to this is when we are grateful for the life we have been given.

This gratitude might be directed toward a greater whole—God, the Universe, underlying reality. Or it might not be directed toward anything in particular—blessings, thanks, or praise forwarded without an address. Maybe gratitude is not the word for you: instead, you feel honored to be part of a larger plan, connected to an underlying pattern.

When we live in this state of gratitude, our entire lives become an act of giving, of generosity. We come into the fullness of heart that brings us into flow.

LEARNING GRATITUDE WITH THE
PRACTICE OF NAIKAN

"I've never met a neurotic person—or a person with a lot of neurotic moments—who was filled with gratitude," says David K. Reynolds, Ph.D. A psychological anthropologist, he has brought to the United States a Japanese approach to behavioral change known as Naikan (translated as "looking inside") which, he says, "is about seeing reality that was previously ignored." The effect of Naikan, which he details in *A Handbook for Constructive Living,* is to cultivate gratitude in people. It has been used in Japan to successfully turn around troubled youths, rehabilitate criminals, and counter addictions. In the United States, as part of Reynolds's Constructive Living program, it is used to help teens at risk, quarreling couples, and management trainees.

In Naikan, you look at life from the viewpoint of being a receiver, seeing everything and everyone in terms of the efforts made on your behalf. A salad in a restaurant is not a collection of greens: it is the outcome of a farmer sowing the seed, the sun shedding its rays, the workers harvesting the crop, the truckers transporting it, the wholesalers marketing it, the restaurant supplier selecting it, the chef preparing it, and the waitress bringing it to your table. All those people have brought you your lunch—and now those greens are contributing to your physical well-being by sharing their nutrients with you. Your shoes, your bed, your car—are all products of thousands of hands. Those items themselves merit your gratitude for the way they serve you by keeping your feet dry, your body rested, your transport ready, and so you treat them with respect: putting your shoes away carefully, making your bed, keeping your car running smoothly.

The outcome of looking at life this way is that we feel part of a vast web of interrelatedness: we feel ourselves the recipient of constant grace. We are filled with wonder that this perfect green salad is sitting in front of us. We see how in fact we have done nothing in our lives by ourselves, and this moves us from "How much can I get out of this situation?" to "How much can I give back?" It seems the least we can do for all we've received.

Naikan is particularly powerful when applied to personal relationships. In Japan, people enter a retreat setting for a ten-day period. For the first couple of hours, they think of their mothers up through the first three years of elementary school. They ask themselves three questions: *What did I receive from my mother? What did I give to my mother? What troubles and difficulties did I cause my mother?* They reflect on specific answers—not "She fixed me food every day," but "She prepared cookies for my class one day," "She bandaged my knee that day I fell off the swing." They briefly report on their memories to a Naikan guide or listener. The next two hours they ask the same questions of the next three years of their life, then junior high, and so on. When they're up to their current age, they start with their father. From there they proceed through everyone in their life who has been significant to them—siblings, teachers, friends, coworkers. By the end, they start to see that everything they are they owe to someone else. They no longer feel isolated but part of a network of caring.

Flow Exercises: Cultivating Gratitude

NAIKAN-BASED EXERCISES, FROM CONSTRUCTIVE LIVING

Daily Naikan. Before going to bed at night, sitting in a quiet place, ponder the day's events and write down the answer to these questions: *What did I receive from others today? What did I give to others today? What troubles and difficulties did*

I cause others today? Be specific; recall and list even trivial items.

You and your parents. Total up the money your parents spent on you from the time you were born until you reached twenty-one, including food, shelter, clothing, presents, education, trips. Then calculate the amount you spent on your parents over the same period. Do the same two steps from age twenty-one to the present. What do you find?

You and your partner. Write a list of fifty things to thank your partner for. Choose five of the items on your list and thank your partner for them. Do this for ten days. Bring home a gift one day a week.

Secret service. Once a week, do something special as an act of service for your partner, parent, sibling, friend—shining their shoes and putting them back, fixing something of theirs that is broken. The only catch is that you can't tell them about it beforehand or afterward—and if they catch you doing it, do something else!

Do secret service for the person you get along with the least. Do this to feel gratitude to the person for the learning they are providing for you and the strength they are building in you.

You and your stuff. Clean out or organize a drawer or closet or purse. As you take each item out, thank it for something specific it has done for you. This will give you a sense of how you're supported not just by people but by things.

You and the essentials of your life. Consider how your car, your computer, your stove, your refrigerator, your stereo serve you, and find a way to demonstrate your appreciation.

WAYS TO COUNT YOUR BLESSINGS

Find the surprise in life. Look around you where you are right now. Look at the same things that you usually see, but with a new eye: Look for the surprise in them. Look at the face of someone you love, see it with wonderment and awe. Pretend you are a child seeing a prized possession for the first time. Take the gift graciously, spend a moment being receptive, then give your appreciation to the giver. Feel the joy that comes from being connected, from the bond of gratefulness.

Consider everything a gift. Whatever comes your way, accept it as it is and appreciate it for what it contributes to your life—say "yes" and "thanks." When you believe that everything has a purpose and that you're here to learn lessons, then this attitude is a natural outgrowth. If you aren't sure those are your beliefs, try saying "yes" and "thanks" for three days and see what happens.

Count your blessings by considering the alternatives. When we start comparing ourselves to others, usually it's upward: we see a luxurious home and ours seems suddenly dowdy, we see a TV star with a fabulous body and ours seems flabby. "Comparison is the source of all misery," said Nietzsche. But if your mind insists on comparing, compare downward. Your house may not be the cover of *House Beautiful,* but it's wonderfully open and airy compared to your college dorm room. So your legs are chubby: look at how well they get you from point to point! And what if you didn't have them!

Say thank you in your journal. Keep a running list of what you're thankful for. Be specific: *the purple rain clouds, getting new windshield wipers just in time, getting the intuitive hint to take my umbrella even though the skies were sunny, not having to water my garden tonight.*

GIVE OF YOURSELF

Generosity is giving from the heart. It makes no demands, seeks no favors. It is energizing and fulfilling. And when you are in flow, it is your nature. Generosity is being in rhythm with the greater plan. It is being connected to others in such a way that "mine" and "yours" are not part of your way of living. To be in flow is to be generous in sharing the essence of yourself.

Alice Mammoser, totally absorbed, leaned intently toward the patient seated opposite her in the tiny office. "I'll bet you have all sorts of energy at night and have trouble going to sleep, but you can't wake up in the morning no matter how hard you try." Her comfortable manner, her complete attention, her kindly face all spoke to Laura, her patient, but what most impressed Laura was how much Alice gave of herself in the next hour. It was as much in Alice's manner as her words: although she had already been at work thirteen hours and had more patients waiting outside, Laura was the most important person in the world to her. Without hurrying, Alice shared her professional knowledge, gave Laura a nutritional program to turn her health around, and spoke of how she took care of herself so she could take care of others. She reassured Laura's mother, hovering anxiously nearby, "I know how it is. I have children, too." And when they were done, they exchanged warm hugs. Laura felt energized and excited: her healing of a malady dating from her teenage years was under way. In the ways that are important, Alice was available—all she is, all she knows, and all she has she gives to others, with no holding back. Alice is generosity in action.

Being generous is being in a feedback loop with the Universe. You get and you give, you give and you get, and what you get is often the opportunity to help others give. Sometimes synchronicities deliver to you precisely what someone else needs.

Flow has a ripple effect. When we are deeply in flow, our generosity is effortlessly manifested in another way: the people around us find that their lives, too, start flowing better. Things fall into place for them, their timing is perfect, and what they need comes their way. Sometimes we have a conscious hand in this by our generous acts, but much of this dynamic is acausal by our ordinary understanding.

Look at your life for the many ways in which you are generous. Think of those dear to you, and how you give of yourself to them. Think of the ways you have given to others at your office or store, in your children's school, at your church or in your community. Think of the ways you've been available to a friend in need or a relative who's in a crunch. Think of when you've gone out of your way to lift someone's spirits or lend a hand to a neighbor.

As you move more into flow, generosity becomes the way you live. You *are* generosity. Mother Teresa and the Dalai Lama personify this way of being: they live in service to others. The high school teacher who never stops caring, the woman who works at the Laundromat and who fills it with welcoming warmth, the pastor or counselor who is always available: they leave you uplifted and energized, feeling better about yourself and life's possibilities.

Generosity has many forms. For Staci Boden, it's "trying to be as present with someone as I can be—that's the best way I can give of myself." For Dan Muse, making himself available to others is his job description as a public servant. And because of his high visibility as an African-American, "I get requests for all kinds of things." He writes many letters of references, helps with job contacts, loans people money, speaks at inner-city schools, serves on boards. "I got a request last week from a fellow I've gotten to know casually who asked me to co-sign for a rental car agreement, using my credit card. I did it!" For Janet Landis, it is submerging her-self in her "calling" of routing out racial antagonism and re-placing it with connection.

We must be mindful of our motives, though. Sometimes what looks like generosity is actually an attempt at control or manipulation or atonement: the giver is trying to get compli-ance, even if unconsciously. The person who cannot receive with an open heart, who fends off honest compliments and refuses to accept gifts, cannot give freely, openly, and hon-estly.

Generosity has many levels. You can give away objects you don't need but someone else can use, such as packing up your old summer clothes for Goodwill. You can give some-one something that you value, such as your only copy of an out-of-print book. Or you may give away what you hold most dear: in a dirt-floored hogan, an elderly Indian woman took from her foot a well-worn, hand-beaded moccasin and gave it to her visitor as a cherished memento of their time to-gether. Think of your gifts and your level of giving.

Even more than objects, the expansion of generosity in-volves giving more and more of yourself. You share openly. That is because true generosity flows from a sense of unity, of oneness: you do not keep track of what people owe you be-cause there's no difference between you and them. As Ram Dass and Paul Gorman write in *How Can I Help?:* "We're not so much helping out because it's me needing to tend to you. We're helping out because it's Us. . . . If one of Us needs help, if one of Our arms gets caught in a door, naturally we use the other of Our arms to set it free."

One way to build generosity is to volunteer regularly at a place where help is needed—a homeless shelter, hospital, se-nior citizen home, tutoring project. As you share yourself with people in need, you'll find your heart opening. Your fears of unknown others melt away without effort. But be-ware of going in with an agenda, of having expectations that because of your work, someone is going to get better. To do so sets you up to judge that person and then yourself, leading to discouragement and burnout. Generosity from the heart asks for no return: as Sathya Sai Baba, a spiritual teacher in India, says, "Hands that serve are holier than lips that pray." He suggests providing service to others not with the idea that you're helping them out of their misery, but with the idea of furthering your own spiritual growth by removing in yourself the barriers that separate you from others. When you do this, you'll find the roles are flipped: the person you're "helping" with mere material aid is helping you out with something much more important—the experience of your deepest self, which brings you into the power of flow.

Flow Exercises: Enhance Your Generosity

LEARN TO RECEIVE

Sit across from a friend. Be silent for a minute or two, and then have the friend tell you something they appreciate or admire about you. Be receptive. Take it in with an empty mind and an open heart. Notice where you are uncomfortable, where you want to deny or discount it. Breathe deeply for a moment, visualizing yourself opening your heart to this gift. Sit with it until you can feel yourself fully accepting it. Show your gratitude by nonverbally saying thanks. Then do the same process for your friend. Repeat the process, going to a deeper level of truth. Watch your bond and connection increase. In generosity, as in gratefulness, the separation between giver and receiver disappears.

OPEN YOUR HEART WITH PRAYER

Praying for others allows your love and generosity to flow and expand. In addition to private prayer, there are public formats in which you can pray for others: they include healing circles, prayer services, and novenas. A Buddhist prayer known as *metta* (loving-kindness) is one approach you can do on your own. You simply pray over and over, as a kind of mantra, "May all beings be happy. May all beings be free of suffering. May all beings be healthy. May all beings dwell in peace." As a meditation practice, visualize sending the prayers first to someone you love, then to someone you feel neutral about, and then to someone you feel challenged by. This type of prayer works particularly well in public places. Looking at people in the street, subway or mall, pray for each one you pass with such phrases as, "May you be happy. May you be free of suffering."

UNDERTAKE ACTION TO INCREASE YOUR GENEROSITY

1. Assess honestly where you are in terms of your own generosity. Are you comfortable with your level of activity? If you died in an hour, would you be happy with how you've served your world? Have you given too much and felt burdened by your own generosity?

2. Make a list of ten options to express generosity. Offer to drive an extra day in the carpool, look after a member of a friend's family, do yard work for a neighbor—these are all generous acts. They can range from quick and undemanding to difficult tasks that require a high degree of self-discipline over a lengthy period of time.

3. Figure out how you could accomplish each option by either talking or writing about it. Weigh each option carefully for its costs and returns. Prioritize each option based on its weight and your available resources. Examine which options are really choices coming from whom you see yourself as being and which ones are ideas that will meet another's expectations.

4. Select which options to act on. Be clear about your criteria for success: How long will you continue? How will

you know when to finish? How will you be able to measure success for yourself? Create a visualization and affirmation to support your choice.

5. Make a commitment to act on these options and do them 100%.

6. Record in your journal and discuss with your flow partner or family how your choices are progressing. Make any necessary adjustments.

7. Acknowledge yourself.

11 GET A POINT OF VIEW FROM THE UNIVERSE

∞

TECHNIQUE #14:

DIVINATION

∞

The word *divination* has the same root as the word *Divine*, from the Latin word *divinus,* which means God. This is apt, because when it's done with care and reverence, divination leads us to closer contact with the Divine and with the divinity within ourselves.

Divination is a practical technique that we can use to align ourselves with flow. It provides information that helps us understand the deeper dynamics of a situation in our life. By understanding how the underlying currents of the moment are moving, we can make a conscious choice to move with it, and this enhances flow and synchronicity. Carl Jung found divination key in his thinking about synchronicity. He had striking truths revealed to him by the I *Ching*, and he saw it as an example of synchronicity in action: It was the coinciding of external events (the throwing of the coins) with an internal event (his question) in a way that was meaningful and that defied cause-and-effect explanation. He believed the I *Ching* and other systems of divination offer a controlled way to tap into the process of meaningful coincidence.

For much of human history, people have sought to divine the patterns in their lives from the environment around them. The passage of clouds across the sky, the flight patterns of birds, the falling of leaves, all held personal meaning and information. As societies developed, they devised techniques to present questions to the Universe. In northern Europe, sticks and stones were carved with symbols known as runes and cast on the ground. In southern Africa, bones and shells were painted or carved and thrown down. In China, turtle shells were tossed into fires to create cracked lines that could be examined for meaning.

Many societies had a central place for oracles, people who would enter into altered states of consciousness to predict the future. In classical Greece and Rome, oracles were an integral part of official decision-making, consulted in peace and particularly in war. In traditional cultures from Siberia to the Pacific Islands, shamans would enter into trance states, commune with magical animals and spirit guides, and return with practical advice.

Western religions—Judaism, Christianity, and Islam—have a history of prophets who foretold and prepared the way for events. Followers of these religions have often found guidance in specific situations by opening their Scriptures at random and reading the phrase in front of them. Eastern religions, which stress the interrelatedness of all things, continue to place divination prominently among their practices. A major text of Confucianism, the I *Ching* is an ancient divination method. In Tibetan Buddhism, for centuries an oracle has advised on matters of state. In Hinduism, Vedic astrology plays such a central role that a marriage will not be arranged unless the charts of the prospective partners show compatibility.

Divination taps into a deeper order. It can help us expand our view of the world and stretch our understanding of what is possible. It can reveal aspects of ourselves or a situation in an exciting new way. It can bring into our conscious awareness truths we already know at a deeper level. If we feel stuck, a divinatory reading can cast light ahead of us and allow us to see the possibility of happiness. If we are facing a major decision, divination can show us the ramifications of our choices from a wider perspective and loosen our attachment to things turning out a certain way. Readings do not always suggest taking the route we had planned—but if we recognize, lying beneath our dismay, an "aha" feeling, a sense of rightness, then it's probably the path that is ultimately best for our growth.

This is not to say divination is for everyone, or that it's useful for all the times in your life. Some of the flowmasters we interviewed for this book have never used it. "Why should I consult anything else? I have myself," said one. Some flowmasters used it at a specific crisis point, some used it on and off, and some use it regularly. It's a matter of personal preference and style. If divination matches your philosophy and feels intuitively right to you, it can be a powerful impetus for growth and expansion. When Staci Boden consulted a psychic for the first time, she was so moved by what she had learned that she cried for three days afterward. She now has a reading every six months, "Not because of the information itself, but because the information pushes me and helps me stretch and move in deeper." She has also taught herself the tarot. "It's a tool to help me get in touch with my intuition. It feels like the information is right on the edge of my consciousness, and the card pushes it so it's clearly right there in front of me."

WHERE TO BEGIN

1. Decide whether to do it yourself or have it done for you.
When you divine on your own, you have a direct experience
of your connection with the greater whole. You put out your
question, the answer comes back, and it is up to you to interpret it for your own use. This builds trust and commitment to
your own process. Going to another person affords the advantage of another person's point of view with an expansive
outlook.

2. See what resonates. As you read through the following
divination options, some techniques, methods, and systems
will click with you and some won't. It's important to follow
those inner messages to select what resonates.

3. Give synchronicity its due. Watch for what comes into
your path via meaningful coincidence. If someone brings out
an *I Ching* book or talks about learning to use the runes, consider that information and look for your relationship to it.
Your desire to know deeper answers will bring the means to
you.

4. Start with silence. By becoming quiet, going deep within,
and coming to that point of connection with something beyond yourself, you can use divination to tap into answers
that your rational mind can't get to. By putting aside your desire for control, you open the space for deeper wisdom.

5. Pose the question. Before you undertake any divination
method, decide what you want to know. Be concise and specific in wording your question.

POSING QUESTIONS ON YOUR OWN

Because divination is brought about by the intersection of your consciousness with outer reality, almost any "technique" can be used: cards, dice, even songs on the radio. There are divination systems on-line on the Internet: you compose your question, click on a number, read the commentary, and interpret the message for your answer. The systems that follow are a sampling of what's simple and easily available. New divination systems are being designed all the time, and a visit to your local bookstore will uncover many more.

I Ching. Perhaps the most venerable system of divination, the *I Ching,* known as the *Chinese Book of Changes,* dates back some 5,000 years. The sixty-four hexagrams on which its interpretations are based were first derived from tossing turtle shells in a fire; yarrow stalks and coins later were used. Incorporating both Confucian and Taoist thought, the *I Ching* is concerned not just with an answer to a specific question but with an understanding of the larger dynamics unfolding in the matter at hand. Jung called it "one of the oldest known methods for grasping a situation as a whole and thus placing the details against a cosmic background." Its language is arcane and flowery, its sensibility practical: it counsels integrity, patience, persistence, and moving when the timing is right. It's uncanny how often it exactly hits the target.

To use the *I Ching,* you need two items: coins to toss and a book of interpretation. The classic version is the translation of Richard Wilhelm's German version; later versions offer more contemporary language. Spend some time in a bookstore to find the one that resonates with you.

Joan Price of Scottsdale, Arizona, a philosophy professor, has used the *I Ching* twenty-five years. "It's not the answer my ego had always wanted to hear, but on a deeper level, if I do as it says and I am patient, in the long run it's always correct." When she was discouraged about her writing, it kept counseling her to "Cross the Great Water," to proceed with her high ambitions. Now, she's a successful writer of children's books and textbooks. "I use it when I can't figure things out logically and realize I have to go to a higher stage and not use the intellectual mind."

Card systems. Systems based on cards offer an easy and convenient way to view and interpret information. The tarot, the oldest and by far the most popular card system, has its contemporary origins in fourteenth century France and corresponds with the Kabbalah, the Jewish mystical tradition, as well as with Egyptian ideas. A tarot deck, similar to a deck of playing cards, comprises a major arcana of twenty-two cards and a minor arcana of forty cards. The cards, bearing richly detailed pictures, feature symbols such as cups, swords, and moons, and lend themselves to reflection and story-telling. Tarot can be used to come up with yes/no answers, but it also offers a wealth of information, often quite specific, on the circumstances surrounding a situation.

Other card systems, much more recent in origin, involve the less complex act of asking a question, drawing a card, and reading and interpreting the result. One of the most popular of these is the Medicine Cards, which are illustrated with forty-four animals used by Native Americans as teachers and guides. Sacred Path Cards cover steps of initiation into a Native American culture and can be used in conjunction with the Medicine Cards.

The runes. The runes are stones or pieces of wood inscribed with symbols. When pulled from a bag or thrown, they reveal the best course of action to take. According to Nordic mythology, a tribe from the North, who were guardians of sacred forest and whose role was to help the oppressed, originated the runes. There is evidence of runes dating back to 1300 B.C., and by the ninth century they had spread through what is now Austria, Germany, and Scandinavia. Like the *I Ching*, the runes reveal the underlying dynamics in a situation and put your decision into a larger context. The most popular book on the runes today is by Ralph Blum, and includes a set of runes in a small brown bag. Those who get deeply into the runes make their own.

Sacred books. One straightforward way people seek direction is by asking a question, praying for guidance, and then randomly opening up a sacred book, such as the Bible or the Torah, and seeking an answer in reading what their eyes or finger first fall upon.

Chits. This is a technique you can use to make a decision on a specific matter: it works best when you use it seriously and resolve to do whatever comes up. To do the chits, align yourself within through meditation or prayer with what to you represents the Divine: God, or Jesus, or Mary, a spiritual master, an angel, your higher self. First, select an object that clearly represents this person or symbol to you—a painting, a photo, a candle. Then contemplate the decision you have to make. Consider all your options and write them out one by one on small slips of paper, the chits. Include options that you are not wild about, as well as one that says, *Await some other alternative*, and one that says *Do not choose this way*—in case this is not the appropriate technique for you to use for this particular decision. Fold up the chits, then meditate or pray until you are calm, peaceful, and connected to your Divine—at minimum, a half hour. Wait for the point at which you feel merged in spirit with that higher energy. Don't rush it: you'll know within when this moment arrives. Then pick up the chits, shake them in your hands and throw them toward the picture or object. The one that lands closest to it is the course of action you follow. A variation on this is to write out on slips of paper only the phrases: *Yes, No, Not at this time*, and *Do not choose this way*. When you toss them, select the chit that falls closest to you. Read it and follow the direction indicated.

Pendulum. This is a variation on the ancient technique of dowsing for water. Take a well-balanced object that hangs from the end of a cord: it might be a crystal dangling from a chain or a pendulum obtained for this purpose. The cord must be held in such a way that the item hangs freely. Ask the pendulum to indicate to you a *yes* response and a *no* response—it might be a back and forth or sideways movement or a clockwise or counter-clockwise circle. After composing and centering yourself, ask your question and watch for the movement. Some people use this method to decide such mundane things as what to eat and what vitamins to take. In earlier times it was used to determine the sex of unborn children. The advantage to the pendulum is that it is fast and versatile; the disadvantage is that it is highly subject to human emotions and error. A strong desire on your part often is enough to move it the way you'd like. To use it accurately, it is important to know your desires well and put them aside during the process.

The Transformation Game. In this board game, which is available in many bookstores and is played with two or more people, you focus on some issue or question in your life. By shaking dice, you move along your "Life Path." That path is yours alone: each player plays their own game on the path in front of them. Depending on your draw from the Life Deck Cards—angels, insights, setbacks, and universal feedback— you move slowly or quickly through succeeding levels: physical, emotional, mental, and spiritual. When you hold the game lightly yet regard it respectfully, it can provide a wealth of metaphorical information on an issue before you at the moment.

POSING QUESTIONS VIA OTHERS

People throughout history have sought out those who have the ability to see beyond the here and now. Sometimes this ability is based on knowledge of an encoded system of esoteric learning, such as astrology or numerology. Sometimes the ability comes from contact with other dimensions of existence, through trances or altered states, such as shamans who work with animal guides, oracles who call on spirit realms, mediums who communicate with spirits, and channelers who pass through the words of various entities. In contemporary American culture, psychics sometimes fill the role of seer, guide, or counselor.

When you want to find options to your current path, learn more about yourself, or see your life from a larger perspective, a divination practitioner might be a useful approach. A good astrologer or psychic or numerologist will leave you with a deeper, more expansive view of yourself: you see yourself in a new light, with greater compassion. You understand better the aspects that drive you and gain new insight into the purpose of hardships you've endured. You have a sense of where you fit in the overall scheme of things, of what your purpose might be.

Understanding the dynamics of the moment, however, is different from seeking to know the future, which has its drawbacks. First of all, the future is constantly changing, depending on your actions, so today's projection of the future is tomorrow's day-old paper destined for the trash can. Also, a prediction of the future raises an interesting dynamic: You can take the information you hear, unconsciously incorporate it into your beliefs, and then act in such a way as to fulfill the prophecy. It's easy to live in a future fantasy, especially if your life at the moment is less than rosy, but in the moment is where change takes place. Then again, sometimes that vision of something brighter gives you the courage to change—so use your best judgment.

This kind of divination is dependent on good practitioners: the wiser and more self-accepting and compassionate they are, the better the psychic material they'll have access to and the more help they'll be to you. Divination practitioners are just as shaped by their personal experiences as you are: They bring both their strengths and limitations into a reading. When you are told something by a psychic that she can't possibly know—say, that your marriage is in trouble—do not conclude that the psychic has a clear, totally untarnished view of the whole picture of your life. She may have the ability to see things you may be blind to or in denial of, but she will also be seeing these things from her own perspective. One psychic may be uncanny on career dynamics, but his own difficulty finding romance may be reflected in that he often mistakenly sees true love in the future of his clients. Another psychic routinely sees the marriage of her clients breaking up, just as hers did. The cleaner practitioners are about their own strengths and foibles, the better their readings will be.

There are several routes to finding a reliable practitioner: word of mouth, recommendations, advertising, and psychic fairs. You might pursue any or all of these—but don't forget to keep your eyes open for synchronicity, which can put the right person directly in your path at the right time.

Word of mouth is the best approach because often the best divination practitioners are almost hidden: they work in a low-key way out of their homes, they don't advertise or give classes, and you only learn of them through others. Have your friends and coworkers ever had a reading? Was it useful? Accurate? It's definitely a good sign if the person recommended to you works full-time as a psychic, if she's been doing it many years, and if she has so many people lining up to see her that it takes you a while to get an appointment.

Go to a local metaphysical bookstore and start asking

around. If you know any shiatsu therapists or other body-workers, ask them for a recommendation. When you hear the same name three or four times, it's worth following up. Psychic fairs in shopping malls are also a place to try a few psychics for relatively little money. That's how Jeff Miller, a Denver travel writer, got his first reading. "I chose a gray-haired woman. She held my palm, closed her eyes, and drifted off into the ozone," he recalls. "Then she said in this eerie voice, 'I see someone standing behind you, someone who is your guardian angel, a person who died in September of 1974.'" Jeff was stunned—his cousin, who had been his college roommate, had died of cancer that very month. "He's watching out for you, because you have allowed him to live his life through you," she said. Now Jeff and his wife see a psychic once or twice a year. Says Jeff: "For $40, you can hear all kinds of fascinating things that make you think about yourself in a new way."

One thing you should not do is walk into a storefront with crystal balls and "psychic reader," "palm reader," or "fortune teller" signs in the window. Often these operators tell people that they have a curse on them or that negative vibrations surround them, and they can bilk terrified customers out of thousands of dollars. Psychics reached on 900-numbers should also be taken with a shakerful of salt. Some ex-employees have told reporters that they were recruited off the streets and given scripts of customer-pleasing generalities to read.

Here are some broad categories in which you're likely to encounter divinatory practitioners:

Psychics. Webster's New World Dictionary defines a psychic as "a person who is supposedly sensitive to forces beyond the physical world." Practicing psychics are unanimous in saying that everyone has the ability to know things beyond the five senses—for instance, by knowing in a flash who's on the other end of the phone before picking it up. But through training and/or by birth, the skills of some people are at a higher level than those of the rest of us.

Many psychics have been "different" since childhood. Nancy Regalmuto of Bellport, New York, for example, was rebuked on the morning of November 22, 1963, for agitatedly telling her first-grade teacher that President Kennedy would be killed later that day. At age five, Angela Hart told a friend on the playground that their friend Joey was going to jump off the seesaw and that Tommy would bang his head and get a bloody nose. When that exact thing happened a few minutes later, her friend looked at her fearfully and said, "You're really weird." Some psychics teach themselves; others get training from psychics who act as mentors, and still others hone their skills in classes.

There are various ways psychics take in information. They might see your situation as symbols in their mind, or as a TV-like scene playing through before their eyes, or they might hear certain words and get a gut feeling of what you're feeling. Sometimes what they "get" requires interpretation; for instance, an image of death may not refer to the body but to the end of a relationship or the death of the ego. Some psychics, to stimulate their intuition, use tarot cards, playing cards, or read palms or tea leaves. Sometimes they focus their attention by holding an object, such as a ring or pendant, that the client usually wears.

No specific training or accreditation is required for someone to work as a psychic, and abilities run the gamut from highly reputable to highly questionable. No psychic gets it all right. Frederick G. Levine had readings from four dozen psychics while writing *Psychic Sourcebook: How to Choose and Use a Psychic.* On average, he says, the psychics were only half accurate about his personality and a quarter accurate about his future. At the high end, a few psychics got his life about 90 percent right.

So it's important to choose a psychic wisely, because more than just your time and money can be at stake. Psychics actually help you create your reality. They say a particular thing, you take it in a particular way, and the two of you have in a sense reshaped your worldview—and that reshapes your life.

Astrology. Astrology is based not on psychic skills but on an intricate, ordered system of knowledge that dates back to the Babylonians of 2000 B.C. Astrologers believe that a chart based on the position of the planets at the place, time, and date of your birth reveals your essential personality characteristics and the general shape of your life. Some attribute this to the electromagnetic energy of the planets on the body at your first emergence into the world; others believe that the planets and your life correspond to each other because they are both part of the same intricate, coordinated ordering of the universe.

Contrary to popular astrological columns, your sun sign alone is of little use: what matters is how the ten planets are positioned in the twelve houses, how they are influenced by the twelve signs, and how they interact with each other. A good chart can be a window into new insights about yourself and a means of self-acceptance; for example, your success in your relationship and your lack of interest in climbing the ladder at your job may make more sense to you when you learn that you have a cluster of planets in the house of partnership and none in the house of career.

Numerology. Somewhat linked to astrology, numerology is a method of divining underlying order through numbers. The Greek philosopher Pythagoras laid down many theories of numerology, as did Chinese thinkers and the ancient writers of the Kabbalah and the Indian Vedas. Numerologists compute the numbers in your life by using your birth date and the letters of your name. Those numbers provide insight into your life path and personal strengths and limitations.

Kinesiology. An emerging approach to divination is that of kinesiology, which involves a practitioner testing the strength of your muscles while asking questions to which you seek answers. The process is viewed as asking your body for answers regarding the emotional and mental data stored in it. For instance, if you have a fear of public speaking, the practitioner will test for when it started by counting backward decade by decade, then year by year, then month by month until the muscle responds. If done by a skilled person, kinesiology can uncover such things buried in your subconscious as prenatal influences, conversations overheard in early childhood, and traumatic rejections.

Channelers. This form of psychic communication involves a spirit or entity from another plane taking over the body of a person and speaking through his mouth. Its origins are in shamanism and in the oracles of classical Rome. Channeling has mushroomed in this country in recent years: More than 1,000 channels are said to live in California, and it's possible in many places to take courses in channeling. Some valuable information has come through channels, most notably the Course in Miracles, yet this is perhaps the murkiest of areas in the psychic realm. There's some outright fraud, and much to be careful of: Even when something supernatural is going on, just because an entity is not in a body doesn't mean it's enlightened. If you consult a channel, the important thing to evaluate is not the means but the message: Do the words leave you elevated and wiser? Do you understand yourself better? Are you encouraged to find your own answers?

TEN WAYS TO SPOT
A PHONY PSYCHIC

Some people who call themselves psychics are flimflam artists. Run away from any so-called psychic who:

1. Says you have a curse that needs removing.

2. Asks for money up-front, more money afterward, or is vague about how much a session will cost.

3. Charges too much. Most psychics charge between $30 and $150. There should be no additional costs.

4. Refuses to let you tape-record the session. What do they have to hide?

5. Advertises as "the most famous" or "the most renowned."

6. Is full of anger, hatred, and arrogance. Their own problems will sabotage your reading.

7. Speaks in generalities. If they say you're a generous person who isn't appreciated, that's a statement almost anyone would feel applies to them.

8. Invokes fear or confusion in you, or acts secretive.

9. Tries to bully you into returning soon. Good psychics don't want their clients emotionally dependent on them.

10. Gives you the creeps. Trust your instincts. If you don't feel comfortable, walk out.

The emphasis in this book is on divination that reveals the gestalt, the underlying dynamics, of a situation or life. Obtaining accurate predictions of the future is very delicate, because readings use the present circumstances as the point from which to look into the future. Tiny changes in situation, attitude, time of day, or any of the factors integral to that specific system changes that point and thus the prediction.

After a reading, do a reality check with your own self-knowledge. Just because something beyond ordinary understanding is being tapped into doesn't mean that human error can't be present to a greater or lesser degree.

When consulting other people, think of them not as oracles, but as consultants hired for their expertise. Listen carefully, sort through the information, keep what is useful, and put the rest away. Ultimately, you and you alone are the authority on your life.

12

WHAT TO DO WHEN THE POWER OF FLOW EBBS

It's happened. There you are one minute, exhilarated by the power of flow, astonished by synchronicity. Never before has life worked so well and been so much fun. You're swimming joyfully with that current, and then—oops! It's gone. No smoothness, no happy surprises: just obstacles and frustrations.

What happened? Where did flow go?

You're not alone. There wasn't a flowmaster we interviewed who didn't sometimes feel out of flow. When John Graham fights with his wife or when they don't get a foundation grant he's worked hard for, he goes "deep into a hole of despair and frustration." Over the years, however, his approach has changed: "What I understand now is that the hole is not the reality: The hole is the place where I am now stuck. It may take a day, or an hour, or a week to get out of it, but I know I've got to get out of it, because I know what is on the outside."

What John and the other flowmasters have learned is that flow never goes away—they only perceive that it does when they are out of sorts with themselves and thus out of

step with the Universe. Flow is always present, always underlying our lives. Whether we experience its full power is up to
us: it relies on the choices we make and actions we take moment by moment.

If you understand flow well enough and live it deeply,
you can immediately pause when it seems to wane, look, listen, and do what you know to do to move back into its
power.

An early warning system can help—and that system is
your own awareness. Be mindful, and you can act quickly to
reverse the tide. Your first clue may be encountering problems: plans fall through, you can't get an appointment, your
sink clogs up, a check doesn't arrive. Look for the messages,
both obvious and metaphorical: What should you be doing
differently? Making new plans? Trying another avenue?
Dealing with a blocked emotion?

Consider the possibility that the problems are your synchronicity. Maybe you're heading down a road that isn't ultimately for your own good or for the greater good. If nothing
seems to be going right, if effort and struggle are the modes
for the day, it might be a sign that a better and wiser dynamic
is at work. Become silent, then move in another direction,
and watch to see if the problems dissipate.

Another early indication is that things just don't click.
Phone calls come at inopportune times, you miss the bus by
seconds, you buy something that you could have gotten at half
price a day later. At previous times in your life these glitches
might have been routine, but once you get used to the power
of flow, they are so unusual that you quickly notice them.

You can also tell that the power of flow is diminishing
when synchronicity falls silent. You might not experience any
coincidences at all, let alone meaningful ones.

When external events aren't flowing in your life, look at
your internal events. In silence, reflect on what could be
blocking your experience of flow. Ask yourself questions like
the ones on the next page.

FLOW CHECKLIST

When you're feeling blocked from flow, ask your-self the following questions and look up the recom-mended techniques as starting points to further growth:

✦ Is there a truth I haven't told myself or another?
   Read *Be Aware*, page 125

✦ Am I spending a lot of time doing something I hate?
   Read *Express Who You Really Are*, page 148.

✦ Am I stuck in a routine?
   Read *Take Risks*, page 191.

✦ Is my level of physical vitality low?
   Read *Appreciate Yourself*, page 206.

✦ Am I trying too hard to make something work?
   Read *Do 100% of What You Know To Do—and Trust*, page 180.

✦ Am I bored with life?
   Read *Practice Mindfulness*, page 173.

✦ Am I frustrated because things aren't going my way fast enough?
   Read *Accept Yourself and Others*, page 139.

✦ Am I resentful about what I don't have in life?
   Read *Express Gratitude*, page 215.

✦ Am I going through a personal crisis?
   Read *Break with Your Old Reality*, page 197.

✦ Am I feeling down on myself?
   Read *Appreciate Yourself*, page 206.

✦ Am I angry at someone for not being who I want them to be?
   Read *Accept Yourself and Others*, page 139.

✦ Are there things to do that I'm avoiding?
   Read *Finish Things and Move On*, page 188.

Use the situation as a learning tool, for these times of ebb are invaluable in illuminating our blocks. They bring to the surface our deepest fears. They point out deficits in our personal attributes. By looking deeper, we can come to understand which of our beliefs and actions have left us constricted and unavailable to the Universe, to others, and to ourselves.

Sometimes the power of flow seems low because we have misunderstandings about how it functions. For example, we might be getting such a kick out of synchronicity that we start focusing on creating it. We forget that we can't create synchronicity as such: we can only create the conditions in ourselves that allow it to happen. Synchronicity does not show up on demand, and if we have pictures of how it should look at certain times, it tends to vanish. The solution lies in defocusing on synchronicity and focusing on the power of flow.

Buoyed by the power of flow, we might also find ourselves getting a little lazy. But flow isn't about sitting back and letting the Universe do it all; rather, it's a participatory sport. Our part is to be open to whatever presents itself, to listen to our inner voice and respond to it, to put ourselves out there, to do all we know to do, and to contribute our part to the greater whole. Then the Universe will volley back to us what we need for our happiness and progress.

Living deeply in flow does not mean that your personal challenges disappear and that things are smooth and easy all of the time. In fact, if you are deeply committed to experiencing high levels of flow, you may find that the Universe has put in front of you, and in dramatic form, exactly what stands between you and that deeper aliveness. When you were a young child, learning the alphabet was a major challenge—but think how monotonous it would be if that were your task for today. The natural order in the Universe presents ever more challenges and opportunities to enhance our experience of flow, to enhance peace, joy, and harmony.

So when an obstacle arises, the Universe is in fact handing us another gift to use mindfully and wisely. For example, the obstacle may be an outer manifestation of our inner doubts or confusions, and we may want to look within: Are we pursuing our course because of what others want or expect from us? Out of old habits and needs? Because it's something we feel we should be doing but don't really want to? By sorting out these desires and drives, we can decide whether to continue on our path or regard the obstacle as a nudge in another direction.

However, if we find on self-examination that what we're doing feels risky but right, that we have clarity and conviction about our direction, then the obstacles we're encountering may be exactly what we need to develop trust, courage, and commitment—flowmaster attributes that enable us to contribute ever more powerfully to the greater good.

Remember that however large the obstacles and tough the situation, flow gives us the inner resources to handle it, because flow gives *us*. When we're in touch with ourselves, we draw great courage and inventiveness from within, and so the bigger the challenge, the more exhilarating it can be. Even when we're stuck in the muck, we have moments of pure joy—because we can see how from that ultimately comes greater clarity and freedom. Because we trust the underlying order of the Universe and the power of flow and know that we will not be tested beyond our strength, we have the ability to get through all that comes our way.

The power of flow operates in an upward spiral. Each time we break through our blockages and come out the other side, we are on a higher level, more integrated and more harmonious. And each time we face the same obstacle, it dissipates faster.

So when the power of flow ebbs, be gentle and kind with yourself. Understand that slow times are every bit as important as fast-moving times. Remind yourself that you're always in flow, always heading toward your destination of

harmony and wholeness, joy and freedom. And try a variation on Carolyn North's solution. When she experiences
what she calls "fallow times," she goes to the library and
takes out a stack of Gothic novels. "I love those crappy romances, I really do," she sighs. When you do something you
love, you open yourself again to the power of flow.

Remember that whatever the situation you're in, how
you choose to handle it is totally up to you. Day by day,
minute by minute, flow is a matter of choice and action—
your choice and your action. The power of flow is highly personal: You create it your own way in each moment.

You alone know best how to chart the path that enhances your attributes of commitment, honesty, courage, passion, immediacy, openness, receptivity, positivity, and trust.
Enjoy the journey, for it is yours to create as you wish. Your
life can be an effortless, joyous dance with the Universe—and
the first step onto the dance floor is yours.

AFTERWORD: BEYOND SYNCHRONICITY

There is a point where metaphors break down, where words fail, where we step through the looking glass and find another world. In the journey you are on, that happens. You have been using synchronicity to give meaning to your life. When meaningful coincidences occur, you notice them, position them, and interpret them as tools for your own transformation. You have experienced an ever-increasing volume of singles, strings, and clusters of them. On a moment-by-moment basis, your life has become sweeter, easier, more intriguing and happier. You find yourself sharing your excitement with others as you learn about yourself as an individual, as a contributor to the group and community, as a spiritual being.

Then one day, you notice that you haven't been talking as much about your synchronicities. When you think back, you realize that you have had just as many of them or even more, but you have come to think of them differently. Instead of signposts and directions, you see them as acknowledgments and confirmations. Instead of pondering the mirrors and lessons of meaningful coincidences, you smile at them and nod thanks. What was astonishing earlier in your journey is now an "of course." The mundane details of your daily life are submerged in the fulfillment of your life mission. When difficulties arise, and they still do, you naturally and immediately see them as part of a bigger picture. You have a certainty about you that is based upon a deeper understanding of yourself, and you don't need words to describe or defend what you know as true.

You trust that the Universe will not deal you a hand that you cannot play; that while you have choice in the game, you do not play it alone; and that is, after all, still a game. We started on this journey together, many pages ago. This book was the guide, synchronicity the compass, and flow the destination. Having now had glimpses of that destination, the guide and compass are no longer as essential. As flow becomes your nature rather than your destination, it sinks from constant view like an underground river, as did synchronicity before it. Although flow is still there, no longer do you see it. For even as a drop of rain cannot separate itself from the ocean into which it has fallen, so can you not separate yourself from flow.

You are flow.

References for Further Study

GENERAL INFORMATION ON FLOW AND SYNCHRONICITY

Aziz, Robert. *C. G. Jung's Psychology of Religion and Synchronicity.* Albany: State University of New York Press, 1990.

Bohm, David. *Unfolding Meaning: A Weekend of Dialogue with David Bohm* (1987 ed.). New York: Routledge-Ark Paperbacks, 1985.

———. *Thought as a System.* New York: Routledge, 1992.

Bolen, Jean Shinoda. *The Tao of Psychology: Synchronicity and the Self.* San Francisco: HarperSanFrancisco, 1979.

Briggs, John, and F. David Peat. *Turbulent Mirror: An Illustrated Guide to Chaos Theory and the Science of Wholeness.* New York: Harper and Row, 1989.

Combs, Allan and Mark Holland. *Synchronicity: Science, Myth and the Trickster.* New York: Paragon House, 1990.

Csikszentmihalyi, Mihaly. *Flow: The Psychology of Optimal Experience.* New York: HarperCollins, 1990.

———. *The Evolving Self: A Psychology for the Third Millennium.* New York: HarperCollins, 1993.

Franz, Marie-Louise Von. *On Divination and Synchronicity: The Psychology of Meaningful Chance*. Santa Rosa, Calif.: Atrium, 1977.

Grasse, Ray. *The Waking Dream: Unlocking the Symbolic Language of Our Lives*. Wheaton, Ill.: Theosophical Publishing House-Quest Books, 1996.

Jung, C. G. *Synchonicity, An Acausal Connecting Principle*. R.F.C. Hull, trans. Princeton, N.J.: Princeton University Press, 1973.

Koestler, Arthur. *The Roots of Coincidence, An Excursion into Parapsychology*. New York: Random House, 1972.

Mansfield, Victor. *Synchronicity, Science, and Soul-Making: Understanding Jungian Synchronicity through Physics, Buddhism, and Philosophy*. Chicago: Open Court, 1995.

North, Carolyn. *Synchronicity: The Anatomy of Coincidence*. Berkeley, Calif.: Regent Press, 1994.

Peat, F. David. *Synchronicity: The Bridge Between Matter and Mind*. New York: Bantam Books, 1987.

Redfield, James. *The Celestine Prophecy: An Adventure*. New York: Warner Books, 1993.

Redfield, James, and Carol Adrienne. *The Celestine Prophecy: An Experiential Guide*. New York: Warner Books, 1995.

Talbot, Michael. *The Holographic Universe*. New York: Harper-Collins, 1991.

Vaughan, Alan. *Incredible Coincidence: The Baffling World of Synchronicity*. New York: Ballantine Books, 1979.

GENERAL INFORMATION ON PERSONAL TRANSFORMATION

Carter-Scott, Cherie. *The New Species*. Farmingdale, N.Y.: Coleman Graphics, 1980.

DeLozier, Judith and John Grinder. *Turtles All the Way Down: Prerequisites to Personal Genius*. Bonny Doon, Calif.: Grinder, DeLozier and Assoc., 1987.

Fowler, James. *Stages of Faith: The Psychology of Human Development and the Quest for Meaning*. San Francisco: Harper and Row, 1981.

Holmes, Ernest. *How to Change Your Life.* Los Angeles: Science of Mind Publications, 1983.

Jung, C. G. *Memories, Dreams, Reflections.* Richard and Clara Winston, trans. New York: Random House, 1963.

Maslow, Abraham H. *The Farther Reaches of Human Nature.* New York: Penguin Books, 1986.

Murphy, Michael. *The Future of the Body.* Los Angeles: Tarcher, 1992.

Myss, Caroline. *Anatomy of the Spirit: The Seven Stages of Power and Healing.* New York: Harmony, 1996.

Ornstein, Robert E. *The Psychology of Consciousness.* New York: Penguin Books, 1973.

Satprem. *Sri Aurobindo or the Adventure of Consciousness.* Luc Venet, trans. New York: Institute for Evolutionary Research, 1970.

Schwartz, Tony. *What Really Matters: Searching for Wisdom in America.* New York: Bantam Books, 1995.

Wilber, Ken. *No Boundary: Eastern and Western Approaches to Personal Growth.* Boulder, Colo.: New Science Library, 1979.

———. *The Spectrum of Consciousness.* Wheaton, Ill.: Quest Books, 1993.

———. *Sex, Ecology, Spirituality: The Spirit of Evolution.* Boston: Shambhala, 1995.

———. *A Brief History of Everything.* Boston: Shambhala, 1996.

Zukav, Gary. *The Seat of the Soul.* New York: Simon & Schuster, 1989.

CHAPTER 6

Gawain, Shakti. *Creative Visualization.* San Rafael, Calif.: New World Library, 1995.

Leonard, George, and Michael Murphy. *The Life We Are Given: A Long-Term Program for Realizing the Potential of Body, Mind, Heart, and Soul.* New York: G.P. Putnam's Sons-Jeremy P. Tarcher, 1995.

Progoff, Ira. *At a Journal Workshop.* New York: Dialogue House Library, 1975.

CHAPTER 7

TECHNIQUE #1: BE AWARE

Andreas, Connirae, with Tamara Andreas. *Core Transformation: Reaching the Wellspring Within.* Moab, Utah: Real People Press, 1994.

Assagioli, Roberto. *The Act of Will.* New York: Penguin Books, 1973.

DeVito, Joseph A. *Human Communication: The Basic Course.* New York: HarperCollins College, 1994.

Ferrucci, Peiro. *What We May Be: Techniques for Psychological and Spiritual Growth Through Psychosynthesis.* Los Angeles: Jeremy P. Tarcher, 1982.

Goleman, Daniel. *Vital Lies, Simple Truths: The Psychology of Self-Deception.* New York: Simon & Schuster, 1985.

———. *Emotional Intelligence: Why It Can Matter More Than IQ for Character, Health, and Life Achievement.* New York: Bantam, Doubleday, Dell, 1995.

Krause, Carol. *How Healthy Is Your Family Tree?: A Complete Guide to Tracing Your Family's Medical and Behavioral Tree.* New York: Fireside, 1995.

Peck, M. Scott. *The Road Less Traveled: A New Psychology of Love, Traditional Values and Spiritual Growth.* New York: Touchstone, 1978.

Riso, Don Richard. *Discovering Your Personality Type: The New Enneagram Questionnaire.* Boston: Houghton Mifflin Company, 1995.

Taylor, Jeremy. *Where People Fly and Water Runs Uphill: Using Dreams to Tap the Wisdom of the Unconscious.* New York: Warner Books, 1992.

TECHNIQUE #2: ACCEPT YOURSELF AND OTHERS

Bodine, Echo L. *Passion to Heal: The Ultimate Guide to Your Healing Journey.* Mill Valley, Calif.: Nataraj Publishing, 1993.

Dixon Monica. *Love the Body You Were Born With: A Ten-Step Workbook for Women.* New York: Perigree, 1996.

Hay, Louise L. *You Can Heal Your Life.* Santa Monica, Calif.: Hay House, 1984.

————. *Heal Your Life Workbook.* Santa Monica, Calif.: Hay House, 1990.

Lerner, Harriet. *The Dance of Anger: A Woman's Guide to Changing the Patterns of Intimate Relationships.* New York: HarperPerennial, 1985.

Santrock, John W., Ann M. Minnett, and Barbara D. Campbell. *The Authoritative Guide to Self-Help Books.* New York: Guilford Press, 1994.

Stone, Hal, and Sidra Winkelman. *Embracing Our Selves.* Marina del Ray, Calif.: Devorss & Company, 1985.

Stone, Hal, and Sidra Stone. *Embracing Your Inner Critic: Turning Self-Criticism into a Creative Asset.* San Francisco: HarperSanFrancisco, 1993.

Williamson, Marianne. *A Return to Love: Reflections on the Principles of a Course in Miracles.* New York: HarperPerennial, 1996.

Wood, Julia T. *Everyday Encounters: An Introduction to Interpersonal Communication.* Belmont, Calif.: Wadsworth, 1996.

TECHNIQUE #3: EXPRESS WHO YOU REALLY ARE

Cameron, Julia. *The Artist's Way: A Spiritual Path to Higher Creativity.* New York: G. P. Putnam's Sons–Jeremy P. Tarcher, 1992.

Csikszentmihalyi, Mihaly. *Creativity, Flow and the Psychology of Discovery and Invention.* New York: HarperCollins, 1996.

Dyer, Wayne W. *Real Magic: Creating Miracles in Everyday Life.* New York: HarperPaperbacks, 1993.

————. *Your Sacred Self: Making the Decision to Be Free.* New York: HarperPaperbacks, 1996.

Edwards, Betty. *Drawing on the Right Side of the Brain.* Los Angeles: Tarcher, 1989.

Hendrix, Harville. *Keeping the Love You Find: A Guide for Singles.* New York: Pocket Books, 1993.

————. *Getting the Love You Want: A Guide for Couples.* New York: Henry Holt, 1988.

Jarow, Rick. *Creating the Work You Love.* Rochester, Vt.: Destiny Books, 1995.

Moore, Thomas. *Care of the Soul: A Guide for Cultivating Depth and Sacredness in Everyday Life*. New York: HarperCollins, 1992.

———. *Soul Mates: Honoring the Mysteries of Love and Relationship*. New York: HarperCollins, 1994.

Occhiogrosso, Peter. *Through the Labyrinth: Stories of the Search for Spiritual Transformation in Everyday Life*. New York: Viking, 1991.

———. *The Joy of Sects: A Spirited Guide to the World's Religious Traditions*. New York: Image Books, 1996.

Sher, Barbara. *Live the Life You Love in Ten Easy Step-By-Step Lessons*. New York: Delacorte Press, 1996.

———, with Barbara Smith. *I Could Do Anything, If I Only Knew What It Was*. New York: Dell, 1995.

Shinn, Florence Scovel. *The Game of Life and How to Play It*. New York: Simon & Schuster, 1980.

Sills, Judith. *Excess Baggage: Getting Out of Your Own Way*. New York: Penguin, 1994.

Tannen, Deborah. *You Just Don't Understand: Women and Men in Conversation*. New York: Ballantine, 1990.

Thompson, Peg. *Finding Your Own Spiritual Path: An Everyday Guidebook*. San Francisco: HarperCollins–HarperSanFrancisco, 1994.

CHAPTER 8

TECHNIQUE #4: CREATE SILENCE

Benson, Herbert. *The Relaxation Response*. New York: William Morrow, 1975.

Dossey, Larry. *Healing Words: The Power of Prayer and the Practice of Medicine*. San Francisco: HarperSanFrancisco, 1993.

Goldstein, Joseph, and Jack Kornfield. *Seeking the Heart of Wisdom: The Path of Insight Meditation*. Boston: Shambhala, 1987.

Harp, David. *The Three Minute Meditator*. Oakland, Calif.: New Harbinger, 1996.

Hyams, Joe. *Zen in the Martial Arts*. Los Angeles: J.P. Tarcher, 1979.

McDonald, Kathleen. *How to Meditate: A Practical Guide*. Boston, Mass.: Wisdom, 1984.

Wilson, Paul. *Instant Calm: Over 100 Easy-to-Use Techniques for Relaxing Mind and Body*. New York: Plume, 1995.

Yount, David. *Breaking Through God's Silence: A Guide to Effective Prayer*. New York: Simon & Schuster, 1996.

TECHNIQUE #5: FOLLOW YOUR INTUITION

Day, Laura. *Practical Intuition: How to Harness the Power of Your Instinct and Make It Work for You*. New York: Villard, 1996.

Goldberg, Philip. *The Intuitive Edge: Understanding and Developing Intuition*. Los Angeles: Jeremy P. Tarcher, 1983.

Vaughan, Frances E. *Awakening Intuition*. New York: Doubleday-Anchor Books, 1979.

TECHNIQUE #6: PRACTICE MINDFULNESS

Brooks, Charles V. W. *Sensory Awareness: The Rediscovery of Experiencing*. Santa Barbara, Calif.: Ross-Erikson Publishers, 1982.

Fryba, Mirko. *The Practice of Happiness: Exercises and Techniques for Developing Mindfulness, Wisdom, and Joy*. Michael H. Kohn, trans. Boston: Shambhala, 1995.

Goldstein, Joseph. *Insight Meditation: The Practice of Freedom*. Boston: Shambhala, 1994.

Hanh, Thich Nhat. *The Miracle of Mindfulness: A Manual on Meditation*. Rev. ed. Mobi Ho, trans. Boston: Beacon Press, 1987.

Kabat-Zinn, John. *Wherever You Go, There You Are: Mindfulness Meditation in Everyday Life*. New York: Hyperion, 1994.

Langer, Ellen J. *Mindfulness*. Reading, Mass.: Addison-Wesley–Merloyd Lawrence, 1989.

CHAPTER 9

TECHNIQUE #7: DO 100% OF WHAT YOU KNOW TO DO— AND TRUST

Assagioli, Roberto. *The Act of Will.* New York: Viking, 1973.

Covey, Stephen R., A. Roger Merrill, and Rebecca R. Merrill. *First Things First.* New York: Simon & Schuster, 1994.

Krystal, Phyllis. *Cutting the Ties That Bind: Growing Up and Moving On.* York Beach, Maine: Samuel Weiser, 1982.

————. *Cutting the Ties That Bind Workbook.* York Beach, Maine: Samuel Weiser, 1995.

Spangler, David. *Everyday Miracles: The Inner Art of Manifestation.* New York: Bantam Books, 1996.

TECHNIQUE #8: FINISH THINGS AND MOVE ON

Flanigan, Beverly. *Forgiving Yourself: A Step-by-Step Guide to Making Peace with Your Mistakes and Getting On with Your Life.* New York: Macmillan, 1996.

Jampolsky, Gerald G., with Patricia Hopkins and William N. Thetford. *Good-Bye to Guilt: Releasing Fear Through Forgiveness.* Toronto: Bantam Books, 1985.

Rechtschaffen, Stephan. *Timeshifting: Creating More Time to Enjoy Your Life.* New York: Doubleday, 1996.

Schlenger, Sunny, and Roberta Roesch. *How to Be Organized in Spite of Yourself: Time and Space Management That Works with Your Personal Style.* New York: Penguin Group-Signet, 1990.

Smedes, Lewis B. *Forgive and Forget: Healing the Hurts We Don't Deserve.* San Francisco: HarperSanFrancisco, 1984.

TECHNIQUE #9: TAKE RISKS

Bateson, Mary Catherine. *Peripheral Visions: Learning Along the Way.* New York: HarperCollins, 1994.

Griffiths, Bede. *A New Vision of Reality: Western Science, Eastern Mysticism and Christian Faith.* Felicity Edwards, Ed. Springfield, Ill.: Templegate Publishers, 1990.

Ilardo, Joseph. *Risk-Taking for Personal Growth: A Step-by-Step Handbook.* Oakland, Calif.: New Harbinger, 1992.

Ross, Jerilyn. *Triumph Over Fear: A Book of Help and Hope for People with Anxiety, Panic Attacks, and Phobias*. New York: Bantam Books, 1994.

Zimbardo, Philip. *Shyness*. Reading, Mass.: Addison-Wesley, 1987.

TECHNIQUE #10: BREAK WITH YOUR OLD REALITY

Andreas, Steve and Connirae. *Change Your Mind and Keep the Change*. Moab, Utah: Real People Press, 1987.

Burmeister, Mary. *Jin Shin Jyutsu Self-Help Book*. Scottsdale, Ariz.: Jin Shin Jyutsu Inc., 1982.

Colgrove, Melba, Harold Bloomfield, and Peter McWilliams. *How to Survive the Loss of a Love*. Los Angleles, Calif.: Prelude Press, 1991.

Kabat-Zinn, Jon. *Full Catastrophe Living: Using the Wisdom of Your Body and Mind to Face Stress, Pain, and Illness*. New York: Delta, 1991.

Miller, Carolyn Godschild. *Creating Miracles: Understanding the Experience of Divine Intervention*. Tiburon, Calif.: H.J. Kramer, 1995.

Seligman, Martin. *Learned Optimism: The Skill to Conquer Life's Obstacles, Large and Small*. New York: Pocket Books, 1990.

Siegel, Bernie S. *Love, Medicine and Miracles*. New York: Harper and Row, 1986.

———. *Peace, Love, and Healing*. New York: Harper and Row, 1989.

Viorst, Judith. *Necessary Losses*. New York: Simon & Schuster, 1986.

Wakefield, Dan. *Expect a Miracle: The Miraculous Things That Happen to Ordinary People*. San Francisco: HarperCollins-HarperSanFrancisco, 1995.

Whitton, Joel L. and Joe Fisher. *Life Between Life*. New York: Warner, 1986.

Wholey, Dennis. *When the Worst That Can Happen Already Has: Conquering Life's Most Difficult Times*. New York: Hyperion, 1992.

CHAPTER 10

TECHNIQUE #11: APPRECIATE YOURSELF

GENERAL

Blackstone, Judith. *The Subtle Self: Personal Growth and Spiritual Practice.* Berkeley, Calif.: North Atlantic Books, 1991.

Canfield, Jack, and Mark Victor Hansen. *The Aladdin Factor.* New York: Berkley Books, 1995.

Chopra, Deepak. *Ageless Body, Timeless Mind: The Quantum Alternative to Growing Old.* New York: Harmony Books, 1993.

———. *Perfect Health: The Complete Mind/Body Guide.* New York: Harmony, 1991.

Cohen, Alan. *The Dragon Doesn't Live Here Anymore.* New York: Fawcett, 1993.

Elgin, Duane. *Voluntary Simplicity: Toward a Way of Life That Is Outwardly Simple, Inwardly Rich.* Rev. ed. New York: Quill, 1993.

Gawain, Shakti, with Laurel King. *Living in the Night: A Guide to Personal and Planetary Transformation.* San Rafael, Calif.: Whatever Publishing, 1986.

Kurtz, Ron. *Body-Centered Psychotherapy: The Hakomi Method.* Mendocino, Calif.: LifeRhythm, 1990.

Leonard, George, and Michael Murphy. *The Life We Are Given: A Long-Term Program for Realizing the Potential of Body, Mind, Heart, and Soul.* New York: G.P. Putnam's Sons–Jeremy P. Tarcher, 1995.

Lerner, Harriet Goldhor. *The Dance of Anger: A Woman's Guide to Changing the Patterns of Intimate Relationships.* New York: Harper and Row-Perennial Library, 1986.

Ornish, Dean. *Dr. Dean Ornish's Program for Reversing Heart Disease.* New York: Ballantine Books, 1991.

Ray, Sondra. *The Only Diet There Is.* Millbrae, Calif.: Celestial Arts, 1981.

Smith, Henry. *Warriorobics Ki Breathing.* Instructional videotapes. New York: Solaris Dance Co.

INSPIRATION

Campbell, Joseph. *The Hero with a Thousand Faces*. Princeton, N.J.: Princeton University Press, 1949.

Castaneda, Carlos. *Journey to Ixtlan: The Lessons of Don Juan*. New York: Washington Square Press, 1972.

Charlton, Hilda. *Saints Alive*. Lake Hill, N.Y.: Golden Quest, 1989.

Chopra, Deepak. *The Way of the Wizard: Twenty Spiritual Lessons in Creating the Life You Want*. New York: Harmony Books, 1995.

Dalai Lama. *Kindness, Clarity, and Insight*. Ithaca, N.Y.: Snow Lion, 1984.

———. *Freedom in Exile: The Autobiography of the Dalai Lama*. New York: HarperCollins, 1990.

Foundation for Inner Peace. *A Course in Miracles*. New York: Foundation for Inner Peace, 1975.

Fox, Matthew, and Rupert Sheldrake. *Natural Grace: Dialogues on Creation, Darkness, and the Soul in Spirituality and Science*. New York: Doubleday, 1996.

Godman, David, ed. *Be As You Are: The Teachings of Sri Ramana Maharshi*. New York: Penguin Books, 1992.

Kapleau, Philip. *The Three Pillars of Zen: Teaching, Practice and Enlightenment*. New York: Anchor Books, 1980.

Krishnamurti, J. *Freedom from the Known*. Mary Lutyens, Ed. New York: Harper and Row, 1969.

Leadbeater, C. W. *A Textbook of Theosophy*. Madras, India: Theosophical Publishing House, 1912.

Mandino, Og. *The Greatest Secret in the World*. New York: Bantam, 1978.

Maslow, Abraham H. *Religions, Values, and Peak Experiences*. New York: Penguin Books, 1986.

Merton, Thomas. *Seeds of Contemplation*. Norfolk, Conn.: New Directions, 1949.

Novak, Philip. *The World's Wisdom: Sacred Texts of the World's Religions*. San Francisco: HarperSanFrancisco, 1994.

Rinpoche, Sogyal, Patrick Gaffney, and Andrew Harvey, eds. *The Tibetan Book of Living and Dying*. New York: Harper-Collins, 1992.

Roof, Jonathan. *Pathways to God: A Study Guide to the Teachings of Sathya Sai Baba*. Faber, Va.: Leela Press, 1991.

St. James, Elaine. *Inner Simplicity: 100 Ways to Regain Peace and Nourish Your Soul*. New York: Hyperion, 1995.

Tsu, Lao. *Tao Te Ching*. Gia-Fu Feng and Jane English, trans. New York: Vintage Books, 1989.

Yogananda, Paramahansa. *Autobiography of a Yogi*. Los Angeles: Self-Realization Fellowship, 1993.

TECHNIQUE #12: EXPRESS GRATITUDE

Reynolds, David K. *A Handbook for Constructive Living*. New York: William Morrow, 1995.

———. *Rainbow Rising from a Stream*. New York: William Morrow, 1992.

Steindl-Rast, Brother David. *Gratefulness, the Heart of Prayer: An Approach to Life in Fullness*. New York: Paulist Press, 1984.

TECHNIQUE #13: GIVE OF YOURSELF

Dass, Ram, and Paul Gorman. *How Can I Help? Stories and Reflections on Service*. New York: Alfred A. Knopf, 1994.

Fromm, Erich. *The Art of Living*. New York: Harper and Row, 1956.

Kohn, Alfie. *The Brighter Side of Human Nature: Altruism and Empathy in Everyday Life*. New York: Basic Books, 1990.

Pilgrim, Peace. *Peace Pilgrim: Her Life and Work in Her Own Words*. Santa Fe, N.M.: Ocean Tree, 1994.

Salzberg, Sharon. *Lovingkindness: The Revolutionary Art of Happiness*. Boston: Shambhala, 1995.

CHAPTER 11

TECHNIQUE #14: DIVINATION

I Ching or Book of Changes. Richard Wilhelm translation. Cary F. Baynes, trans. Princeton, N.J.: Princeton University Press-Bollingen Series XIX, 1976.

Blum, Ralph. *The Book of Runes.* New York: St. Martin's Press, 1982.

Levine, Frederick G. *Psychic Sourcebook: How to Choose and Use a Psychic.* New York: Warner Books, 1988.

Sams, Jamie, and David Carson. *Medicine Cards: The Discovery of Power Through the Ways of Animals.* Santa Fe, N.M.: Bear & Company, 1988.

World Atlas of Divination: The Systems, Where They Originate, How They Work. John Matthews, consult. ed. Boston: Little, Brown and Company, 1992.

Acknowledgments

Synchronicity and flow are sometimes seen most clearly in retrospect, and they were in evidence in 1973 on our first collaboration, a Colorado gubernatorial campaign for which Charlene was the film producer and Meg the media director. Everything magically fell together to allow us to produce a happy-go-lucky television spot that was key in our candidate's victory.

In the following years, our career paths diverged: Charlene went into business and academia in Denver, Meg worked on a newspaper in New Jersey and lived in New York. But what increasingly converged over the years were our psychological and spiritual paths, which involved personal growth seminars, meditation, and trips to holy places. Charlene incorporated her insights into her teaching in personal growth, corporate, and university settings, and Meg used it to give greater depth to her writing.

In the summer of 1993, an amazing chain of synchronicities led directly to the writing of this book. We had planned to travel around South India for a month. Meg got

there first, and was meditating at the ashram of Sathya Sai
Baba in Bangalore when she had a vivid sensation of being in,
of all places, the main temple in Lhasa, Tibet: she could hear
it, smell it, feel it. She got a clear understanding that we were
supposed to go there, and an even stranger inner message: We
were to let the Universe take care of the details. What did
that mean? When Charlene arrived a few days later, she
laughed at the news: It had always been her dream to go to
Tibet. A few days earlier, a friend had invited her to accom-
pany him there the next year, but she knew intuitively that
she would have already been there by then.

So we headed toward Kathmandu, Nepal, to see if we
could get into Tibet that way. It was a long shot: Everyone
told us that because of Chinese visa requirements and travel
complications, trips into Tibet—if we could get in at all—required many months of advance planning. Communications
being what they are in that part of the world, we couldn't do
that from South India. Instead, we did what we had planned
to do all along: we visited a temple town and a seaside resort,
staying at each place until it seemed time to go on. We were
delayed by canceled flights, and by the time we finally flew
into Nepal, we learned that we had only one working day to
get a Chinese visa and a plane ticket on the only available
flight to Tibet. But we were immediately directed to a hot-
shot travel agency that could work miracles, and—another
miracle!—it took American Express. A day later, we were on
that plane, winging past Mount Everest toward Lhasa.

The week that followed seemed blessed every step of
the way. We traveled by Jeep around the countryside with a
Tibetan guide, drinking tea with families, breathing in the
musky incense of ancient temples. We were moved by the for-
titude of the Tibetan people: their warm hearts and wide,
open smiles gave us faith that despite the brutality of Chinese
rule, what is essential about their culture remains untouched.
In fact, cannot be touched.

Since the temples have been allowed to open again, they

are usually thronged with laughing, praying pilgrims and pulsating with the chants of monks. But to our dismay, the Jokhang Temple in Lhasa was closed the day we were there, the last day of our trip. Our guide managed to get us in somehow, and so we were virtually alone in the temple among the ancient statues and flickering butter lamps. There, Meg's meditation and Charlene's lifelong dream came to pass: we sat down in the silence and prayed.

The next day, heading back to Nepal, a Tibetan businessman agitatedly approached Charlene at the airport. He was having a panic attack and thought he was going to die on the flight back to his home in Kathmandu, and he sought out Charlene for help because, he said, he saw the Dalai Lama all around her. As the plane winged south, Charlene sat next to him and gently calmed him as he thrashed around. At one point, a mantra was going through her mind; she looked down and saw his lips moving silently to it. Two days later, after Meg had left for home, his family tracked Charlene down. She was able to get him out of a mental hospital and under the care of a doctor who prescribed effective medication. For a month, she lived with his family in Kathmandu, and she had an honored place: He considered her his mother from a past life. Oddly enough, he was born in Tibet in 1964, six months after, in Colorado, Charlene's infant son had been taken from her by a rare form of meningitis. Furthermore, his name is Sonam—son am.

He had a twenty-two-year-old sister, Tsering, who felt her destiny was in the States. Although young single Tibetan women seldom are given American visas, she received one with Charlene's help: it turned out that the U.S. embassy official in Kathmandu had once taught—by coincidence, of course—at the same campus Charlene did, the University of Colorado at Denver.

In the States, Tsering studied briefly in Denver and then joined friends in New York City, where she worked sixty-hour weeks in Chinatown for a pittance and lived in a crowded apartment in a dangerous neighborhood. She fell ill, and the city's Tibetan refugee coordinator, a relative of the Dalai Lama, allowed her to stay at his home to recuperate while he was away. When he returned, destiny took its course, and they are now married. This all happened in accord with a vivid childhood dream of Tsering: she knew she would meet her Tibetan husband in America.

It was in trying to understand more deeply these experiences of ours that this book was born. Looking back, we saw how the synchronicities seemed to flow out of an inner space in which we followed our inner voice, trusted in a larger plan, and allowed things to unfold. Is this always the way it works, we wondered? Does synchronicity always flow from, well, flow?

We wrote a book proposal to examine these questions, and through clusters of synchronicities, within weeks we found a wonderful publisher and the perfect agent. Although the research and writing has been long and arduous, we've been graced throughout by the loving support of many people—our flow messengers.

We'd like to thank, first of all, the hundreds of people who gave of their time and experiences to shape the content of this book—including the flowmasters, focus group participants, and people who filled out magazine and newspaper questionnaires. We were continually impressed by their insights and moved by the depth of their sharing: this book just begins to do justice to the richness of material.

Our good friends in Denver, upstate New York, and New York City gave us advice and support thoughout the process—encouraging us, giving us feedback, showing up at our door with chocolate cake. Mary Lundstrom and Kathy Donovan typed the 1,000 pages of tape transcripts with dedication and provided us with their valuable insights; Laura Belitz designed a snazzy web page on the Internet (http://www.FlowPower.com).

David Spangler, Rick Jarow, and Earl Davis shared with

us their rich perspectives on flow and synchronicity, perspectives that proceed from their creative and expansive takes on life.

The deep insights and practical advice of Gary Smith have greatly enriched the book; and we're grateful to Suzie Rodriguez-Hunter, who cheerleaded us through the rigors of writing. MaryAnn Wrobleski's nurturing and Camille Fine's inspiration lightened our days.

Muriel Nellis, our agent and godmother, is one of the best communicators we've met, and her sage counsel steered us wonderfully through the twists and turns of the publishing process.

Most of all, we thank Wendy Hubbert, our editor at Crown Publishing, who had an unflagging enthusiasm for the book and who expertly coached us through the unfamiliar process of writing it. Her wise influence is evident in the book's structure and tone. This book would not be in your hands without her devotion to it.

And finally, we thank our families, whose love has sustained us and provided the bedrock on which this book was built: Laura, Michael, Jamie, Dale Belitz and Gram; Josie, Rick, Allison, Collin, Mary, Cary, Matt, Linda, Leif, Katrina, Corianne, Amy, Jim, John, and Richard Lundstrom.

Index

If you would like to share your flow experiences or participate in further research on flow and synchronicity, you can visit this book's web site:

http://www.FlowPower.com

Or write either:

Charlene Belitz
Synchronicity Studies
P.O. Box 370885
Denver, CO 80237

Meg Lundstrom
Synchronicity Studies
P.O. Box 236
Palenville, NY 12463

About the Authors

Charlene Belitz teaches human communication studies at the University of Denver and the University of Colorado at Denver. She has led hundreds of communication and transformational seminars in corporate, academic, and personal development settings.

Meg Lundstrom, a widely traveled magazine writer and former newspaper reporter, has written extensively about self-development approaches and the human search for meaning in relationships, work, and spirituality. She lives in Saugerties, New York, and New York City.